Genesis and Exodus

Genesis and Exodus

A Portrait of
the Benson Family

DAVID WILLIAMS

Hamish Hamilton: *London*

First published in Great Britain 1979
by Hamish Hamilton Ltd
Garden House 57–59 Long Acre London WC2E 9JZ

Copyright © 1979 by David Williams

British Library Cataloguing in Publication Data
Williams, David
  Genesis and Exodus.
  1. Benson family
  I. Title
  929'.2'0942   CS439.B/
ISBN 0 241 10190 5

Printed in Great Britain by
Ebenezer Baylis & Son Ltd, The Trinity Press, Worcester and London

Contents

List of illustrations

Between pages 132 and 133

THE BENSONS

CHRISTOPHER BENSON
of Pateley Bridge ('Old Christopher')

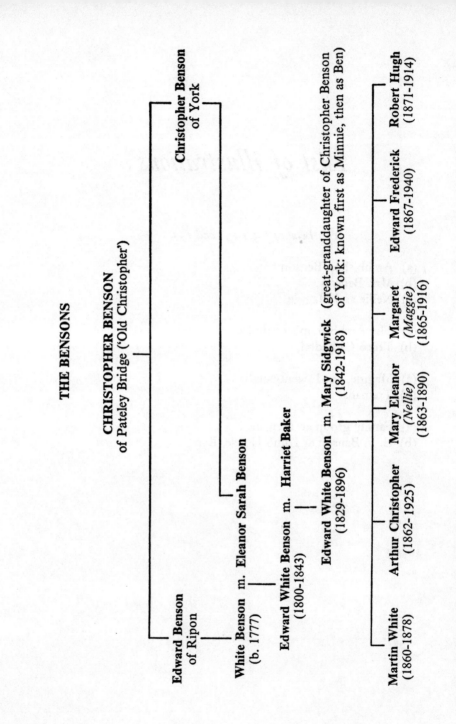

Edward Benson
of Ripon

Christopher Benson
of York

White Benson m. **Eleanor Sarah Benson**
(b. 1777)

Edward White Benson m. **Harriet Baker**
(1800-1843)

Edward White Benson m. **Mary Sidgwick** (great-granddaughter of Christopher Benson
(1829-1896)   (1842-1918)   of York: known first as Minnie, then as Ben)

Martin White
(1860-1878)

Arthur Christopher
(1862-1925)

Mary Eleanor
(*Nellie*)
(1863-1890)

Margaret
(*Maggie*)
(1865-1916)

Edward Frederick
(1867-1940)

Robert Hugh
(1871-1914)

Preliminary

'HAPPY FAMILIES are all alike; every unhappy family is unhappy in its own way.' This opening sentence of Tolstoy's *Anna Karenina* has been much quoted and admired. Like many of the generalized pronouncements of this writer, however, it tries and fails to make a virtue of oversimplification. Any distillation of wisdom about families needs to be so qualified that it becomes blurred and useless as a contribution to our knowledge about ourselves.

'Every unhappy family is unhappy in its own way'—this though we may accept. There is scarcely a limit to the variations of method by which people contrive to make each other miserable. But 'Happy families are all alike'? This is indeed a large assumption.

The two generations of the Benson family studied in this book would certainly, in the eyes of their contemporaries, have been considered a happy family. Death visited them untimely of course, but then, up to the early 1920s, there was scarcely a family in the land that was not so visited. The death of Martin Benson while still a boy at Winchester, and of Nellie Benson at the age of twenty-seven, cannot be counted as making for family unhappiness. If they were to be so counted happy families would be rare indeed. (All the same, it has to be said that the death of his eldest, treasured son stuck in the throat of the then Bishop of Truro to the very end of his days.)

So the Bensons were 'happy'. They came from sound middle-class Yorkshire stock which produced lawyers, clerics, academics.

1*

(The Sidgwick side—Mary Benson's side, that is—was slightly the more distinguished of the two.) They rose to high places, carried upwards on Edward's sustaining wings. They wrote loving letters to each other. They commemorated each other in numerous books which are fragrant with me-to-you admiration, but which fail to tell quite the whole truth. They hurry to each other's death-beds. Arthur, in the late autumn of 1914, leaves the pure if chilly air of Cambridge to reach the Bishop's House in murky Salford, where Hugh, only forty-three, is making his last stand and preparing to receive his viaticum. ' "Arthur, this is the end!" I knelt down near the bed, and I knew somehow that we understood each other well, that he wanted no word or demonstration, but was just glad I was with him. . . .'

And yet, although there was always amongst them this very private closeness, there were also deep divisions. There were also mysterious sexual inadequacies which meant that, out of a second generation of six, not one single Benson of the third generation was ever produced. Admittedly they produced much in compensation, much of it brilliant, yet none of it, perhaps, quite of the first class. Why was it so? Did the fault lie with the parents? Speaking of them both, Arthur said 'She [Mary Sidgwick] was afraid of Papa and I don't wonder.' But that won't really do either. Mary, once she had reached her belated maturity, was never afraid of her husband Edward Benson, not even when he had become a decidedly autocratic Primate of All England.

So the Bensons have their mysteries, and, in common with vast numbers of families once you begin to look at them closely, their very particular sort of fascination.

Acknowledgments

I offer my most grateful thanks for help of various kinds, all most generously given, to the following (in alphabetical order): The Bodleian Library, the Cambridge University Library, John and Marjorie Haynes, John Kerry, the London Library (where would any of us be without it?), Roger Machell, Dr. David Newsome, Tony Reavell, Ludovick Stewart, Mr. and Mrs. Charles Tomlin.

I

Dear Little Minnie

'BY THE LAST HALF of the eighteenth century they were very substantial people.' This was how Fred Benson described his father's forebears, and in claiming so much he is certainly not overstating his case. They never climbed into the grandee class, but they were not nobodies either. George Benson (1699–1762), though not directly in line, was of the family, and had in his time a certain fame. He was a Calvinist divine who wrote fluently about sin and about the Kingdom of God. He married, but was childless. Of the same family too was Robert Benson, later Lord Bingley (1676–1731), a much less holy man. Indeed Sir John Reresby wrote dismissively of him as 'a man of mean extraction and little worth'. Still, he was briefly Chancellor of the Exchequer in Queen Anne's time and 'Gentleman Johnny' Burgoyne, better at writing comedies than commanding armies, was his godson.

The family property was in the Yorkshire dales, and Edward Benson, great-grandfather of Edward White Benson, was by great good luck able to add considerably to it. His neighbour, Francis White, was a bachelor and a crony, and when he died he left a good share of his considerable wealth to Edward. To serve the family as a reminder and as a tribute, Edward called his son White, and White turned out to be something of a black sheep— not jet black by any means, but falling somewhat short of the solid Benson respectability. He became an infantry officer, shared in the dissipations of Prince William Frederick, Duke of Gloucester, wasted his fortune, married his first cousin Eleanor, who was rich too, wasted hers, and fell fatally from his horse in 1806 leaving a widow and young son not well provided for.

This son, called Edward White, grew up serious-minded and hard-up. For him there were to be no junketings with royalty and no commission in a good regiment; he had neither the inclination nor the means. Indeed he had to abandon any idea of being a member of the landed class, and instead descend to the grade of manufacturer. He sold his remaining piece of property in York and started a factory in Birmingham. He was notably good at chemistry and had discovered a new method of making white lead. The setting up of his factory took all the capital he had, but there was, he knew, a good demand for white lead, and who better than he to satisfy it? With his wife Harriet, a sister of a Manchester man, Sir Thomas Baker, he installed himself at 72 Lombard Street, Birmingham, and here, as a relief from producing white lead, begot seven children and wrote a *Meditation on the Works of God* which was ruminative and reverential.

In 1843 the business failed and Edward White Benson died. At the age of fourteen, Edward White Benson the second, the eldest, promising son of his numerous family, was left fatherless—but not irresponsible and very far from incapable. Earlier, at the age of eleven, this young Edward White had been entered at King Edward's School, Birmingham, and, from 1838 to 1847, the headmaster of the school was James Prince Lee, a small, intent man having eyes that could intimidate.

Lee is important, not only for the influence which he exercised upon his pupil, an influence which remained strong throughout Benson's life, but also for his right to be recognized as representative of much—some of it good, some of it bad—that was influential in mid-Victorian thinking about education. In 1830, at the age of twenty-six, he had been one of Arnold's first appointments to Rugby. During his eight years there he thoroughly satisfied Arnold. He was passionately religious, classically learned, and could entrance the idlest and most careless of boys with his sustained eloquence. He showed courtesy to his pupils so long as they were attentive, but if they fell short, small though he was he could flog. His furies indeed were as passionate as his religious convictions, and these might charitably be ascribed to his physical sufferings. Neuralgia attacked him, inflamed eyes plagued him. He took laudanum to soothe his pains. He was indeed, like so many of his own and the succeeding generation, a laudanum addict. In support of his application to the governors of King Edward's School he submitted thirty-one testimonials, which is indeed a staggering quantity of testimonials. Arnold's was the one that mattered, and Arnold's did not let him down. Amongst much else, Arnold said: 'His activity of body and mind is unwearied: his interest in his profession intense: and his manner with boys is at once firm and courteous. They would never, I think, put him in a passion,—they would find him always kind; but they would know that he would be minded.'

They would indeed know that he would be minded, and there would certainly be occasions, in spite of Arnold's certainty, when they would put him in a passion. Edward White Benson, a model pupil, would never have experienced the fires of a Lee thwarted, disobeyed or disgusted. Benson was intelligent, worked hard at his books, and above all was, even at so early an age, a dedicated and single-minded Christian. Keble's Assize Sermon on National Apostasy had been preached on 14 July 1833. In February 1841, during Benson's first year at the school, Newman had published Number 90 of *Tracts for the Times*. By the time of White Benson's death in 1843 Tractarianism was blowing hard across the land, and herding intelligent, bookish youngsters into devout clusters. Westcott and Lightfoot, fellow-pupils of Benson's at King Edward's School, both like Benson intensely religious, both to succeed in due time to the Bishopric of Durham, caught like him the liturgical fervour inspired by Newman. (And here they were not putting their feet exactly into the prints left by their admired headmaster, Lee, whose churchmanship always remained broad and Arnoldian.) The young Benson, indeed, went so far as to set up for himself, in his father's now disused white lead factory, an Oratory in which he said his Canonical Hours, probably with Lightfoot sometimes taking part as well, Westcott too perhaps though not so certainly—he was four years older. The seven young Bensons were not rich—though not of course poor either in the savage Victorian way. The widowed Harriet had her portion; the Manchester Bakers were substantial people; and there were plentiful Benson relatives still living in some style up in Yorkshire. The young Benson walked into town from Birmingham Heath, where his mother now had a house, to Barry's grand new Gothic school in New Street which had been opened in 1838.

From the outside it looked, so Westcott assured his readers in the first School Magazine dated September 1842, like King's College Chapel in Cambridge, and Birmingham folk aged fifty or more will remember it because it stood on that New Street site, very black by then but still imposing, until 1935. By then though its impressiveness could no longer be accepted as sufficient counterweight to its unsuitability as a place to teach people in the twentieth century. Big School was thirty-four yards long and twelve wide and fifteen high. Prince Lee taught at a regal desk at one end; the Rev. Sidney Gedge, his second master, taught from the other end also occupying a regal, though less regal desk; subsidiary groups behaved themselves in between. School architects of the time did not design for matiness and free movement. King Edward's School was not Rugby of course. The sons of gentlemen mingled with the sons of tradespeople; for the most part it was a day-school, so that Lee was not, as Arnold was, in command right through the twenty-four hours. The tenets of Anglicanism could not be adhered to universally. Jews attended. So even did Unitarians. 'I offer Religious Instruction,' Lee said, adding sadly, 'if they will not take it, I cannot help it.'

But he certainly saw to it that his pupils were well taught in the secular sense, and that they worked. The record of success amongst those of his pupils who went on to the university, especially to Cambridge, was impressive. But what of Edward White Benson? Would he be afforded the opportunity to get his First in the tripos? Harriet Benson was a widow; money was tight; there were six children younger than Edward. There was a feeling, especially strong amongst the Manchester Bakers, that he should go straight into commerce, and take some of the burden off his mother's shoulders. There would be a career open to him; the Bakers, if not the Yorkshire Bensons, could ensure so much.

But never, not even in adolescence, was Benson the meek and biddable type. He knew that his scholarship would be equal to any demands which Cambridge might make upon it. Furthermore, the cramped and lowly life lived at Birmingham Heath was not by any means the only life he knew. During his holidays he visited Yorkshire relatives. A great-aunt had married William Sidgwick, and now lived on, in some state, at Skipton Castle. Life there was gracious and not too much hampered by obtrusive rules. 'My aunt is not at all strict,' he told his mother in 1844, 'except that I am obliged to eat bread and butter with a knife and fork.' His aunt took the good things of life for granted, did nothing in particular, but did it in the grand style. Benson did not learn to despise the humbler ways of living enforced on him in Birmingham—his Christian conscience, never off guard, would see to that—but he did become aware that he came from stock that lived far differently. His aunt's sons, both bachelors in early middle age, had already given up gainful occupations in order to live idle, quirky lives in the castle. John, an elder great-uncle lived in a splendid house at Stonegappe, which was remote, without a railway, and which the centuries seemed to have passed by. Young Benson would return home in the autumn to workaday Birmingham with his head filled with lordly notions. Impressions gained on such visits as these, combined with his wish to take holy orders, would have made the thought of a business life distasteful; and he had the strength of mind, even at so early an age, to resist pressures on him which were probably strong. In 1848 he went up to Trinity College, Cambridge, as a subsizar, leaving behind a hard-pressed mother to bring up six children.

During his first year his mother wrote to him to say that if business was too drab and drossy for him it was not for her. She still held the rights of a patent process, to do with cobalt, left by her dead husband. She thought she might make something of it. Life with six dependent children was after all costly. Benson, caught up in the excitements of Higher Things, was alarmed at this proposal. A mother going into trade, however hard-pressed, seemed to him a most distasteful prospect. He wrote and told her so. 'I do hope and trust you will keep out of it. It will do me so much harm here, and my sisters so much harm for ever! I trust that the scheme may be abandoned once and for all.'

It would be a mistake to think that Benson was simply being sanctimonious and objectionable. The climate of the time he was living in has to be taken into account. It was a rockhard, stratified society; a tiny handful of grandees who knew each other and were for the most part more or less distantly related; some of these were dissolute and self-indulgent; others were high-minded, intense. Below these were the landed, comfortably off who split into three divisions depending on the way they looked at religion: the Evangelicals, the Tractarians, and the broad Modernists who might be termed Arnoldian. Benson belonged among the

Arnoldians. After these came Trade, a populous group, outwardly respectful towards religious observance but not deeply committed. It was the group which grew steadily in power and influence throughout the Victorian period, and the graph of its rise keeps step pretty closely with the climb of Joseph Chamberlain, born in 1836, to the top. Underneath all these were the hordes of accepting poor. Nowhere, except among those high-minded and intense grandees, had a social conscience emerged as a strong force. The emphasis for the most part was on last things, on the notion of the Kingdom of God, on the beckoning rewards waiting for all in the hereafter. If you kept a firm hold on your certainty about the good things to come, what, relatively, did it matter that you suffered pain and penury in the fleeting Now? So Harriet Benson struggled on in Birmingham, and Benson plunged deeper into his classics at Trinity, and was whirled aloft by the ecstasies of theological discussion. During these early years at any rate there was no flickering in his faith.

He proved himself worthy of more than a subsizarship. The fellows made him a sizar, and not long after that he moved upwards again. He became a scholar of Trinity. And, provided his mother did as she was told on important matters, he was wholly ready to work hard to help her. He managed to get tutoring work and shared the proceeds with her. But now Harriet took another big decision, and this time not under instructions. She invested a good deal of what capital she had in a railway company. She chose her moment badly. 1848 was the year of the crash of George Hudson, the Railway King. Shareholders became frightened. Flotations collapsed. Harriet lost her money and became very poor indeed.

Then death, that frequent visitor to Victorian families, took a sudden sharp interest in the affairs of the unfortunate widow. Two of the children, both girls, caught typhus fever. She wrote to her eldest brilliant son telling him the news and begging him to keep away for fear lest he should become infected. Benson seems to have seen the wisdom of this. But further news came hurrying towards him. Harriet, the girl nearest to him in age, had died. This time his mother did not renew her urgings that he should keep away. He made preparations to leave Trinity, to leave Lightfoot, to leave learning—not permanently, perhaps, but at any rate as a temporary measure.

But sorrows did not come to the Birmingham house that year single spies; they came in battalions. Prostrate with grief and with unrelieved, unsuccessful nursing, Mrs. Benson went to bed with another daughter, with the dead Harriet lying in another room. Sleepless during the night, she felt a compulsion to look on her eldest daughter again. Having done this she appeared calmer and readier to sleep. In the morning she was lying very quietly, and the young child beside her could not wake her. Indeed she had passed beyond waking, and when Benson arrived he had a double funeral to see to, and he also found himself suddenly head of a family almost entirely without resources. The family had to be shared out amongst relatives, and a Baker uncle, rich and unmarried, told Benson he was prepared to adopt the youngest brother.

This was generous, a piece of good fortune to be seized. Or so one might think. But Benson, surprisingly, did not look at it like that at all. He saw a difficulty. Baker was a Unitarian. The religious upbringing of the young Charles Benson had been without taint. Even at this dire stage in the family's affairs, Benson was not prepared to take the risk of pollution. To the generous Baker he wrote a letter which to us must sound unbelievably pompous and self-righteous. To put the young Charles under the guidance and protection of a Unitarian was not to be thought of. Letters went to and fro, but Benson was not to be moved. His final letter must be given at some length because it contains a fair statement of where Benson stood on religious matters not only at the age of twenty-one when he wrote it—an age when extreme positions are joyfully taken up—but also all through his life. 'My religious principle,' Baker was told, 'is not a thing of tender feelings, warm, comforting notions, unproved prejudices, but it consists of full and perfect conviction, absolute belief, rules to regulate my life, and tests by which I believe myself bound to try every question the greatest and the least.' And then he went on to say why he had decided that a younger brother should be refused a safe and comfortable haven in Manchester. 'I shall constantly hereafter as a Priest in the English Church, if God will, several times in every service proclaim "Glory be to the Father and to the Son, and to the Holy Ghost": I shall offer humble prayer on my own behalf and on behalf of the Church at large to my Redeemer—with what conscience or with what countenance if ever memory should suggest that in one person's case, and his the dearest that could be, I had robbed those Divine persons of the worship and the praise that should have proceeded from his heart, his mind, his lips, his whole life? Whom could you more rightly brand as Hypocrite than him whose professions should be so loud, whose actions so discrepant? This is a very serious matter, and I hope you will not think bitterly either of the young man's presumption, or the young churchman's bigotry. Bigot, thus far, a conscientious Christian must be.'

This is a letter worth pondering. It throws so much light both on the good and on the insufferable side of Edward White Benson. His absolutely unshakeable faith—even though there came one blow later on so severe as almost to wreck it—gave him a strength and a purposefulness which drove him on—to power certainly but also to wide-ranging and altruistic achievement. That same faith could turn him into a bully—a difficult man to live up to and at the same time a difficult man to live with. His pride in his bigotry startles. Who was he to fling away a life-line meant, after all, not for him but for a third party—even though that third party happened to be a brother and a younger one? His description of himself as offering 'humble prayer' is funnier than he means it to be. Humility was never a garment that fitted Edward White Benson well.

The certainty of 'I shall constantly hereafter as a Priest . . .' is something else that surprises. Entry into the priesthood meant coming down from Trinity with a degree. His scholarship would not be enough to support him until his finals, let alone provide against his other commitments so confidently entered into as head of the family. But luck, in the person of Francis Martin, bursar of Trinity, now did him a very good turn.

The friendships between wealthy unmarried men of middle age and handsome youngsters (EWB was very handsome indeed, if perhaps a little short in the leg), are not thought of in the same way now as they were 130 years ago. We would say now that Francis Martin plunged into a homosexual affair with EWB which lasted long and which was handsomely profitable to the younger partner. But to think in this way would be to misunderstand completely the climate of the period. In 1849 the rule requiring the celibacy of Oxbridge dons still remained absolute. 'Cuthbert Bede', otherwise Edward Bradley, author of the

Adventures of Mr Verdant Green, wrote a mock medieval ballad on the subject in the next decade when the celibates were beginning to become vocal and restive. He imagines a Fellow of Trinity, who . . .

> 'dreams of a bright-eyed, browne-haired girl. . . .
>
> She has no fortune, save hersen,
>   Though that is a treasure, I trow,
> Yet not enow for ye keepynge of house,
>   As times and taxes goe.
>
> And he has nought but his Fellowshyppe,
>   And not marrye on that he maye:
> For gin he marries, his Fellowshyppe
>   He loses for ever and aye . . .'

There is no evidence at all that 'Cuthbert Bede' was thinking of Francis Martin as he wrote his ballad, but there were plenty of dons in those days, in Trinity and elsewhere, tormented by not knowing quite what to do with their sexuality; and certainly Francis Martin was one of them. He was rich, could have thrown his fellowship in the Master's face, and gone a-whoring in the Haymarket, or, more likely, in upper-crust London drawing-rooms. But Martin was a scholar; the graciousness of life in Trinity, even in those relatively uncosseted days, would have made his bursar's niche a hard one to relinquish; and, yes, that constantly renewed supply of vigorous, eager and talented young men—this also would have been a strong allurement. And EWB was indeed a very special allurement. He had a splendid head, a mobile mouth, was greatly gifted, was so dominating in an effortless way, would be, no doubt of it, a leader. Francis Martin grew quite passionately fond of him, and it is likely that the phrase 'unnatural vice' never for one moment entered his mind. It is even likelier that such a monstrous thing as a homosexual attachment was never so much as remotely contemplated by EWB.

For all that it was for Benson, suddenly stripped of almost all resources and equally suddenly responsible for numerous dependants, a very fortunate infatuation indeed. Not merely did he find himself not obliged to quit the university, he was instead installed in new, much more comfortable, rooms in college. What he needed, what sometimes he could even have done without, was readily paid for. During those infinitely long vacations Martin took him travelling; if he was ill, Martin fussed over him. Martin's concern for him was, in fact, immediate, practical and limitless. It extended to the whole family; it extended through life. Benson's sisters found themselves with sizeable dowries provided from Martin's funds. Could he ever have found all this devotion, both practical and emotional, excessive? There is no evidence at all that he did. Did his friends mock? There is no evidence of this either. Lightfoot, his capacious mind intent upon higher things, would probably not have noticed. Benson wrote inconsiderable little poems, read them to Martin, and received admiration for them.

He took a first in the Classical Tripos of 1852, and won the Chancellor's gold medal. He was staying at Clifton when Martin, defying in his enthusiasm all the difficulties of cross-country journeys, brought him the news and Benson notes in his diary that the delighted Bursar of Trinity 'was folding my hand all around into all shapes'. Clifton was at this time the home of Mrs. William Sidgwick, a widow and a cousin of Benson's. She had four children, William, Henry, Arthur and a daughter, Mary, the youngest of the four, born in 1842. Her husband had been headmaster of Skipton Grammar School, and his now orphaned offspring quartet were formidable. Arthur became a Rugby master, Henry, nine years younger than Benson, was Professor of Moral Philosophy at Cambridge from 1883 till his death in 1900, and Mary became Benson's wife—a more testing task and work-load, be it said, than either Arthur's or Henry's. On the occasion of this stay of his at Clifton in 1852, twenty-three years of age, a thumping academic success, probably and naturally very full of himself and of his prospects, Benson made an entry in his diary to us so astonishing it needs to be quoted at some length: 'Mrs Sidgwick's little daughter, Mary, is this year eleven years old. From a very young child great parts and peculiarly strong affection have been discernible in her, with a great delicacy of feeling. She is remarkably persevering and though (naturally) lacking the taste for dry sorts of knowledge, which her brother Henry, whom she most resembles, had from an infant, she has much fondness for histories, above all the ancient, and a most striking love for poetry, and taste in fine poetry, and has a wonderful deal of it committed (always of her own inclination) to memory. As I have always been very fond of her and she of me with the love of a little sister, and as I have heard of her fondness for me commented on by many persons, and have been told that I was the only person at whose departure she ever cried, as a child, and how diligent she has always been in reading books which I have mentioned to her, and in learning pieces of poetry which I have admired, it is not strange that I, who from the circumstances of my family am not likely to marry for many years to come, and who find in myself a growing distaste for forming friendships (fit to be so called) among new acquaintances and who am fond indeed (if not too fond) of little endearments, and who also know my weakness for falling suddenly in love, in the common sense of the word, and have already gone too far more than once in these things and have therefore reason to fear that I might on some sudden occasion be led . . . [a cryptic language takes over at this point for a little while] . . . it is not strange that I should have thought first of the possibility that some day dear little Minnie might become my wife. . . .'

There is much here to puzzle the ordinary reader, as well as, perhaps, to delight the psychologist. Is he anchoring himself to a young child in order that he should be held back from a plunge into sexual adventures? Or has he already had sexual adventures and is, for some reason, feeling ashamed of them and of himself ('my weakness for falling suddenly in love')? A hesitant Yes, and a much more confident No are the answers, in that order to these two questions. The hesitancy of the affirmative arises of course from the fact that the whole notion is so bizarre. It is, we have to remember, simply a private diary entry, so could Benson simply have been just fantasizing? Well, the diary has more to say: 'Whether such an idea ever struck the guileless little thing herself I cannot tell. I should think it most unlikely. Yet I could not help being surprised one night when she was half lying on a sofa on which I sat, by the following conversation. MINNIE: Edward, how long will it be before I am as tall as if I was standing on that stool? EDWARD: I don't very well know, Minnie, five years perhaps. MINNIE: When I am twenty I shall be taller than that? MINNIE: When I am twenty, how old shall you be? EDWARD: Thirty-two. MINNIE: Thirty-two! Edward, I shan't look so little compared to you, shall I, when I'm twenty and you're thirty-two, as I do now that I'm eleven and you're twenty-three? EDWARD:

No, no, you won't, Minnie. . . . This unexpected close shot made me blush indeed, and the palms of my hands grew very hot.'

Indeed the young Benson seems to have been so bowled over by Minnie that he went to the length of talking to Mrs. Sidgwick about her. Perhaps as the widow of a headmaster she had grown accustomed to strange posturings and stranger emotional out-pourings from over-excited young men. She does not seem to have shown any sense of outrage, but contented herself with making the point that there was plenty of time ahead in which he might meet more mature young women and change his mind. As for Minnie herself, would she, at the age she had arrived at, have any notion of what he was talking about?

A year went by, with moves and changes. Benson, supported by Prince Lee, was invited by Goulburn, headmaster of Rugby, to teach the sixth form at the school for one hour a day, and to assume in addition responsibility for fifty private pupils from School House. Benson accepted. Mrs. William Sidgwick decided during the same year to move from Clifton, and the cousin and widow of the Master of Skipton Grammar School settled in Rugby in order to be near her sons, Henry and Arthur, who were being educated there. She took the Blue House and was far from lonely. Her eldest son William, shortly to win a scholarship to Christ Church, was in and out; then came Henry and Arthur with still a long way to go; cousin Edward Sidgwick, in due course to become a solicitor, was also at the school. Benson's sister Ada, clever, attractive, strong-minded, had been brought into harbour at Blue House too (there was no taint of Unitarianism in Mrs. William Sidgwick's churchmanship). Still this hospitable lady had room for more. Her sister, Henrietta Crofts, 'a lady of masculine appearance, with a deep voice, moods of dark depres-sion and a most incongruous sense of humour', had also her room and her place at table. Finally, there was Benson himself, the new young Rugby master, still not ordained and so able to cultivate his dress sense. For Sunday chapel at Rugby he wore light pearl-grey trousers, a blue frock-coat, collars rising to mid-cheek, expansive silk tie tied in a hard knot and much fluffed out at the ends and decorated with birds like toucans or bit-baskets filled with flowers. Lilac gloves and silk bachelor's gown and cap completed an eye-catching picture. And the gown, of course, would have usefully served as concealment for the shortness of the legs. Was Minnie impressed? Certainly he still wanted her to be, and persuaded the indulgent Mrs. William Sidgwick to speak to the child about what was still very much on his mind.

Benson's hour of teaching in school came in the morning. In the afternoons he rode on horseback all over Warwickshire (he was a keen horseman all his days), and Minnie, on her pony, used sometimes to go with him for part of the way. It was during these rides that he screwed up enough courage to decide that a serious talk with Minnie had by now become necessary and right. In an astonishing passage he noted it all down in his diary. 'In our rides, those charming rides, many little things occurred which made me believe that she saw something of my thoughts, and so at last the day came and I spoke to her. Let me try to recall each circumstance: the arm-chair in which I sat, how she sat as usual on my knee, a little fair girl of twelve with her earnest look, and how I said that I wanted to speak to her of something serious, and then got quietly to the thing, and asked her if she thought it would ever come to pass that we should be married. Instantly, without a word, a rush of tears fell down her cheeks, and I really for the moment was afraid. I told her that it was often in my thoughts, and that I believed that I should never love anyone so much as I should love her if she grew up as it seemed likely. But that I thought her too young to make any promise, only I wished to say so much to her, and if she felt the same, she might promise years hence but not now. She made no attempt to promise, and said nothing silly or childish, but affected me very much by quietly laying the ends of my handkerchief together and tying them in a knot, and quietly putting them into my hand. . . .'

It is a gruesome passage, but perhaps not so gruesome then as it seems to us now. The Victorian child, we need to remember, was very much thought of as the Victorian grown-up only not yet quite so large. John Stuart Mill began the study of classical Greek at the age of three, and in his *Autobiography* tells us himself that he 'never was a boy'. The children of the submerged nine-tenths of the population, with no pretensions to culture or even to the most elementary sort of education, were nevertheless obliged as a matter of course to bear a share in the physical labourings of their parents. They could make their way along the dark tunnellings of coal-mines without having to adopt that shuffling stoop so irksome to the fully grown. A chimney-sweep liked extremely young assistants because they weren't so liable to get stuck in the flues.

Yet all the same, Benson's phrase 'and then got quietly to the thing' can't avoid sounding sinister; and he must have been aware, if only half-consciously, that there was something quite shocking in what he was doing—or why should he choose the shame-faced vagueness of 'the thing'? The 'rush of tears' is perhaps simply Victorian, and a child's recognition of what would be considered the accepted thing to do. The tying of the handkerchief is a moving little bit of business. The child would know that something very serious was happening to her and reached for a child's play-symbol as the only way she knew of reacting to it.

The insistent question to be asked is: why did Mrs. Sidgwick not protect her daughter from Benson's absurd *schwärmerei*? Benson was certainly not acting behind her back; he was far too 'honourable' for that. But why a woman as intelligent as Mrs. Sidgwick should have given her approval is difficult indeed to understand. The answer must be that she, like so many others of her time, could see no clear distinction between childhood and adulthood. Mary Sidgwick, in her thirties and by now the wife of a successful, swiftly rising man, put down some revealing notes about the beginnings and the progress of this betrothal-in-advance, and the first one is amongst the most revealing of all: 'Mother rather feared than loved.' One must conclude from this that Mrs. Sidgwick and Benson between them had come to some understanding beforehand and that the child had been made aware that anything other than some gesture of acceptance on her part would have been frowned upon. There are other comments by Mary Sidgwick (Minnie, as Benson called her) which offer much enlightenment about her feelings over the ensuing seven years, but these can be more usefully considered a little later on.

Benson was now a fellow of Trinity and a Rugby master. For the fellowship he had had to wait a year because he came behind Lightfoot and Hort. But election duly followed in 1853. Faithful to Arnold's policies, Rugby maintained a strong, and well-paid staff. Goulburn's headmastership lasted till 1858, when he left to become a prebendary of St. Paul's and chaplain to Queen Victoria. Frederick Temple succeeded him, but by then, of course, Benson's seven years of waiting were nearly up. The staff was of course churchy in the extreme (Benson would have liked that) and very many were to become strong Victorian establishment figures: Highton, later Principal of Cheltenham College, R. B. Mayor, a Canon of St. Alban's, G. G. Bradley who became Dean of Westminster in 1881, J. C. Shairp, a close friend of Clough's and a Professor of Poetry at Oxford, T. S. Evans, Professor of Greek at Durham University, Charles Evans, Headmaster of King Edward's School, Birmingham, Beardmore Compton, Vicar of All Saints, Margaret Street and Prebendary of St. Paul's, T. W. Jex-Blake, Dean of Wells, A. G. Butler, Headmaster of Haileybury and then Vice-Provost of Oriel, C. B. Hutchinson, Canon of Canterbury . . . all zealous Christians rather than climbers, but still, Victorian England being what it was, they floated up—not undeservedly.

The ceremony of ordination followed for Benson in January 1854, and it was conducted, fully in accordance with the wishes of both, by Prince Lee, Benson's old headmaster, who by now had become the first Bishop of Manchester. (Prince Lee's temperament was quite disastrously unepiscopal; he was much better when dealing with boys.) Benson refused the offer of a Rugby boarding-house. This seems at first sight odd, because he would have been far better off as a house-master and there were demands upon his resources from the younger members of his family. He refused presumably because he enjoyed the life at Mrs. Sidgwick's Blue House and the proximity of Minnie whose development, both mental, spiritual and physical, he was, situated as he was, in the very best position to supervise. The lack of a boarding-house also left him a freer agent in the holidays. He travelled with Lightfoot, visited France and Italy, and in Rome was presented to Pio Nono. From Rome, on the last day of 1854, he wrote to his Minnie, who was still only twelve: '. . . the Pope was there. He sat in a great canopy on one side, there were 40 or 50 Cardinals all in their scarlet and white, for they had been staying on since the Council, and the scene was very grand. . . .'

Once back in Rugby he kept her at it. She must be fattened up like a turkey for Christmas. And more important than anything else, because she far outstripped a turkey in intelligence and was very sharp indeed, her mind must be seen to. Architecture, arithmetic, a serious attitude to life in general because she tended to be frisky—these were things to be cultivated. In 1857 he was not himself at all; he suffered neuralgia and pains of all sorts and was advised to give up Rugby and take up a full-time tutorship at Trinity which was now on offer. Yet he stayed where he was. Minnie's *Lehrjahre* were still very much in the forefront of his mind; and also by now there was the imminent retirement of Goulburn and the prospect of the arrival of Temple as headmaster, a lifelong friend and someone he knew he could work with.

It was probably on Temple's recommendation that Benson from extremely genteel poverty got his first real lift towards the majestic height he was eventually to reach. He was invited to become the first headmaster of Wellington College. The idea of such a new foundation came out of the busy head of the Prince Consort. The great Duke should be commemorated within a decade of his death, and how better than by founding a boarding-school which should offer, very cheaply, to the sons of army officers absolved prematurely by death of their parental responsi-bilities, an education which should compete on equal terms with the sort offered by Winchester, Eton, Rugby, Marlborough and the others? The school was planted in Berkshire heathland, the red brick looked very new, and the intake, by the terms of the endow-ment (which was, by the way, in no way generous), not of the kind likely to make swift and certain scholars of Balliol or Trinity. The place would probably develop into an unalleviated army class —solid, dependable chaps but with no Lightfoot among them to carry a banner and lead them through the complexities of the classical Greek verb.

Benson, with his drive, his certainties, and his ability to get his own way, probably felt confident from the very outset of his capacity to change a somewhat inauspicious beginning. On 20 March 1858 he wrote to Lightfoot to say that he had been offered, and had accepted, this pioneering job. The school, he said, was very much the Prince Consort's darling, and was not yet ready for opening. He wrote also to Minnie, and described his interview in the House of Lords. Prince Albert had been there. So had Lords Lansdowne and Derby. So had Sidney Herbert—in fact very grand grandees indeed had been there, and he had been appointed. So far as he could see he had been the only person up for interview. What was more, they were prepared to antedate his salary by three months—that is, they were going to pay him £200 straight away—'which is very handsome'. The headmastership, therefore, was to be worth £800 a year; and there was, of course, to

be a house—not a particularly gracious one as it turned out, but
still roomy and responsive doubtless to a woman's touches. He
wasn't to take up residence till January 1859, but was to spend the
intervening summer studying German and Prussian school
methods. (This, doubtless, would have been a stipulation of the
Prince Consort's.) Arriving therefore in Germany with *hochwohl-
geborne* recommendations, Benson was admitted to the best
society. He dined with Prince and Princess Frederick William at
Potsdam, and Baron Stockmar himself was present. Princess
Frederick William naturally knew Balmoral very well, and if
Benson did not know Balmoral, he did at least know Abergeldie
Castle which was not at all far away. Before he had gone up to
Trinity from King Edward's School, in that very hard-up summer
of 1848, he had managed to get a stop-gap job tutoring two boys
whose father had leased Abergeldie, and it was during that summer
that Victoria and Albert had taken the lease of Balmoral House.

He duly studied German educational methods, but doesn't
seem to have been at all impressed. This would have been a
disappointment kept to himself and his close friends, and not
something to be communicated to the Prince Consort. After he
had got back Benson wrote to Lightfoot about it on 26 October.
It certainly is not a letter by a man fired by new thoughts, new
visions. 'My tour was dullish work, tho' not uninteresting when
contemplated from a sufficient distance, nor uninstructive from
the same standpoint, but the fact was that I was *in school* all the
holidays.

'. . . The general gist of [my impressions] . . . I want to discuss
with you. . . . The vast superiority of English over German
classical schools, and (save a few giants in Germany) scholars also
—i.e. our run of scholars vastly superior, in sense, in feeling and
extent of reading to theirs.

'Their conceit is however unbounded (like ours). But they
know nothing of English education and told me gravely, and
refused to disown or give up, the most wondrous fictions about
our schools.

'My glimpses of 2 Courts were v. funny and v. pleasant.'

Well, that, anyway, must have been something.

By now, of course, Minnie was nubile. And Benson, with £800
a year plus house immediately in prospect, could talk to her not as
an extremely insufferable young man who had half-hypnotized a

girl-child into the symbolic tying of a knot in a handkerchief, but
as a responsible man of thirty with a well-paid job immediately
ahead. And he could talk to an extremely intelligent young woman
in her eighteenth year who had been intensively schooled by a
king among schoolmasters. Minnie knew much about the life of
Scipio Africanus; did she know as much about the physical
realities of being married to a mightily energetic, and almost
certainly sex-starved young man of thirty?

Very soon she was to know—even though Mrs. Sidgwick
('Mother rather feared than loved') had perhaps not found the
words to explain to her. On 23 June 1859 Edward White Benson
and Mary Sidgwick were married by Frederick Temple, who was
himself to succeed the about-to-be-married man as Archbishop
of Canterbury in 1896. They were married in the old church at
Rugby, and spent their honeymoon in Switzerland. Minnie, the
very young Minnie, had already for seven years—Benson himself
makes this quite clear—been able, if unknowingly, to preserve him
in the path of sexual righteousness.

2

A Passion of Tears

BUT ALL WAS NOT WELL with Minnie. The first of the auto-
biographical jottings she put down many years later has already
been noted. There were many others. Not even when she is young
woman enough to know what her Edward means by the word
'intentions' does she show any genuine signs of somebody in
love. He dominated her. She thought he was splendid, but 'Ed.
coming fear of him—love? always a strain—never the love which
casteth out fear'—this does not strike the glad, confident, morning
note. She wanted him to approve of her because she was frightened if ever he showed disapproval. Mrs. Sidgwick's conviction
that it was perfectly natural and easy for even a young female to be
genuinely in love with a person so obviously suitable as Edward
was plain to see. And as the relationship went slowly on, and
Minnie slowly matured, the exact nature of her anguish became
clearer to her. 'A terrible time. Dreary, helpless—from the first
the most fatal thing was the strain on my conscience and the
position towards Edward and Mama. He had been allowed to tell
me but was not allowed to speak but he *did*—and more hand-
embrace—etc. all weights on my conscience—and which did I
love best? it was not love that was growing for him. Oh the 1000
difficulties and complications! I lacked courage to bear his dark
looks—gloom—but I see now I *did not* love him. . . .'

And the older she grew the more certain she appeared to become about her emotional coolness towards him. 'Settling about
engagement and marriage. Still no *real* love, but influence. I knew
not God and his influence was the strongest I knew.' And 'his'

influence here is of course Edward's, because Minnie had neither
the understanding nor the possessing of Edward's all-consuming
religious feeling.

The last entry before her marriage has pathos; she is a small
twig caught at last in the irresistible pluck of the millstream. 'Then
towards March came engagement known—elation—sense of
being interesting—daily letters, but alas! no *real* what I know now
to be love . . . I was happiest when I knew E. happy and yet wasn't
with him . . . I read novels and eat oranges in the face of mighty
mysteries . . . so childishly, confidently, without stay or guide,
though trusting in God . . . only childish in understanding, I
married that June morning.'

She wrote him letters, love-letters, of the approved type, but
they were bookish and didn't at all come from the heart. Benson's
to her—and perhaps he too was not all that much clearer about
what he was embarking on—are at any rate, as one would expect,
much more specific. 'By this day week we shall sleep in Paris,
married life with its untried bliss will be a reality.'

The probabilities are that it was all very far from blissful.
Minnie's gasping, unshaped little memories point that way.
'Wedding night. Folkestone crossing. Oh how my heart sank. I
daren't let it. No wonder. An utter child, with *no* stay on God.
No real reference to Him in all my actions. Danced and sang
into matrimony, with a loving but exacting, a believing and therefore expecting spirit, a much stronger, much more passionate!
and whom I didn't really love. I wonder I didn't go more
wrong.'

Arthur Benson, who long afterwards wrote the official biography of his father, approaches the situation much more circum-
spectly, is remote and cloudy, shies away from his mother's
central phrases—'. . . a loving but exacting, a believing and therefore expecting spirit, a much stronger, much more passionate!'
Arthur is composing a pious monument to a Prince of the Church
and is careful to keep to a seemly tone. 'There was not a single
thought or plan or feeling which he did not share with her: and
from first to last her whole life and energies were devoted to
him. For many years she was his sole secretary. He consulted her
about everything, depended upon her judgment in a most unusual
way, and wrote little for public utterance which he did not submit
to her criticism. My father had an intense need of loving and being

loved; his moods of depression, of dark discouragement, required a buoyant vitality in his immediate circle.'

'An intense need of loving and being loved'—the second part of that is beyond question right. The active 'loving' part—well, in a way perhaps that is right too. But it had to be Edward Benson's way of loving. He could never very easily come at any understanding of the feelings, intense, genuine, sometimes inarticulate, of other people, even of other people whom he quite genuinely cherished. This blindness—and it is blindness, not neglect—is a useful disability in anyone setting forth—if not with any deliberate consciousness setting forth—on a grandly successful career.

Minnie acted out her part obediently and most capably—she had, after all, a much stronger, much subtler intelligence than her husband—along the lines described by Arthur in his biography. She had more to add to those little jotted memories of her honeymoon, and with what rueful clarity she recalls the situation. 'Paris. The first hard word—abt. the washing. But let me try and think how hard it was for Ed. He restrained his passionate nature for 7 years and then got *me*! this unloving, childish, weak unstable child! Ah God, pity him! misery—Knowing that I felt nothing of what I knew people ought to feel.' (Is her sympathy misplaced here? Would Edward Benson have found it possible to imagine himself into the feelings of a shy young female, with homosexual tendencies she would be quite unaware of, as she was tossed and gored? It is unlikely.) 'Knowing,' she goes on, 'how disappointing this must be to Ed., how evidently disappointed he was—trying to be rapturous, not succeeding, feeling so inexpressibly lonely and young, but *how* hard for him! full of religious and emotional thoughts and yearnings—they had never woke in me. I have learnt about love through friendship. How I cried at Paris! poor lonely child, having lived in the present only, living in the present still. The nights!—I can't think how I lived.' Fred Benson, her third son, when he came upon these notes long afterwards, made use of them, but not full use of them, in his book about his mother; but he does admit she 'danced and sang into matrimony with a loving . . . spirit . . . whom I didn't really love'. And all through the book Fred's sympathies are with his mother. '. . . he [his father] pounced on a fault (quite rightly) with a view to its correction; she (quite rightly), without condoning the sin, would set to work to comfort the sinner.'

There can be no doubt that very few young girls would have found Benson other than formidable. He was a man armed with certainties. His Christianity was somehow so totally unqualified as to be in a sense mindless. He swept along, brushing obstacles and objections aside, his swift advance checked only by his periodic bouts of melancholia, the glooms; and then it was for his Minnie, endlessly devoted but never really loving, to support him through his black mood. 'My father had an intense need of loving and being loved': these words of Arthur Benson, smoothest and discreetest of biographers, need repeating. But he does add, with a hint perhaps of sharpness in his tone, '. . . his moods of depression, of dark discouragement, required a buoyant vitality in his immediate circle'. Edward Benson, Arthur is in effect saying, was a very trying man indeed.

Were they sad to see him move on from Rugby to this rather new, rather unorthodox job, begun after he had expressed the greatest contempt for the German educational methods which he had inspected on his exploratory tour and which the Prince Consort had thought might prove so inspirational? The memorialists whom Arthur invited to contribute to his biography at this point emphasize his zeal, admire his energy, are amazed at his drive; but there are hints too that he could be a violent man. Lee Warner, afterwards a Rugby master, but a boy there in Benson's time, wrote: 'I have seen him commit grave mistakes in his discipline. Once he threatened to kick a boy downstairs.' 'He would call me up after tutor lessons if he saw that his impatience had frightened me, and make it up.' '. . . on another occasion he caned a boy without giving him time to explain; but on each occasion he publicly expressed his sorrow, so that, chastened himself, he more than recovered his position.'

So that was all right. How highly characteristic of Benson it is, by the way, that he should want to express his sorrow in public. In the good as well as the bad sense, Benson was always a very public man.

After the honeymoon they moved into the Master's Lodge at Wellington. They stayed there for fourteen years, from 1859 to 1873, and it was during those years that Benson established himself nationally as a coming man, a man to be reckoned with. He was only forty-four when he came to the end of his tenure, but no one by then had any doubt that here was someone certain to go fast and far.

He faced a difficult job. Wellington had no long history, no fame, no phalanx of grandee old boys willing to fight its battles in any difficult or dangerous situations which might arise. . . . Its too-bright red brick was new; its situation in those days, on the Surrey heathland, was remote. A marsh to the north Benson managed to convert into bathing-places; he tried to soften the Haworth-parsonage-harshness by a lavish planting of rhododendrons which liked the soil and situation and flourished mightily. The bare and daunting rigour of the place was, however, difficult to smooth away. The Prince Consort, who visited his child frequently in the early days, felt it, at the College's north-east corner particularly. Surveying the premises from this point one day he stopped suddenly in the manner of one who has suddenly thought of something. 'You want some tall trees there—poplars, I think.' And he dug his walking-stick into the ground half a dozen times, prod, prod, prod. The accompanying Benson turned immediately to an attendant to say: 'Put some marks into those holes.' And so, in due time, pages in the footsteps of Wenceslas, the poplars grew. Professor Munro said equivocally that the place reminded him of a Spanish convent. The kindest adjective Arthur Benson could find was 'stately'; but he was worried by 'a small walled garden to the east, with a rockery of broken carvings from the stoneyards, overlooked by a tall chimney vomiting smoke, very terrible to childish minds'. But the Queen herself came to open it, and they started with eighty boys.

The question of a uniform for them exercised distinguished minds, but again it was the Prince Consort who issued the clinching directive. He disliked the quasi-academic-ecclesiastical dress which was still clung to in many of the great English schools. It was, he thought, 'a badge of their monastic origin' and for that reason not well adapted, one supposes, to his rather shaky Lutheranism. A uniform of dark green was chosen. It had brass buttons and the trousers were plaid. The cap reminded one of the kind worn by postmen in the mid-century: it had red lines and a gilt crown over the forehead. The boys disliked it. Lord Sackville Cecil and the Hon. A. W. Charteris, both early pupils, found themselves, when loafing around the station, being handed used tickets by alighting passengers. Albertine infallibility did not include dress-sense, and he was man enough to admit this. Something less reminiscent of the working classes was devised.

The pupils did not necessarily come from stately homes where large libraries and Latin and Greek would have been since toddler days an ambience taken for granted. Placing some of these beginners in 1859 presented problems. Frederick Temple helped Benson in the initial sorting. 'Well,' said Temple to the first Hero's Son that came up, 'come and tell us what you know.' The boy was fat and ruddy, had a strong Scots accent, and scented mischief and traps on every side. He stuck to silence as the safest course. 'You've learned a little Greek, I daresay,' Temple prompted. 'No, sir, I don't think I've learned any Greek.' 'Well, Latin, then— Latin Delectus, Latin Grammar?' Feeling that his tactics were succeeding and thus emboldened, 'No,' the young Scot said again. 'I don't think I've learned any Latin! 'Did you ever do any algebra or Euclid?' This was going really well. 'Never sir. Never heard of 'em!' 'Well, arithmetic then?' Did the boy detect a tiny flush of impatience? 'I'm not sure, sir, that I know any arithmetic.' 'But you know some History and Geography?' 'No, sir, I don't think I know either.' Temple was beginning to feel he'd had enough. 'But you know *something*! You must have been taught *something* at your last school?' A straight denial here might go against him, the boy must have felt. 'I'm not sure, however,' he said, 'that I know anything.'

Benson was good at overcoming difficulties. He was a dynamo. He overcame these. He was an autocrat. If the place was to fail, it would fail through his own shortcomings; if it was to succeed, then the glory would be his. By the original constitution, matters concerning the estate, the catering and the general domestic arrangements were put in the hands of a secretary and a steward who were responsible not to Benson but to the Governors. But 'divide and rule' was not in his nature. The pleasure of being sole arbiter outweighed the strains arising from shouldering a disproportionate burden of work and responsibility. In 1867 he sent the Governors his manifesto: in Wellington College he must be almighty in all departments, and if the Governors could not accept Benson's notions of centralized power, then Benson would go. The Governors bowed to his wishes. Immediately, as if sensing his wish for an outward and visible sign, a flagstaff blew down, and Benson, whilst his Steward disagreed, gave orders for its replacement. And as the flag again fluttered, seven wild swans appeared on the lake. It was an omen.

As a headmaster he was fierce and terrifying: a great beater. He had been a Rugby master and knew that it was idle to shut your eyes and pretend that impurity amongst adolescent boys was a mirage. He caused barbed wire to be nailed round the tops of the dormitory partitions, taking the view that it was better to be safe than sorry. Educational thinking in the 1970s turns away in revulsion from this. We are aware, perhaps too much aware, of one of the great occupational dangers of headmastering: the imperceptible acquisition of a numbing self-righteousness. 'What, boy? You *lied*?' Then comes a pause for the inevitable 'Yessir'. And then: 'Go to my study to await my [retributive] coming'. It sounds like an altogether too easy, and too quickly assumed exercise of judicial powers. Yet one must see the headmaster's difficulty: his grip on a crowd of lively youngsters must be seen to be tight. The headmaster knows very well that if that grip is not immediately made manifest, his flock may rumble him for the faltering, fallible human creature he is, and they will be lost to him for ever. Really his hold is always, must always, be based upon an illusion. Benson, especially the young Benson, fully understood this. Witness the critical incident in 1866 when fireworks were let off against orders and the prefects, unable to nose out the offenders, decided to keep the whole school in for a half-holiday, and occupy them with the writing of lines, a much more pointless occupation than the picking of oakum. Benson was very reluctant to agree to this. He knew the prefects were being high-handed. He knew the school thought they were being high-handed. He feared it might, on this occasion, refuse to bow to authority. Benson asked that all masters should be on duty on the chosen afternoon in case of trouble. Benson himself could not keep himself aloof, but went, with a bundle of exercises from the sixth form, ostensibly for marking, to sit with Penny, his secretary, in his office. 'Penny,' he told him, 'I think this is the most critical day in the history of the College.' Penny, a senior master in College as well as secretary, thought so too. Both men felt the tension in each other until the news came that the calling-over had gone off without incident and that all had dispersed to school-rooms. There was still though the ticklish period between the end of detention and the final locking-up at 5.45. '. . . we took off our caps and gowns,' Penny says, 'and went for a short walk in the College grounds, taking care to be on the turf when the boys came rushing forth about 5.30 p.m. They were very excited, and reminded us of an angry swarm of bees which cannot make up its mind to settle anywhere. Some few took to punt-about, but there was a good deal of shouting and cheering and rough horse-play, apparently made with a view to attracting our attention. We however continued to walk up and down as if nothing unusual was happening, and presently they all dispersed into the College. . . .' Benson's backing of his prefects in their unjustified exercise of authority—so characteristic of the very young—Benson's bluff, in fact, had worked. Had he the right to feel pleased with himself? Any Victorian headmaster would have given a thumping Yes in answer to the question. Amongst their 1978 counterparts there would be a far from unanimous reaction.

Benson, at any rate, was enabled to go his masterful way. Arthur Benson says: 'Some old pupil has said that it was an awful sight to see the Headmaster fold his gown round him and cane a liar before the school. Awful, no doubt, it was; but the reason for his extreme severity to that particular fault lay, I believe, in the fact that it had been his own boyish temptation, and was therefore to be relentlessly combated in others.' This is a squalid reason for violence, and Arthur, whilst careful to say nothing directly, makes us aware that he considers it so. He goes on: 'But his severity had in it something painful, because it was with him, though he did not fully realise it, so unnecessary: he could have ruled by the tongue, and yet he did believe in and use corporal punishment to a conspicuous degree.'

Of course the position he found himself in, his tasks, were difficult and testing. He was a man who had come up from almost nowhere, yet he had to deal with and win over on his Governing Body magnates of the first order. On the death of the Prince Consort in 1861, Lord Derby became President of the Governors. Albert had been President at the time of Benson's appointment; in 1866 Derby was to become Prime Minister again. These were men who expected and got a high quality of service from those whom they were set over; they were not the sort of men to tolerate high-handedness from anybody. And Benson was always a man to whom high-handedness came naturally. He *must* make a success of

Wellington, a success of some kind, and preferably an academic success of the sort achieved by Rugby or Winchester or of his own King Edward's School—but his customers were on the whole sturdy and slow to study, not brilliant achievers like Lightfoot or Clough.

Benson too, it must be remembered, was operating from a very insecure personal base. He was poor—poor, that is, by the standards of those he was now mixing with. To find himself obliged to give up his job from lack of success would have wounded much more than his pride. He would have no private estate to retreat to, no private means to rely on, no study in which he could work on his *Life of St. Cyprian*, secure in a well-run household, the meals regular and sufficient, the children—they came along rapidly—supervised by ladies impeccably qualified.

The black bouts of melancholy and depression which he always suffered from, but more alarmingly and more frequently in these early days of his first testing job, were partly the result of the genes he was born with, but made worse, undoubtedly, by the trickiness of his situation as headmaster of a new school with a reputation all to make and with a Board of Governors which looked upon great expectations as a natural background to their existence. 'I believe,' Arthur Benson says, 'that he never attended a meeting of the Governors without saying gravely to my mother that this time he expected to receive his dismissal.' It was natural, perhaps, that he should grow morbidly suspicious, develop certainties that he was not being backed up by his staff. One of these was once told, in joky triumph, by a boy that he had dodged call-over and had escaped for the afternoon to the Ascot races. The master, himself not unnaturally considering it a little tale worth a little laughter, told a colleague about it. And so, inevitably, Benson got to hear of it. The master was summoned to the presence and experienced the awfulness of Benson's wrath. 'Want of honour and loyalty, inveterate love of gossip, unfitness for any position of responsibility. . . .' The young man had never passed through so disagreeable an experience. Penny, closer to Benson than the rest of the staff, knew all about these moods. '. . . one morning he came in to me evidently deeply depressed. I asked what was the matter and if he had had bad news. No; but he was feeling utterly baffled. His work here did not prosper. The Governors as a body hostile and on the look-out for the first sign of failure in his administration.

Worse than all, the boys he had to teach were so heavy and unintellectual, he found the Sixth a dead weight which it was impossible to bear up against. And here he burst into tears. . . .'

Those frequent Victorian tears shed by members of the then dominant sex were the almost expected accompaniment of that 'manliness' they all set so much store by. Perhaps they relieved Benson's tensions: certainly they were not the signs of weakness or of approaching collapse. His little turn would soon be over. Confidence, mastery, a sense of purpose fulfilled or at any moment about to be fulfilled soon came flooding back. A. W. Verrall, who was a boy at Wellington from 1865 to 1869, who was a scholar of distinction and became in due time Senior Tutor of Trinity College, Cambridge, was induced by Arthur Benson, when he came to write his father's biography, to make a contribution of memories of Benson as headmaster (Arthur Benson's biography is very much of a composite job, a piecing together of tributes from all sources with Arthur satisfying himself with the role of collator.) Verrall's portrait is full scale, and done with care and insight. 'As a Headmaster and always, to my eyes, he was, first of all, an unsurpassable actor of noble parts; and this he was by virtue of two qualities, first, the extraordinary range of his social and personal interests, and secondly, his high estimate of spectacular function as an index and monitor of such interests, a visible picture of society, directly corrective through physical sensation to narrowness, lowness and selfishness.' Does this boil down to Verrall's saying that Benson was a show-off and a climber? Are we to take 'the extraordinary range of his social and personal interests' as Verrall's quiet way of saying that Benson laboured energetically to cultivate people who would help him up to worldly eminence? Too much should not be made of this. Verrall was not a malicious man. But all the same he is perhaps just hesitating dislike. 'Very remarkable was his management of Speech Day. . . . The personages with whom he had to act . . . made a group in rank and power out of all proportion to the scene and to the natural height of his own office. . . . Yet I never saw, either then or for that matter afterwards any personage (with one single exception)'—this was Derby—'over whom, if and so far as it was proper, the Headmaster could not easily take the lead.'

But this getting on with the great was not, Verrall feels sure,

something done calculatingly. Benson had small intuitive understanding of people, whether they were youngsters, or members of
his own family, or grand and venerable elders. But he was, none
the less, passionately and unaffectedly *interested* in people. '. . . the
affairs of each person seemed to be more interesting in the eyes of
Benson, to look altogether larger and more significant, than the
agent himself esteemed them. . . .'

He was not popular amongst the boys. He beat them too much,
and he expected too much from them. When he taught he tended
always to be too much of the grammarian and the verbalist. He
cut great literature a bit too much down to his own size. The
young gentlemen got a little tired of his love of pomp and circumstance. He had roseate visions of the wonderful world he was
about to create, and these were so real to him that he often spoke
and acted, quite sincerely, as if they had already happened. One
sine qua non of every successful headmaster he did unquestionably
possess, and Verrall's sharp eye notes it unerringly. 'One quality
he had without which the most equal justice is in domestic
government the most pedantically absurd. He could ignore, without seeming not to know. . . .' This is indeed an important part of
the confidence trickery which it is needful to practise in the
government of the young when they are, as it were, always on
the edge of full awareness of the potentially overwhelming
strength of their numbers. Or at any rate in Benson's time, and
for a long while afterwards, it *was* an important part. Now that
schoolmasters and schoolmistresses have deliberately invited
their charges to rumble them, things may be wildly different.

At all events Wellington grew and prospered, and Minnie
struggled hard to keep up with him. She remained tactful through
his moods of deep gloom; she willingly took blame on herself
when he testily found fault with her. It should be remembered
that a boarding-school headmaster's wife, when she is only
twenty-one, has to learn to carry a burden disproportionate to
her years. It has to be kept in mind that Benson was not a rich
man. He had no personal funds to fall back on, to give him
confidence. He still had younger brothers and sisters more or less
dependant on him. The housekeeping side at Wellington was very
much in Minnie's hands—a large and responsible job requiring
experience. She wrote in her diary: 'I was very bad about bills. I
knew it was the one thing he dreaded and disliked—but I disliked

the doing of them, and dreaded the gloom'—she meant *his* gloom
—'they always brought and so, cowardly and improvident, I put
them off and lived in the present.' She had plenty of excuses besides her youth. She had babies. They were married in late June
1859, and Martin White Benson, her eldest son, was born on
19 August 1860. Arthur Christopher was born in 1862, Mary
Eleanor in October 1863, Margaret in 1865, Edward Frederick in
1867, and finally Robert Hugh in 1871. All of them therefore came
during the Wellington days, which did not come to an end until
1873. If Benson was not for one moment idle all that while,
Minnie as well must have been kept hard at it.

Benson's attitude to his children resembled his attitude to all his
other undertakings; he loved them very much, but in a glazed,
absolutist sort of way. He would lead and they follow. He knew
the way. As soon as they could get about on their feet he delighted
in taking them for walks in the fir woods round Wellington. Once it
got to about 1872, when they were all, except young Robert Hugh,
mature enough not only to walk but to put their thoughts into
some sort of words, they passed one day a flock of sheep with their
bells tinkling. This, he thought, was an occasion for co-operative
poetry, with himself, of course, as the ultimate shaper. It came
out hymn-like, and with a characteristic emphasis on the
führerprinzip:

> As the flocks together keep,
> With the leader of the sheep,
> So may we our Leader love,
> Safe and faithful forward move,
> Choose no thorny dangerous way,
> But by our gentle Shepherd stay.

> If we miss his warning look,
> He will use his guiding crook.
> Welcome check and welcome pain
> That brings us to his side again,
> 'Neath the shadow of the rock
> Where the Shepherd rests his flock.

There is a bit of not unintentional confusion here perhaps between
the Almighty and the Headmaster of Wellington College. He
liked so much to be in control of things and people, to be the
manager.

Minnie was his stay and comfort. He relied on her, not so much for advice about what he should do as for confirmation that what he had decided to do was beyond question the right course of action. She supplied this need. She was very young, utterly loyal, and easily overborne. He took her on a holiday early on, before her frequent pregnancies made her too much of a burden. This was to France southward as far as the Spanish frontier. Martin, his almost too loving friend and benefactor from Trinity, was of the party and perhaps, from his abundance, contributed more than his strict share towards the expenses. She should keep a full and detailed diary of all they saw and experienced, he instructed; and indeed that is what she did. Fred, writing his memories of his mother long afterwards, noted that 'she put down with incredible care all that interested not herself, but my father'. He dragged her about from church to church, from cathedral to cathedral, from altar to altar. Minnie was not greatly interested in ecclesiastical architecture. Successfully she concealed this flaw in her perceptive capabilities, and concealed also from him the immense physical weariness that stole on her through the long succeeding days. It was Sunday when they found themselves at Angers. They went to mass at the cathedral, and then back to the hotel for a more seemly Anglican service. But there were three more visits to the cathedral that day. Neither Nones nor Vespers nor Compline were missed. Next morning they were out again early bound for the cathedral, and then on from there to the church of the Holy Trinity. 'A very curious and interesting place,' Minnie dutifully notes, 'which I will not attempt to describe. Edward made a minute plan of the vaulting.' Poor Minnie, what did she do while Edward made a minute plan of the vaulting? One hopes that perhaps somewhere near, so that she should be under his eye, there was a bench under a tree. Oh, all those cathedrals. In the one at Bordeaux 'the triforium windows were larger than those in the clerestory'. There is an exhausted deadness about this entry. What Minnie wanted to say was: 'The triforium windows were larger than those in the clerestory and I do not give a damn.' But she suppressed the wish. Once Edward fell asleep on a wall whilst taking a brief break from his investigations. She put the fact down. She must have known perfectly well that this was not the sort of diary-entry Benson had in mind for his Minnie. But it went in—a tiny, rather moving hint at rebellion.

Mary Sidgwick acts throughout, in her relations with her husband, like a woman hypnotized. It is difficult for us, a hundred years on, to understand how someone of such extremely high intelligence as she had, could act consistently in such a spirit of total abnegation of herself, but she did, none the less, hold on to her inner, private certainties, and later on these were to make themselves felt.

He ruled by fear. He dominated. He strode about. He could allow passionate fury to overcome him. There is no one alive now to tell us what it was like to be a boy at Wellington in his day. But General Sir Ian Hamilton, born in 1853, can write of his experiences there quite without any show of outrage, that, because he could not overcome a habit of being late in school, Benson flogged him every day over a period of weeks. 'When I went to the bathing lake and stripped I became the cynosure and stupor of the crowd. The blues of the previous week had changed to green and yellow, whilst along the ribs under my arm—where the point of the cane curled—the stripes were dark purple.' Did Benson think this was right? Of course he did. He was a man corseted in frozen attitudes. Prince Lee had flogged—not Benson, certainly, because Benson as a schoolboy never stepped across the lines of perfect propriety—but certainly plenty of others. And so Benson flogged. Did he enjoy it? It was a question it would not have occurred to him to put to himself. But at any rate the flogging would have afforded a release for his fury that anyone, mature or immature, should diverge from the code of conduct laid down by Benson as the only code that could possibly satisfy the requirements of Almighty God.

He was not mean or vindictive—except of course that he could become infuriated by Minnie's overspending and financial flightiness. He wanted Wellington boys to grow up to be Christian gentlemen. He wanted them to work hard enough at their classics to make it possible, in a little while, for Trinity College, Cambridge, to admit them as classical scholars. When serious wrongdoing occurred at the school he was horrified and upset. Minnie notes one particular instance. She is carefully vague about the nature of the boy's crime, so that it seems reasonable to suppose that he had been satisfying his sexual impulses in the only way that seemed open to him.

'He [Benson] always felt most keenly anything that went wrong in the school, or at any serious fault in a boy: I remember well one special time; there had been great trouble about a boy; it was clear the offence could not be passed over, and that the boy must not remain in the school. There were several terrible interviews with the boy and his parents. The parents were broken-hearted, but bowed to the decision. He told me how terrible it was to see the meeting between the boy and his father; I don't remember any words now, but there was no severity, only deep grief. At last they took the boy away. That afternoon my husband and I started for a long walk, as usual, and went to Caesar's Camp, about three miles off, talking of all of this. There were magnificent Roman fortifications there, covered with fern. We sat down here as we always did, and in a few minutes he burst into a passion of tears. . . .'

Those manly Victorian tears again; how they recur. What was Benson crying for? A lost soul? But then surely, if he was, in the model of his Master, a fisher of men—and Benson would always want to claim that for himself—was it not his duty to try hard for some reclaiming, and not simply take the surely easier way of simply banishing into the outer darkness? Was it intensity of regret that human beings should so fail to come up to his standards? But if he took on so for a reason such as this, was he not himself being guilty of the sin of pride? Were they perhaps tears that flowed from a motive he was not himself in any way conscious of? Was he really asking for sympathy and understanding and love from Minnie? Did he want her to tell him how absolutely right he had been? This, I think, comes nearer to it. It is possible to detect, in Minnie's account of the affair, a certain reserve. Of course Edward was *right*. Edward was always right. But 'it was clear the offence could not be passed over'—she doesn't seem to be quite committing herself here. Clear to whom? To Edward certainly, but to her? Had she been in charge of affairs, you feel, there might not have been such tantrums, such a multiplication of broken-heartedness. No single word of this would have been uttered by her during that walk to the magnificent (and instructive) Roman fortifications. But it is possible that Benson, girt about with certainties as he was, might have become aware of a tiny querying, an almost imperceptible scratching at his defences. This would have been shattering to him, an eagerly taken cue for an emotional outburst.

The school grew and prospered. Parents were grateful for his firm leadership. His own family grew too—and the babies did not die in the common Victorian way. Perhaps the keen aromatic airs of the Berkshire heathland hardened them up. The headmaster's house became too small for comfort, especially as Ada Benson, Edward's sister, used to visit not infrequently. Ada was domineering, not a woman perfectly suited to spread sweetness and light in a crowded house. Edward, comfortably used by now to his immature Minnie, found that Ada took some of the shine out of his role as Master of all he surveyed. In 1865 he built a new Master's Lodge.

It was to his own planning and design. There was a large central hall, and round it on the first floor a gallery led to the bedrooms. He chose pitch pine for the woodwork, a type of décor then much in fashion. In his biography of his father Arthur Benson keeps pretty faithfully to the accepted tone of his time: the tone of unctuous panegyric. On the subject of the new Master's Lodge, however, which he must first have toddled into at the age of five, he lets himself go. 'The fittings were of pitch pine, then held to be a beautiful wood, the entrances and hall were distempered with a light lilac wash, supposed to be bright and cheerful, but inexpressibly dreary and inharmonious.'

On the whole Edward was a man who understood himself less well even than most—which is to say much. There are moments when he pauses to look at himself appraisingly, but these moments are rare. One of them comes in a letter he wrote to Minnie from Wellington (perhaps she was away visiting) in 1861. '. . . I wish I were more fit for my work. It is too great a work for me. I am not as keen and yet not as loving as I ought to be. The burden of all things seems to make me fidgetty from head to foot, so that I feel little comfort in leisure. I want a greater soul and a calmer way of looking at things. Where am I to get it? It seems to dwell in some books and to penetrate me while I am feeding on them—but Puff! it all goes when the clock strikes. I wonder if one will age into it, or fatten into it. I only wish it would come somehow—for I don't seem to have the spare minutes to philosophize myself into it. . . .'

Here he writes perceptively about himself—and, incidentally, about that quality of restless unease which is enormously more widespread amongst people today than it was in Benson's time.

Like many capable of violent activity and feverish enthusiasms, he was subject to moods of deep depression. No one, when he was in the middle of one of these, could persuade him that Wellington College wasn't swiftly travelling the primrose path to the ever-lasting bonfire. The boys were idlers, knavish and corrupt; the masters, young men for the most part, were no better. They *smoked*. Masters did, and boys did, and Benson, who detested smoking, knew that they did, and furthermore was convinced that both teachers and taught were in collusion to keep the evil fact from him. In his earlier days—in his Wellington time, that is —his moods tended to express themselves in bitingly ferocious attacks upon other people. His tongue lashed masters who condoned minor schoolboy crime—and Benson's nose for the scent of crime on his pupils was as keen as a hound's for the track of a terrified hare.

'I cannot think,' he said once, 'what makes my teaching here so ineffectual. I can only say that it was very different at Rugby.' Benson certainly had Arnold's vigour and drive; what he did not have was Arnold's intellectual power. Realization that this was so came to him only slowly and painfully.

The new Master's Lodge was, not unexpectedly, only the second of Benson's building priorities. The first was the Chapel. By the time the Prince Consort died in 1861 the income from fees was beginning already to grow substantially. Now was the time to begin building something beautiful which should be the focal point of a Christian School. He told the Governors—Derby now was President—that he had been able to persuade some of his friends to promise useful subscriptions. He got them to agree. But the place would have to be small—smaller, Benson warned them, than would satisfy the needs of Wellington once it had grown to its full intake. But he rightly felt that to make a beginning was the most important thing of all, and he flung himself into plans and preparations with the usual Bensonian brio. He was always a man to be captain of all he surveyed. So now he saw to the architecture, he saw to the stained-glass windows. Lord Redesdale, an unconventional dresser, was one of the Governors who could, on occasion, cause trouble. '. . . looking in his buff waistcoat, blue coat, gilt buttons, pumps and white tie, for all the world like a decent serving man, [he] recommended a transept. And the tide seemed to be setting that way to Scott's dismay

[Scott was the architect] and mine. But Lord R. has a happy knack of urging something very strenuously, and then retiring to the fire with a paper—and so his cause went. . . .' And Benson again got his way. Mr. Bingley and Mr. Butcher did the stone-carvings, and Benson watched them at it with the critical intentness of a works foreman before the days of shop-floor solidarity. He told Bingley his work was conventional, and Bingley felt strong enough on the point to go all the way up to London to consult Scott about whether he should take his orders from Benson. After that there came another pleased note in Benson's diary: 'Mr. Scott said he [Bingley] was in all respects to do what I wished.' Everybody at Wellington did as Benson wished.

He and his young family made friends round about. Clear of his glooms, Benson was always good at taking the lead in strenuous sociability. He came to be familiar with the disconcerting ways of Soapy Sam Wilberforce, Bishop of Oxford, who came to take his confirmations, and also, on 16 July 1863, to dedicate the completed Chapel. But not even Benson's dash and confidence could make any impression on Soapy Sam's startlingly personal way of conducting his life and affairs. Benson's first meeting with him was at the Bishop's London lodgings in Ryder Street, where Wilberforce had asked him to call to make arrangements for the coming visit. Arthur Benson describes his father's answering of the episcopal summons with a certain relish. 'My father, at some inconvenience to himself, went off by an early train, and was at the house at the time fixed. He waited for nearly an hour looking over some composition he had taken with him to employ himself. At the end of that time he heard a footstep slowly descending the stairs. The door was opened, and the Bishop came in, walking delicately, with a look of intense preoccupation, carrying in his hand an immense quarto Bible, which he deposited on a small table, and leaned his elbow upon it. My father always said that he had no doubt he had been reading it, and that it was convenient to him to bring it downstairs with him. But at the same time it had an indescribably theatrical air. He then asked one or two questions which my father answered to the best of his ability, with the depressing consciousness that the Bishop was not paying the slightest attention. In the middle of one of his answers the Bishop suddenly looked at his watch and said that he feared he had an engagement,—"a directors' meeting", my father used to opine,—

but that if he could wait until his return he had several suggestions to make. The Bishop then left the room in a state of abstraction, but returned in a moment with some letters which he opened and then said in his most engaging manner that he was terribly pressed for time, and that if my father could possibly in his absence answer one or two of the letters for him, it would be of great service to him. My father expressed himself delighted'—how strange that his tricky and violent temper should not have raised its cobra-head at this, if not, indeed, at some earlier, moment. It shows how wonderfully Benson's eagerness to have Wilberforce consecrate his new Chapel could strengthen his self-control—'and the Bishop indicated the nature of the replies desired. He then went away, laid them out on the table and directed the envelopes. A couple of hours passed; my father had had no food since the early breakfast, but he did not like to go. The Bishop at last returned; my father showed him the letters. "I am infinitely obliged to you" said the Bishop, and began putting them into the envelopes as fast as he could. My father said, "Won't you just look at them to see that they are what you would desire?" "I am sure they are delightful—perfection," said the Bishop with a benignant smile, and sealed them up. Then he asked a few more vague questions, and then graciously dismissed my father, who lunched at a coffee-house and returned home in haste. . . .'

A trying morning, but worth it, perhaps, because Soapy Sam did indeed come to consecrate Benson's new Chapel. Now Wellington College had its focal point; and it had all been Benson's work; and his school could now forge forward confident and complete. Wilberforce, brought down to Berkshire the day before, was still however capable of giving Benson cause for alarm. They were using Benson's own library as a vestry, and Wilberforce came in rather late, put on his robes, and then asked for a pen, ink and blotting-paper. 'They were provided; he then took out of his pocket a MS sermon, only half-finished, and began to write in a bold hand, quite oblivious of the conversation and movements of the clergy present. Presently a messenger came in to say that the Royalties had taken their places and that everyone was waiting. The Bishop was told; he smiled and said, "I daresay they can give me a few minutes," and wrote on, till my father was in despair. Then he deliberately blotted his MS, and signified that he was ready.'

But Soapy Sam was good at a deadline. The sermon passed successfully under even Benson's scrutiny, a sermon-fancier if ever there was one. A noble piece of Christian rhetoric, he thought, stately yet practical. . . .

Minnie did her best to keep up with him. She coped, not unsuccessfully, with the whirl and the social glitter which life with Benson involved. She was, after all, a very intelligent woman indeed, and once her firstborn, Martin—named after Benson's Trinity benefactor—had arrived, she grew somewhat in ease and self-reliance. Edward, she knew by now, had his weaknesses; his need of her was far far greater than her need of him. As a mature matron of twenty-three she entertained the widowed Queen, when she came down to see how Benson was forwarding Albert's purposes. The Queen toured the school, saw the maids emptying the slops, thought the tuckshop provided too much in the way of sweetstuffs. She then finished up at the new pitchpine Lodge where Minnie, in fullest fig, was ready to receive her. Minnie had turned the best spare bedroom into a sort of powder-room and had had a can of hot water put there all ready with a cosy over it to keep it warm in case the Queen's schedule should run late. Martin and Arthur and an infant girl were on view, and Martin told her she had a very funny bonnet. Minnie had poise by now though, and could laugh this off. It was as well, perhaps, that Benson was not present at the little encounter. The expanding family gathered friends around them too. Apart from the dark times Benson was a great social man, an unsurpassable actor of noble parts.

They became friendly with the Kingsleys,[1] who, at Eversley, were not far away. He was unconventional, wore a suit of rough grey cloth, with knickerbockers, and a black tie. Benson told him about his strenuous, investigative holidays abroad; and Kingsley told him that *his* notion of the way to relax after the daily round was 'to lie all day, of course, with your belly on a hot flat stone like a l-lizard in the sun, and think about nothing'. All

---

[1] Charles Kingsley (1819–75) was rector of Eversley in Hampshire from 1844 until his death. He was a gifted and prolific writer; his Christianity was of a very different kind from EWB's, having a socialist and populist slant far from wholly derived from the thought and writing of Carlyle and F. D. Maurice. His views on how human beings should conduct themselves sexually were 'liberated' in a man of his time and upbringing – and quite surprisingly so in a man of his cloth. 'A hearty, athletic, carnivorous clergyman' Professor Haight calls him.

this would have been baffling to Benson, and Kingsley's sudden fantastic outbursts at the dinner-table would have tested Minnie's hostess-tact. But she was learning. And Benson's handsome looks must have taken Kingsley's fancy as they had taken Henry Martin's, because Maurice, the Kingsley's eldest son, was entrusted to Benson's care at the school. Minnie would have been attracted by Mrs. Kingsley's gypsy good looks, and admired, from a modest and discreet distance, her dashing unconventionality. 'This is Grenfell,' Mrs. Kingsley told Minnie as she introduced her dark, younger son. 'He is going to be a Civil Engineer! He knows a great deal about Engineering already, but not much about civility.'

Kingsleys and Bensons got into the way of dining together at monthly intervals, and Minnie noted in her diary that these were meetings that gave them both 'extreme satisfaction'. When it was the Bensons' turn to entertain, Mrs. Kingsley used to say she felt 'on the heights'. The headmaster, still under forty, was so handsome, especially when astride a horse, which was a favourite pose, and to listen to the two men talking about education was wonderful. Of course, whether the talk was of education or of religion, Edward's positions were always much more conventional, much more predictable than Charles's; but that handsome physical presence was in itself worth so much. 'My husband,' Minnie noted, 'had been pleading with her [Mrs. Kingsley] once to get a better governess for the children—and specially that the youngest boy should be properly *grounded*—it was so important, he said, to lose no time so that he might be brought up to the standard of his age without pressure or cramming. Mrs. Kingsley looked gravely at him with her beautiful mouth twitching with humour. "Dear A—," she said, "I am sure we should all break our hearts if she were to go away—but she couldn't ground a gnat." Once when they had been talking again on the subject of conversation and Mr. Kingsley had vehemently stated that he believed everything connected with mind and brain to be a "fungoid growth on the body", Mrs. Kingsley closed the discussion by saying, "After all, Mr. Benson, the *body's* the thing, isn't it?" '

Did Kingsley ever properly understand where Benson stood, either on education or religion? It is doubtful. There can be no doubt that Benson's intentions, as a schoolmaster, were always to edge away from the suitable training of the sound, solid,

practical and perhaps wooden-headed types—which had undoubtedly been much in Prince Albert's mind when he was
formulating his ideas about the place—and to turn the school
more in the direction of Rugby, where the brilliant, classically-
minded few were forcibly fed like geese in Gascony. And there can
equally be no doubt that the governors themselves were not
entirely behind Benson in his determination to shape Wellington
into a model Victorian public school. Disraeli, for example, one of
the governing body, did not like what he saw, lost interest and at-
etnded only one policy meeting. Kingsley likewise would have had
very different notions of the way a school should be run. 'Their
friendship was very strong and enduring,' Minnie says, but adds:
'It was not founded on agreement only, for they often differed, but
the freshness and originality and intensity of Mr. Kingsley
delighted my husband to the core, and there was great affection
between them.'

As for religion—well this might be an appropriate moment to
consider that strange phenomenon—Benson's churchmanship.
That decade, the 1860s, was one of violent excitement and agitation about religious matters: the ferment was everywhere and it is
difficult for us now to understand it. As G. M. Young put it forty
years ago: 'At no time since the seventeenth century had English
society been so much preoccupied with problems of doctrine and
Church order: at no time had the Establishment been so keenly
assailed, or so angrily divided within itself. A misjudged appointment to a bishopric or deanery might influence a bye-election, or
provoke a cabinet crisis. Church policy could shake a Government.'

Bradlaugh was pamphleteering under the name of 'Iconoclast';
Leslie Stephen, a young don at Trinity Hall, 'became convinced
among other things that Noah's Flood was a fiction . . . and that
it was wrong for me to read the story as if it were sacred truth. So
I had to give up my position at Trinity Hall. Upon my stating in
the summer of 1862 that I could no longer take part in the chapel
services, I resigned my tutorship at the request of the Master.'
Bishop Colenso was removed from his see of Natal by Bishop
Gray of Cape Town because he had become convinced of similar
improbabilities in the scriptures. 'Do you believe all that?' a Zulu
member of his flock had asked him, and Colenso, searching in his
heart, found that the answer had to be No. His candour caused

outrage and conflict. Science was beating upward on a strong
wing, and people reasonably calling themselves rationalists, were
looking aloft and admiring. Matthew Arnold, although he had
listened to all that robust and confident sermonizing in Rugby
Chapel in the late 1830s, found uncertainties creeping up on him
on every side. The robust cohesiveness of human society was
crumbling away. Man in general, like Mrs. Gummidge in particular, was 'a lone lorn creetur', and when, in 1867, he published his
New Poems, there was one particularly beautiful acknowledgement
of disquietude called 'Dover Beach'. Who now possessed eyes
sharp enough to see divine purposes rising up in front of them,
clear, sharp, reassuring and resplendent—like Table Mountain
rising out of Table Bay on a clear bright morning? '. . . we are
here as on a darkling plain,' he wrote,/'Swept with confused
alarms of struggle and flight,/Where ignorant armies clash by
night.' Even the Privy Council felt obliged to wriggle and to
indicate, if only tentatively, an escape-route. Although Scripture
contained the Word of God, the Privy Council thought, it was
not *in itself* (my italics) the Word of God. The Church of England,
tenacious occupier of the middle ground, now felt itself pushed
and pulled in contrary directions by extremists. People like Bradlaugh or G. W. Foote were of course simply unspeakable. But
what was to be done about Newman and the Tractarians?
Weren't they far more dangerous by virtue of their very holiness?
And had not Newman written in 1862: 'I do profess *ex animo* that
the thought of the Anglican service makes me shiver'?

The point about Benson is that if the question the Zulu put to
Bishop Colenso had been put to him, he could have replied,
instantly and without qualification, 'Yes, I do believe all that.' He
was never a mystic in the manner of George Herbert. He was
religious, in a practical, almost thoughtless, way; he believed in
the way a man believes a four-legged chair will support him as he
lowers himself into it. That letter he wrote to the Unitarian Baker-
relative all that while ago when he was still an undergraduate and
suddenly the sole provider of the needs of a large family can stand
as a final statement of his position. He was a middle-of-the-road
Anglican, with a liking for ceremonial because he was 'an
'unsurpassable actor of noble parts'. The Gorham Judgment,
which pronounced that no priest was under obligation to believe
in Baptismal Regeneration, caused no ripple in Wellington.

Benson felt neither relief nor outrage on account of it. It did not seem to matter. People excitedly thought him a High Churchman; people just as excitedly thought him a Latitudinarian. He was both. He was neither. He swept grandly and intently along licking Wellington into shape, noting that controversy was flapping about in rather an ugly way but not being really concerned. When *Essays and Reviews*, a collection of pieces by contentious theologians, appeared in 1860, a long letter appeared in the newspaper the *Record*, alleging that the Headmaster of Wellington College had presented a copy of the book to the boys' library. Benson wrote a correction; he had presented it to the Masters' Library, a place barred to boys; and he added that he thought 'the nature of the Masters' profession made it desirable that they should study works of very various tendencies. . . .'

Arthur, describing all this, adds: 'It is curious to note how difficult it is at this date to define exactly his ecclesiastical views.' It was difficult not only at this but at all dates. A female parent wrote to one of the Governors to complain that she smelt whiffs of Tractarianism in Wellington College Chapel. The Governor sent the letter along to Benson, inviting a reply. He got one. '. . . You know how anxious we are to give no just offence. We must have *system* in a school, where order and discipline is everything; but if anyone could point out a more unobjectionable model I should be happy to follow it. I think nothing of such matters myself, and think it wrong and foolish to offend conscience by trifles. I am myself neither High, nor Low, nor Broad Church, though I hear myself by turns consigned to all—as often to one as to another. . . .' Long after Benson was dead, Hugh, his youngest son, tried to mark out the religious ground upon which his father stood, but had to confess to lack of success. Benson's flexibility worried the much more absolute Hugh. 'Now I am perfectly convinced that my father did not believe himself inconsistent—that he had, in fact, principles which reconciled to his own mind these apparent contradictions. Yet I never knew, and do not now know, what they were. For, though he loved nothing better than to be consulted by his children on religious matters, as a matter of fact he was not very approachable by timid minds. I used always to be a little afraid of showing ignorance, and still more of shocking him. Never once, in a genuine difficulty, did I find him anything but utterly tender and considerate; yet his intense personality and his almost fierce faith continually produced in me the illusion that he would think it unfilial for me to do anything except acquiesce instantly in his judgment; the result was that I was often completely at a loss as to what that judgment was. . . .' Benson's moral stance young Hugh found equally puzzling. 'He had a very great sense of the duty of obedience,' he wryly says. But was this really quite enough? Should there not be grades of wrongdoing? Lying, thieving, cruelty—these were abominable and Benson was instantly prepared to cast them down into the pit of Hell. 'But beyond these,' Hugh says, 'practically all other sins seemed to me about the same; to climb over wire fences . . . by putting one's feet anywhere except at the point where the wire pierced the upright railings—(my father bade me always do this to avoid stretching the wire)—seemed to me about as wicked as to lose my temper, to sulk, or to be guilty of meanness. In this way, to some degree, one's appreciation of morality was, I think, a little dulled. . . .' Benson's ability to inspire awe and fear in his own children was felt by all of them except perhaps Fred, who was the toughest of them, and could mock. But Arthur, who wrote the official biography and who was himself a large and important man, had to admit: 'It was always a certain strain to be long alone with him.' So perhaps we ought to say, in order to sum up this side of him, that he was, perhaps to the end, a headmasterly churchman rather than a holy churchman.

Apart from the Kingsleys, the important new friends of the Wellington days were the many Wordsworths. John Wordsworth, son of Christopher Wordsworth, was born in 1843 and in the middle 1860s did duty for a time at Wellington as sixth form classics master; it was through him that Benson came to know his father, then Archdeacon of Westminster. In 1868 Disraeli made Christopher the offer of the Bishopric of Lincoln. The Archdeacon was staying with the Bensons when the offer was received, and, characteristically, he dithered. His was not a particularly strong mind and what there was of it did not much run on earthly things like bishoprics. He wrote a refusal, but Benson, twenty-two years the younger, put this aside as feeble, and the result was that late in 1868 Christopher Wordsworth became Bishop of Lincoln.

The new Bishop had a daughter, Elizabeth, who was twenty-eight at the time of his translation. Minnie was just one year younger, and had a surer understanding of herself by now. She was the mother of three sons and two daughters. Only Hugh, born in 1871, remained to be, perhaps reluctantly, conceived. Elizabeth Wordsworth attracted her, and, in her private writing, Minnie was frank with herself about it. 'Oh my vanity! . . . I thought she was thinking of and looking at me when far other and nobler things occupied her.' What these nobler things were we can only guess at, but Edward Benson, at thirty-nine, was still a man to take a woman's eye; but he was not, either at thirty-nine or at any age, a man upon whom sexual desire made urgent demands. And there were other Wordsworths, many other Wordsworths, besides Elizabeth. Christopher, holy and unworldly as everyone assured everyone else he was, had his quiver full. There was Mrs. Wordsworth, placid and affable; there were Mary and Priscilla, Susan and Dora—'sisterly spirits' Arthur calls them—and John, of course, later to be Bishop of Salisbury, but now Benson's appointee and the bringer of the two families together. Finally there was the second, youngest Christopher, studious, still at Cambridge this one, and also intending holy orders, like all the male Wordsworths apart from the great pantheistic Progenitor who was himself at this time only eighteen years dead.

Certainly Elizabeth Wordsworth looked at Benson very closely indeed. Both families took holidays together, at Whitby in 1869 and Ambleside in 1870. 'In those days,' Elizabeth says, 'he was, I believe, the youngest-looking of Headmasters, and this look of youth lasted quite into middle age . . . I think I should say that eagerness, fervour perhaps would be a better word, was his main characteristic. I always used to notice the size of his eyeballs, which when he was excited, showed more than in an ordinary man's face. He had the hands too of an enthusiast, every finger full of character and vigour. It was a pleasure to see him handle anything. . . .' And you feel that if only Minnie would conveniently die, Elizabeth would like very much that Benson should handle her.

Once Bishop of Lincoln, Wordsworth made Benson his chaplain, and Elizabeth notes, with what undercurrents of feeling one may only imagine: 'When he first appeared in his chaplain's scarf in the Chapel at Wellington College it was popularly supposed by the 4th form boys that Mrs. Benson had died in the night and that he had promptly adopted this method of going into mourning for her. So at least the story runs (*ben trovato*).'

By 1869 there can be no doubt that Benson was beginning to have had enough of Wellington. He was offered the living of Dorking but this he refused. It was worth £500 a year and this was not enough for a man who had to live by what he earned. By accepting a Canonry he could have made do, but that he would not consider because accepting a Canonry would have meant condoning pluralism, a practice he always strongly disapproved of. Also in 1869 Temple ceased being Headmaster of Rugby in order to become Bishop of Exeter. Had he wished, Benson could without doubt have succeeded him at Rugby; but it had become clear to him that he did not want to spend all his life schoolmastering. In his debatings with himself over whether or not to accept Rugby it was Elizabeth Wordsworth, rather than Minnie, whom he made his confidante.

Minnie, indeed, had lost her liveliness and even her dependability. She had, it must be remembered, been bearing children with testing Victorian frequency; and Edward's dominating qualities, his pauseless energy, his religious certainties which she could not feel—a young woman of twenty-six was being subjected to pressures strong enough and persistent enough to turn her into a neurotic. Edward undoubtedly took the greatest interest in his children; he took them instructive walks; he was their lord, master and shepherd. Minnie felt herself pushed, not of set purpose but simply in the nature of things, into the role of elder sister rather than that of mother. Suppressed rebelliousness must have smouldered. After all she was very far indeed from being a naturally submissive nobody. The very young children were quite aware, as they always are, of the unspoken tussles between the parents on the question of the usefulness of strict sternness in the bringing up of the young at all stages. Fred, writing long afterwards when he himself was an old man, remembered it all exactly as it was. '. . . his ways were different from hers: if people had done wrong, he was stern with them. No doubt that was quite right, for he was anxious for their sakes that they should not err again, and if they were well scolded, that would help them to keep straight. But her plan was otherwise: if anyone was suffering even for his own fault, her instinct was first of all to make him happy again at once, and after that it was time to see about being good. "And though he was right," she wrote, "I was right too. . . ." '

A gap of four years separated the coming of Fred in 1867 and the birth of her last child, Robert Hugh, in 1871. During those years she was not perhaps so constantly under his influence because his close connections with Wordsworth took him frequently to his fine palace of Riseholme, near Lincoln. Minnie tended to stay at home. On 31 March 1869 he wrote her a long letter, describing the enthronement, and concluded: 'Your most loving husband—with regrets after all that I didn't bring you by might.' But she remained invalidish and at home. On 4 January 1870 he wrote to her again, this time from Borrowdale; he was there holidaying with Lightfoot and Westcott—after another little stay at Riseholme. The Wordsworths, all the Wordsworths, clearly enchanted him. 'I can't tell you,' he told Minnie, 'the inexpressible calm sweet sisterliness of the four at Riseholme. If you had been there it would have been *perfect*. Mrs. Wordsworth is so busy and motherly affectionate and the Bishop not only kissed me but put his arm round. To have so sunk into the bosom of such a house and to feel that they not only love one, but love one with all one's faults which must be nearly as well known to them as to you, that is a thing which ought to encourage one to higher ways of feeling. And then those two friends here [Westcott and Lightfoot]. But of all blessings you are the crown. Do keep yourself well and strong that you may be a blessing always: if you were to have ill-health what good would my life do me?'

So there it was. It was Minnie's duty to shake off any megrims because what would Edward do without her? But by March 1871 she had conceived again. Benson kept busily at it both by night and day. The Church was opening her arms to him wider and wider; he had turned down the headmastership even of Rugby and this could mean only one thing; he was certain that a life of the grandest ecclesiasticism lay open before him. In July 1871, with Minnie already beginning to be heavy with Hugh, he went to Windsor to preach before the Queen. He wrote to Elizabeth Wordsworth, telling her all about it. 'Last Sunday I had a singular and interesting change. I went to Windsor to preach to the Queen and saw something of and *much admired* Mr. Gladstone. His eyes alone afford sufficient reason for his being Prime Minister, and we talked of anything and everything (except cathedrals), as if he had not another thought in his mind except to know all the knowable in literature. Court is a formidable atmosphere no doubt, only peculiar circumstances could flourish there, but they have a peculiar grace of their own.' Benson was pleased. He had made a favourable impression on the man, above all others, who counted.

But it would not be right either to think of Benson as a worldly, ambitious man in any calculating way. It was just, somehow, that he happened to do the right things and say the right things when it was crucially important that the right things should be done and said.

After Hugh's birth in November 1871 Minnie became very ill indeed. Her malady was one which Victorian medicine could do little about. She slept badly, she had giddy fits, occasionally she lost her memory. She went off to the Wordsworths to try to recuperate amid the splendours of Riseholme. But it was only right, Edward felt, that she should be in her place at Wellington for Speech Day, and so back she came, in very poor shape indeed. Her brother Arthur Sidgwick, seeing her about then, felt very worried indeed about the way she was looking. Did he perhaps think that Edward was showing a certain lack of concern? At any rate he suggested that Minnie go right away from the whirl of Wellington. Why not a recuperative period abroad with Edward's crippled younger brother Christopher and his wife Agnes whose father held a professorship at Oxford? The Christopher Bensons lived in Wiesbaden which would be reposeful and, comparatively, irreligious. It had not been a marriage which Edward had approved of, but he was in a whirl of decision-making by then and probably because of this managed to lay aside his managing ways for long enough to express his abstracted consent. So Minnie went. And indeed her intention might well have been never to come back to him. A woman, a Miss Hall, was boarding with the Christopher Bensons, and Minnie's emotions were aroused. Could it have happened, she wondered in her diary long afterwards, 'if I had loved God then? . . . gradually the bonds drew round—fascination possessed me then the other fault. Thou knowest I will not even write it. . . .' She wanted to stay on over Christmas (1872). Edward thought she should be home for the festival, thought she was being extravagant in sending presents to the children, and expressed himself on these points to her in tones of headmasterly reproof. This caused her to slip back again into her neurasthenia, and there was no question of her being able to be home in time for Christmas. Miss Hall was a sympathetic nurse.

3

My Dear Wife Mends Slowly

IN THE MIDDLE of all this Bishop Wordsworth offered Benson the Chancellorship of Lincoln Cathedral. For someone in Benson's position, headmaster of a thriving public school built up from nothing by his own labours, earning £2,000 a year which was in those days handsome enough, accepted on all sides as a coming man, an ecclesiastical presence, the job was an astonishingly modest one; it meant really that he was to train, and lecture to, candidates for holy orders. True, a Canonry went with it, but all the same by going to Lincoln he would be halving his salary. Why was he so attracted by such a prospect? Well, it must always be remembered that Benson was never a careerist in the sense that he carefully and calculatingly mapped out a route to the summit. He liked the recognition that success brings—who does not?— but it had to be success in a venture he considered important. There is no doubt that he was a naturally gifted teacher in the manner that was considered proper and purposeful in his time— which doesn't at all mean, of course, that a hundred years later his methods would not encounter the fiercest opposition. Among his many certainties there was none more unshakeable than this; he did believe in the enormous influence of teaching, of up-bringing, on a human being. To have a hand in this process was a vocation worth following; and at Lincoln he would be dealing with mature people dedicated to serve the Anglican faith— whereas at Wellington there had always been so many, however hard he had tried, who were stupid and indolent and not dis-inclined to sin. So he accepted. Bishop Wordsworth made the offer on 9 December; on the 12th he wrote to accept—so it was quick work. 'My two counsellors,' he told Wordsworth, 'are of one mind. . . . My third and best counsellor is not in England [Minnie was far away in Wiesbaden, with Miss Hall to look after her] but has so always and eagerly lived the every thought of a Cathedral home, that I know I may leave the communication of that opinion to another day. . . .' How sure of her he always was, and how hard—too hard?—she tried to respond.

On 9 January 1872 he paid a visit to an old school-friend. This was Purbrick, who, twenty-four years before, had left King Edward's School, Birmingham, for Christ Church when Benson had gone on to Trinity. Almost immediately Purbrick had become a Roman Catholic, and was now Rector of Stonyhurst. Benson's description of his visit is interesting especially as showing the robustness of his Anglicanism as well as his belief in the abiding strength of school influences, however variously adulthood may shape the man. 'Yesterday after a long tiring journey I arrived at Stonyhurst. It was too dark to see my route from Whalley but we were going uphill all the way. It rained vehemently. I began to read Cyprian's *De Lapsis* as I left Birmingham by L.N.W. and finished it with the last flicker of my reading-lamp as I neared the College and saw its lights. . . . He [Purbrick] wears his cassock and a sort of unbecoming sleeveless gown—grey socks and slippers made his humanity very cosy and close—and as we sat in large heavy old oak chairs with our feet over a blazing fire, it seemed as if 24 years were rolled back and we were sitting as once we sat in my study, night after night, at school, talking the talk which after all more than anything has made him what he is and me what I am. . . .' Here surely is the explanation of why he should find the offer of the Chancellorship of Lincoln so instantly acceptable. He would be taking part in the moulding of human character. Here at Stonyhurst he could walk and talk with Purbrick and 'feel that his faith and mine put no barrier between us in love . . .' while at the same time his robust Anglicanism could express itself without any feeling of constraint. '. . . After service he [Purbrick] dropped on his knees and said one Pater and three Aves for the Pope. It is thus that one suddenly pulls up to wonder if we are beings of the same sphere. So after, we passed through a sort of cloister dimly lighted with fathers and boys on their knees before an image with a little light before it, "to which" (Father Purbrick afterwards

told me) "the boys have here a special devotion." Think of the
Wellington College or Birmingham boys transformed into this!
I was amazed to hear this baseless nonsense, this mathematics
applied to things eternal, gravely poured out by an honest
believing gentleman. . . . I hate using hard words'—this, on Benson's part, is simply to use thoughtlessly a form of words; he used
hard words often and relished using them—'but if superstition
means the holding fast with blind eyes to that which has no
meaning in itself . . . then it is superstition to have been driven
to this lonely eating, this whispered consecration. . . .' Yet all this
robust rejection, this quite purposeful misunderstanding of all
that Purbrick was up to, in no way weakened the bonds of
friendship formed with the Jesuit in that Birmingham school a
quarter of a century earlier. 'The sight and company and converse
on many dear things of my dear friend is more delightful than I
can say; I walk beside him and feel that his faith and mine put no
barrier between us in love. And then suddenly he says something
that would incline me to say "are you ill?" so completely it seems
to belong to a world where reasoning is mere sequence of
words. . . .' Benson was not, then or ever, an ecumenically-
minded man. He was a dictatorially-minded man.

He did not finally give up Wellington until the end of the
summer term 1873, and all this while he had to do without his
Minnie. Arthur Benson, writing the official biography of his
father, keeps very quiet about it. 'My mother was ill at the time
we moved, and was much away. . . .' That is about all we get from
him. And yet the marriage of Mary Sidgwick and Edward Benson
must during these months have begun to look very shaky indeed.
That it should totally fail was of course inconceivable. A man in
Benson's position, holding the unqualified views which he held,
simply could not have allowed it. But he must have been under
great strain, and so of course must Minnie. Her diary entry
summing up the Wiesbaden episodes is vague and confused and
full of mental stress. 'I haven't gone and I can't fully into the way
I wronged my dear ones here [in Lincoln by now]—I lost my
head—and blessed be Thy name O Lord, I came to grief. The
letter—ah! my husband's pain—what he bore, how lovingly, how
quietly—our *talk* my wilful misery—my letter to her. Ah Lord,
how blind thou allowedst me to get.' It is easy to understand her
'how quietly'. Edward would have understood the need for

desperate tact, the extremest discretion. Any whisper of troubles of this domestic kind would have been ruinous to him. For fourteen years he had been taking his wife too much for granted, had been treating a highly intelligent woman, overstrained by too frequent child-bearing, as if she was still the eleven-year-old child he had decided, so astonishingly well in advance, to marry. That final, lonely summer term at Wellington, with all its ceremonies and emotional leave-takings, must have been testing indeed. Yet he got through it in the seemliest, stateliest fashion. At Speech Day the new Duke of Wellington, an inarticulate man, tried in public utterance to put Benson's achievement into words. His effects were blurred, to put it mildly, but after lunch he said it all again to the headmaster privately. 'Made a hash of it—knew I should. Always do. But I really did try to say something this time. When the money was subscribed for a Memorial after my father's death, I and my family hoped that there would be a fine monument set up in his memory in every considerable town in England. And you can fancy what our feelings were when we found that it was going to be lumped together and a Charity School built with it where scrubby little orphans would be maintained and educated. . . . What good would that have been to us or to them? By great good fortune the Governors found you . . . and now *you* have made the College what it is . . . one of the finest Public Schools in England. . . . There,' his Grace dug Benson in the ribs with his elbow, 'that's my speech. . . . But Lord when I stood up to speak it all ran out at my heels.'[1] Whether this patrician stuff was exactly what Benson wanted to hear is something to guess about, but probably it was. There was worldliness in him (a bit), and other-worldliness too (a lot), the latter of a kind difficult for us now to understand. What were his thoughts about the millions of sub-human poor all around him? He must have known, much better than the second Duke of Wellington, all about them. After all he had been brought up in Birmingham, not in poverty certainly but in circumstances which his Grace would have described, had he been able to find the words, as considerably reduced. Only a year or two before that summer of 1873 he had been up in Manchester for the funeral of his old headmaster,

---

[1] his account comes from the memories of the Rev. C. W. Penny, one of Benson's assistant masters at Wellington, and is quoted by Arthur Benson in his biography of his father (Macmillan 1900, p. 357, Vol. I.)

Prince Lee. There he would have seen plenty of scrubby young-sters, orphans and other. He did not wilfully disregard the appal-ling conditions in which the vast majority of his fellow-country-men were condemned to live; it was simply that he passed his days before the social conscience had blazed into life. Material well-being, did it matter so much? Benson, quite sincerely, would probably have answered No. Think of him pounding northwards in the winter cold towards Stonyhurst and reading the words of St. Cyprian by the failing light of his personal little oil-lamp. The Victorians were accustomed to discomforts and nastinesses and sudden death. They had most of them smelt the stinking Thames, were inured to the swift pouncings of typhus and cholera—the second Duke of Wellington just as surely as any scrubby orphan.

On the last Sunday of the summer term of 1873 Benson preached his parting sermon before the school. The peroration was long; it was intended to leave its mark, and on many it did. It is as good a statement of the strength (and, not by Benson's in-tention, of the weakness) of the Victorian public school as we shall find. '. . . how can I thank God for His works of grace, for the unfolding of high principle and the expansion of strength and the kindling of Christian fire? for such power there has been in our prefectural order. . . .' It is the voice of the Arnold of the 1830s still sounding strongly over thirty years on. '. . . I have seen near a thousand men go away to labour in their turn where and as duty summoned and God ordained. . . .' These were the men who very soon indeed would be exercising dominion over the greatest empire the world has ever known. And on and on Benson went, to the last ringing paragraph of all. Will the systems we have arranged, he asks, work as adaptably to the needs of 700 years to come as those of the past? 'Yes, if ours is built on humanity's best, on a true perception of humanity's needs, on . . . eager acceptance of God's work in man and through man. . . . If we trust the same cornerstone . . . so shall we be part of the Living Temple of God. . . . So shall your hearts beat with energy. . . . For you will be men. You will seek Purity, that the souls and bodies you offer to those you love . . . may be white and un-spotted. . . . But that these things may be, you must fix eye and heart unflinchingly on Christ and his Reproach; you must adore it, you must achieve it, for there is no treasure like the Reproach of Christ, understood, loved and lived.'

3

Arthur Benson was eleven by then, and says he was affected almost to tears, and many other eyes were wet, he assures us. And then after the evening service—a hot summer night, it was, with little puffs of wind, the whole school waited in the Quadrangle to say goodbye to him, and Minnie at last was back, and before going out Benson waited in his stall for his family to gather round. Then he shook hands with his colleagues and walked through the cloister lined with boys who silently stretched out their hands to be shaken. 'My father,' Arthur says, 'walked along with quick steps, his surplice and hood swayed by the wind which blew in through the grilles of the cloister, his face streaming with tears. In the court he was cheered by a crowd of boys; he smiled and waved his hand; at the door by the Masters' library leading out towards the Lodge, as he unlocked it, a number of Prefects who were gathered there pressed forwards. "Goodbye, my dear, dear fellows," he said falteringly; and as he went out into the dusk, I remember a cry of "God bless you, sir." ' General Sir Ian Hamilton, the black and blue and green of his bruises faded, would have missed it by a year or more because he was twenty by then. Or perhaps, for an occasion so thick with complex crowd emotion, he came back; youngsters of the middle and upper class of his generation had a way of taking their hidings in good part.

On the whole we find scenes and sentiments such as these difficult to understand—and distasteful. Had Benson really decided what he meant by 'humanity's needs'? Certainly he had. Fulfilment in the hereafter—everything sublunary should fall in contentedly behind that primary objective. Did the great majority of his young congregation understand what he meant by those two words? Certainly they didn't. They were young and hugely preoccupied with the needs of their flesh, but they responded, with vague emotional sympathy, to their headmaster's words because they were of their age, and the spirit of an age, in ninety-nine per cent of cases, is overwhelmingly stronger than the spirit of any single individual. Ought Benson to have drawn so straight and confident a line between humanity's manifest and woeful material needs, and humanity's (equally genuine) spiritual needs? But the capacity of able and devoted people to ignore what might push a system out of shape is the great Victorian mystery and perhaps also the secret of the great Victorian strength. Were they wise not to keep on all the time about the living conditions of the miners at (say)

Eastwood colliery, but instead to devote themselves to their devotions and simply hope that the larger hope would come good in good time? Was David Herbert Lawrence more unhappy, less unhappy, than his father? There are no quick answers to these questions. Beth would have had no answers at all.

Beth (Elizabeth Cooper) has so far made no appearance in these pages, but she has an important place in any history of the Benson family. She was born in 1818 and died in 1911. She is one of the vast army of nameless ones ('Beth', after all, is scarcely identifiable), whose ninety-three years of existence would count for nothing at all if it wasn't for the fact that she became attached to the family of a highly important public man who produced a numerous and variously talented family. When she was fifteen she went to the Sidgwicks as nursemaid and general domestic helper. After 1841 she was Minnie's nurse, and when Minnie married she was taken along, as one takes along one's personal belongings to a new house, to be the nurse of Minnie's children. She spent seventy-eight years in the service of the family, saw all the children of Minnie and Edward grow up, and, when Minnie had her long and strange breakdown at the end of the time at Wellington, took charge of a young family in a way that was quite beyond the capacity of the much preoccupied Benson. Arthur, writing in his mother's house on a warm June evening in 1905 (Beth was eighty-seven by then) noted in his diary: 'Dear old Beth comes trotting up with a rose which she has tied for me. Well, I have had another very happy day, and am grateful.' Dear old Beth.

The Chancellery at Lincoln was a fine grand ancient house ('one of the most beautiful it has ever been my lot to live in', Arthur said), and Benson, as new Chancellor, was immediately willing to recognize that here his work was to lie not only in preaching the Word to the affluent and to the at any rate nominally converted. He charged into what we would call welfare like a knight on a galloping horse. He started night schools for the men and lads of the city. There were bible classes for mechanics employed at the works of Clayton Shuttleworth and Robey. With those flashing, compelling eyes of his he asked for money to support what he was doing, and mostly the money was forthcoming. He even overcame the reluctance of two old ladies. 'We give this to you, Mr. Chancellor, to show our regard for you, but for our parts, Patty and I prefer an ignorant poor.'

He conducted a mission at the church of St. Peter-at-Arches in 1876. A Tory by nature, Benson found himself mixing with, and even enjoying mixing with, the artisans. The working classes were dazzled. Benson was a brilliant talker and Minnie, restored now though changed—the subservient, self-reproachful Minnie of Wellington days had gone for good—was as brilliant as he was and seemed to find the work at Lincoln bracing. Physically Lincoln may not have been as exhilarating as the Berkshire heathland, but for her the enclosed life at Wellington was not without its stuffiness.

And by now of course the children had developed, or were beginning to develop, personalities of their own. Martin, the eldest, born in August 1860, was thirteen; Hugh, the youngest, born in November 1871, was twenty months. Arthur Christopher, born in 1862, was eleven, Mary Eleanor was ten, or almost (born October 1863), Margaret (Maggie) was eight, Edward Frederick (Fred) was six. The Chancellery gardens were a perfect place for children, with innumerable outbuildings to excite curiosity and relics from past centuries and the ancient wall of the close to ensure that it was a fine and private place. Benson plunged vigorously as usual into re-decorations and alterations. He was a man who always loved to express himself through solid shapes and objects, through patterns and designs, through the work of his hands.

The move, the uprooting, with no Minnie beside him to give support, must have required all his fortitude. In 1874, when things had settled down somewhat, he wrote to Canon Wickenden, one of his oldest friends from Trinity days: 'I am beginning to look on the months hitherto as a sort of illness. So many anxieties, so many uncertainties, so many wonders whether one had done rightly or quixotically. Now as one gets to work clouds drift away. . . .' But the clouds were lying thick and dark and heavy on him in that autumn of 1873, with Minnie still behaving as the wife of an ingrained and notable ecclesiastic never should, and with a crowd of young children leaping around him and clamouring for the attention which he was always willing, often glad, to give. He used to take them on long strenuous walks, more in an attempt to clear his own fits of black depression than to slacken the steam-pressure of their energies. Arthur Benson remembered one of these walks—a walk 'which we took with my father when he had got the house fairly straight. He was then suffering from the reaction of the change, regretting that he had ever given up Wellington, feeling that the new surroundings would never suit him, and in deep depression. We went all down the long High Street of Lincoln, with its great stone archways, Bars properly called, across the road, and the quaint towers of its churches, St. Peter-at-Arches, St. Peter-at-Gowts and the rest. On a hill near Canwick we saw what seemed to be a fountain rising in great jerks into the air; we went off to explore this and found at last that it was the white sails of an unseen windmill. Then we turned, and the glories of Lincoln burst upon us— Castle and Cathedral in all their stately glories above the streaming smoke of myriad chimneys. My father's eyes filled with tears and he said, "Well, we must try to live up to that!" '

Benson's tears are not always easily explained. These though are understandable enough. He had launched himself out of success and stability into something new. Was Minnie, the sweet biddable child he had married, deeper and more mysterious, and suddenly more independent than he had ever dreamt? His certainties were slipping away from him. The windmill was a Quixote-windmill. And then suddenly the swing round, and the sight of one of the most beautiful buildings in Europe, and the consolation that he belonged to it, a reviving conviction that he had a purpose in this new place and that he had talents and energies enough to fulfil it.

Slowly things began to go right again. Minnie came back, but Lincoln did not at first please her; the new people she had to learn to know were not stimulating. For Edward, an absolute ruler in his own domain for fourteen years, the taking of several steps down the ladder—as the eyes of this world saw the ladder anyway—was painful and difficult. The natural, growing assertiveness of his children was at times a trial. Canon Crowfoot, seeing much of him at this time, noted: 'The children were all growing up full of great promise. In one year his eldest boy [that was Martin] was head of the Winchester scholars, and his second boy [Arthur] high in the Eton list. The sisters were not a whit behind their brothers in intellect and power. Nothing struck me so much as the intense reverence, which, as a father, he felt for his children. He spoke sometimes with awe and trembling, lest his own strong will and that stubborn temper, with which his own life was one perpetual struggle, should do some wrong to them. It was a very beautiful and characteristic trait. He felt that they were his, and yet not his, but only lent.' Crowfoot writes of course as a man controlled by the modes of thought and feeling current in his time (we are all transit-passengers, and must, even the most forceful and imaginatively enlightened among us, submit in large measure to this control), but Crowfoot writes very perceptively in this passage all the same. Not many who knew Benson had greater insight into the mind and motives of this complicated man.

Before J. W. Blakesley in particular Benson had to learn to curb his pride. Blakesley was Dean of Lincoln, and therefore monarch of all he surveyed just as surely as Benson had been at Wellington. Blakesley had a good mind, dry and keen and critical. He could see a joke, and make one. He could, and did, deflate Benson's wild enthusiasms. Benson wrote to Cubitt, MP for West Surrey and an old friend from Wellington days: 'The Dean is *very* able, not enthusiastic, but anxious for good things. I think this somewhat cynical soberness will make us all careful to do *well* what we do . . .' Benson deserves praise for writing like this. Note the 'us all'. This is manfully put in by an arrogant man to indicate, however obliquely, that he is trying hard to accept, and accept willingly, a subordinate role. And he succeeded. He deferred, but he was not quenched. When Blakesley died in 1885, Benson was in the third year of his Primacy and wrote fairly and generously of the Dean. 'He was a very delicate and choice scholar. Not of an ecclesiastical turn of mind, but very valuable to ecclesiastics by his application of a critical measure of justifiableness to all they did and proposed. "What do you mean exactly?" "What are your exact grounds?" "What is the exact effect which you believe your proposal will have?" He did me much good, because I always determined that I would in the last resort obey him in all Cathedral matters, however little I liked doing so.'

In 1874 Wickenden, one of his Wellington masters, sent him one of his own water colours of the College. His letter of thanks, written on 16 March is far from formal and has an ending more personal than was usual with him. 'We are getting much happier. I've been intending to write and tell you for some two or three weeks. We have been through a bad time.' And to Westcott in the same year: 'My dear wife mends slowly. . . .' The Chancellery building was ancient and beautiful, but it was dilapidated and

there were alterations which had to be seen to. Mission-work—
he came quickly to see his new job as primarily involving this
—presented problems. He had to learn how to talk effectively to
people who, though docile enough, were not academic, had no
training in the handling of abstractions. He did learn how to do
this, and before his short Lincoln stay was up had made a brilliant
success of it, but at the beginning it was hard. 'I feel . . . far too
keenly the sense of the electric message to be sent, and its power
both to speak and to read—and of the fulness with which it has
been given—and that I am a machine charged to transmit it—and
that the field is before me in this glorious place—and that I stand
like a Leyden jar, which somehow no charging with electricity
will charge—or bring anything out thereof but a feeble snap. . . .'
But Benson had batteries inside him strong enough in the end to
swing the most sluggish engine into life. Lincoln got beneficial
shock treatment. Benson's energy triumphed.

But 'My dear wife mends slowly'. This was the painfullest
thing about 1874. The child he had chosen and educated, the
extremely young woman he had married, the only woman he
ever looked at sexually even though there must have been throngs
of women who looked at *him* sexually because he had the handsomest face in the world—the devoted headmaster's wife who
had managed for fourteen years to conceal from him her inability
to accept the Christian faith which was the driving force and *sine
qua non* of his life: what had happened to her? Why had she not
been with him when he had decided to switch from his successful
conduct of a job that gave prestige and held out promise in order
to accept something subordinate at half the salary? She knew, she
must have known, that he relied upon her as upon nobody else.
And then when she did finally come back, she seemed for the first
time reluctant to share his enthusiasms and his certainties. She was
grown-up now. She had had experiences other than child-bearing.
There had been Miss Hall—and others. She did not find theological students at all as much fun as Wellington boys. And then
there was the disturbing business of Mrs. Mylne. For Benson,
almost certainly, the name of Miss Hall was entirely unimportant,
a name glanced at in a letter and then forgotten. But Mrs. Mylne
was different. Mrs. Mylne was the wife of one of the theological
students, a middle-aged person who had received the call a full
twenty years after his fellow-students. His wife was similarly

middle-aged. Both of them belonged—belonged fiercely—to the Evangelical wing of the Church of England, and this in itself was displeasing to Benson who himself favoured the line of long-dead Archbishop Laud, liked even the pomps and ceremonies of the Tractarians, but who none the less always recognized as paramount the importance of a united front and deplored extremist splinter-groups whether of one side or of the other. All that though was relatively unimportant. What mattered, what chiefly worried Benson was that Minnie, cool in her reaction to Lincoln social life in general, became attached to Mrs. Mylne in a quite total way which Benson found disturbing—unnatural even.

In her diary she recognized that she was not supporting in the way she should, Edward's efforts at establishing good and fruitful relations with his students. She was also obliged to admit that old Wiesbaden emotions, which she had hardly known how to handle, could survive transplantation. 'Then came . . . Alice Swan—the old, ungoverned desire. . . .' And then—to put everything right perhaps?—came Mrs. Mylne.

Minnie called her Tau, and Tau was—this was the important, new thing—'Thy Messenger, O Lord of Hosts, my beloved Tau —and I did not know her at first—played even with my human love for her and hers for me—felt it coming—felt how different places were when she was there—but played, played and all the while Thou hadst sent her, and she has led me to Thee.' In other words the large, unkempt grounds of the Chancellery in which she and Mrs. Mylne strolled—perhaps hand in hand, no whisper has come down—became for Minnie a Pauline Road to Damascus. She suddenly knew that God, Edward's God who for so long had been mysterious to her, was real, was someone Whom you could talk to confidingly in the second person singular, could pray to in the intimate, suited-to-the-minute Evangelical way which took no account of rubrics and rites and rules laid down in the thirty-nine articles or even in the Book of Common Prayer itself—how could Cranmer, burnt, martyred, humane Archbishop though he had been, know anything of Minnie's private problems, her personal anguish? It was not, would never be, Edward's kind of religion, of course, but she clung to it for the rest of her long life. In the darkest single moment of all their time together—this still lay ahead—it gave her a strength, a capacity for acceptance, which eluded Edward and almost smashed his world.

By 1876 Benson's will to success was well on the way to re-establishing his mastery of most situations. He taught himself to preach, and to preach magnificently, to all sorts and conditions of men and not simply to schoolboys or to academics. He proved triumphantly his belief that education was the right of everybody and not an elegant plaything for the privileged. He established night schools and these were for men as well as for boys, and the men and boys trusted him and worked for him because he gave them, unaffectedly and uncondescendingly, all that he had. He became very impatient about churchiness and frills. He became widely known, much sought after. He was offered great places—the Hulsean Professorship of Divinity at Cambridge, the Bishopric of Calcutta; and he refused them. The Bishopric was turned down in brisk and practical fashion. 'Six children from sixteen to four years old are surely not meant to be left in the wilderness—and the *promise* is to those who give up *delights*, not to those who forsake duties.' He was learning to give good reasons for doing the right things. (He took a poor view, anyway, of colonial bishops. 'I've had a Colonial Bishop lately,' he tells Wickenden, 'who has utterly sicked me . . . it's the buckles—tights—and Aprons that ruin the Colonial Church—*and* the loops of the hats.') The Hulsean Professorship he found harder to forgo, but he honestly doubted whether his scholarship was up to it, and he hated pluralism even of the most dignified kind, and Lincoln was beginning to challenge his energies in the way he liked, to monopolize him. Here he was for the first time becoming everybody's schoolmaster, and discovering that going out to fight against illiteracy filled you with the same warm feeling as going out to fight against sin. He wrote to Westcott on 10 March 1876: 'The Mission here has left really an *awful* impression on all minds here. The assiduous thirst of the people is most touching. Their crowds, their eagerness, the way in which they remained praying after the Services in silence, give me an impression I cannot shake off. We are so wretchedly armed with what they want. . . .' And later in the same letter managed a bit of self-analysis he would not have been capable of five years earlier. '. . . I fear it was very bad that I did not stay and read Philosophy after my degree and I shall never get over it. But this is a useless wail. If you can tell me any direction in which to read, what I can do to get my straying and vainly anxious unsubstantial thoughts into order and strength,

3*

even at this eleventh hour, how grateful I should be. . . .' Here
Benson rightly sees that positiveness in a man, an outstanding
ability to get things done, can still none the less conceal 'straying
and vainly anxious unsubstantial thoughts'.

Of course all through this period the change in Minnie must
have been hanging over him, baffling him. He was forty-four,
doing better work, he felt sure, than he had ever done in his life,
so why should Minnie—not leave him, oh far from that, yet
somehow, for the first time, choose to put a distance between
herself and him? He did not know that Minnie was privately
communicating with herself about their relations. She was failing
him, she admitted that. She was untidy and unpunctual and spent
more money than she should. She would do her best, under this
new God she had been helped to discover, to do better on all these
points. But Sidgwick people, she knew now, were unbridgeably
different from Benson people. 'I think I have got into the habit of
merely grumbling . . . that his ways and thoughts and feelings
weren't exactly suitable to me. I have expected that Christianity
would do away with necessity of *accommodating* myself to him.' By
this presumably she meant that Conversion would have given her
the freedom to go her own way without feeling guilty about it. But
Conversion had not after all quite meant that. The necessity of
accommodating herself—a grim little phrase, coming from this
cool, sweet-natured woman—still remained, she now saw—and
would always remain. Edward was not obtuse. He would recognize
immediately the difference between this new surface union and
the old total one. At the end of March 1876 he sent her an
enormous letter—where she had gone to, Arthur Benson does
not say—in which he tried to grapple with this newly acquired
religion of hers and his own which for so long (he thought) had
done for both of them. In it he sounds tortuous and a bit lost—
as he very rarely was. He also sounds more than a bit desperate
—as he certainly could be when his bouts of melancholia blanketed
him. Minnie has grown tired of being subjected to a spiritual and
moral bully. He recognizes this but, understandably, finds it
exceedingly hard to put into words. '. . . you know what self-
condemnation I feel. . . . While I have really and warmly believed,
and thoroughly realized (I think I may venture to say) the truths
of the unseen and the persons of that world, as actually taking
part in this, still, (I know not yet fully *why*) the facts which gave

me such happiness and strength . . . have not till lately, if even now, reacted . . . on my temper, my pride, my resentment, my self-government, or my opinion of myself . . . my notion has had in it a world of confidence in a naturally religious disposition, as if it had been a character formed and shaped by God, while it was not. This has been a snare of a most serious kind, and I have for years trusted to the religious sentiment to mould the life, without using anything like a careful interior *discipline*. The lost ground I have to make up is *awful*. It is therefore I who want your prayers, more than you mine. . . .' This is an admission, indirect and reluctant, of seventeen years of taking her for granted. And having got it out somehow, he rushes off into anguished sermonizing; but then he realizes that he must come down from the pulpit, and simply appeal. His words are true, he assures her, 'if only I could beat my music out'; and then the final assurance: 'I am afraid this is all awkward—but it is a true endeavour to express how earnestly I will carry out your wishes. And *you* for me? . . .'

And so, on this new basis, the two came together again, but now they always approached each other more carefully, and Minnie, in her thirty-seventh year by now and possessed of a first-class, if comparatively untrained, mind, began, I think, to become the stronger of the two.

Benson found it more and more easy to forget his personal problems, faced with all the challenges that Lincoln offered. He came to see that the Wellington pattern of schoolmastering was not the only one. One of his helpers found it impossible to keep control in his night-school class. It is almost impossible to give effective advice to anyone plagued with a problem of this kind. It is all so much a matter of instinct and of touch. Yet what Benson told the sufferer is right, and as helpful as helpfulness in such matters can be. '. . . But of course the roughness, the callousness, the indifference to learning, are just the very things which we want to replace by different spirits. They are rather the bad material which we have to work up, and we can't complain of it any more than the ironworker of the hardness and stubbornness of the iron he has to hammer into shape. This is what we have to evangelise, first civilising it into capability of evangelisation. . . .'

And there was all the awful drinking to contend with. The

Victorian urban poor drank because of the greyness, featureless-
ness and unalterability of their lives. The Trinity-Rugby-and-
Wellington Benson now found this fact pushed up hard under
his nose. He wrote to Lightfoot, browsing unperturbed—a bit
too unperturbed?—on the tranquil uplands of scholarship: 'I
send you the new iron—my prospectus about Temperance.
You'll think I meddle with "ower many things"—but you
couldn't help it if you lived in a place like this. It's awful to see
so much wit and work take to drink and death. My Working
Men's Bible Class is very nice, but the people who come to it are
every way better than their master, so that does no new *good*.'

He was in his fourth year at Lincoln. He was tired, but eager to
go on. He had learned much there—about himself, about others—
more perhaps than in all the previous forty years of his life.

4

My Life is Behind My Light

THEN, on a morning in the winter of 1876, he came early to breakfast and saw the post already arrived, and told himself, so he said afterwards, that there was something important there lying in wait for him. And yes, there was a letter from Disraeli who was inviting him—as Prince Lee in 1848 had been invited before him—to be Bishop of a new see. Cornwall was to be separated from the too large diocese of Exeter; would Benson consent to become the first Bishop of Truro?

He did not find the decision easy. Things at Lincoln were beginning to hum—and it was mostly his doing. He had been there only a short while. Truro would mean much more in salary —£3,000 a year; but there would be a great deal more to find out of it. There was no house, let alone a *sufficient* house, as he put it. The Great Western Railway had, in 1876, only just crossed the Tamar, so a Bishop would absolutely need a carriage and pair, with all the outlay that meant. He would be expected to subscribe widely and generously. 'Bishops who do not *give* subscriptions,' he told Westcott, 'are not able to *raise* subscriptions.' Would he be able to get on with Cornishmen? Somebody told him there was a natural enmity between Yorkshiremen and Cornishmen. Would he, having reached the age he had—forty-seven—be stuck there for good? Would he want to be stuck there for good?

But quickly he brushed the doubts and the questions aside. Before the year was out he had made up his mind. He would be the first Bishop Cornwall had had for itself since—AD 936, he thought. His Working Men's Bible Class gave him a parting gift of a set of dessert dishes made of bronzed metal from the Coleby mines. They got the material themselves and worked at it in their limited free time. It was, of all the many presents he received on leaving Lincoln, the one he most prized.

They made their move in the summer of 1877, and Minnie told Susan Wordsworth she felt wretched and rebellious. Any sight of Mrs. Mylne from now on would mean a long, long journey. Finding a suitable house had not proved as difficult as Benson had feared. First and most important, a fund had been raised to help him with the finances of any new house; and then Richard Vautier, vicar of Kenwyn, a parish within a short walk's distance of the centre of Truro, wanted to go on extended leave. His vicarage was large, a graceful country house in fact and set in its own parkland. Vautier put it at Benson's disposal, and the fundraisers made considerable extensions possible: a library, a private chapel, a new drive, two new wings. He had his Palace, and he called it Lis Escop, which is Cornish for Bishop's Court.

More and more, however, as Benson bounced round on terrible roads from parish to parish, getting to know, and making himself known to, his new domain, he found himself, as indeed did all the family, in a foreign land. Cornwall was Celtic. 'Lis Escop' needed translating. Here, as in Wales, nonconformity in the 1870s was strong, and everywhere was putting the Church of England on the defensive. In April, Benson had been consecrated by Archbishop Tait, with a tremendous splendour of ceremonial, in St. Paul's Cathedral. Now here he was, all muddied and bewildered, like Dr. Slop arriving at Shandy Hall on the most protracted of all obstetrical missions. He was in a new world— or rather a very old one. In one place he found the vicar's sister reading the lessons in a deep bass voice. Somewhere else they were still talking about a curate-in-charge who had had to be chained to the altar-rails for the duration of the reading of the service because in no other way could he be prevented from making a dash for the open air betweenwhiles. Churches were dedicated to strange saints he had never heard of: St. Uny, St. Ia, St. Carantoc, St. Feock and St. Erme. In such places it was no use talking the language of the moderate English high church. If the nonconformists had largely won the Cornish people over, then Benson must brush up on his nonconformity. He did so. Never, either at the beginning of his ministry or ever, did he try to act as

if dissent was not there. Those missions which he had so successfully conducted in Lincoln were now a great help to him; he was
already more than halfway proficient in speaking a new language;
he had already begun to understand ways of thought quite outside the scope of Westcott, or Lightfoot—or the Duke of
Wellington. In Truro, at his first Diocesan Conference in 1877, he
made it quite clear where he stood. It was the Church Established,
remote and uncaring, that was to blame, not the Cornishmen.
Dissent and disunion 'began in days when our own energy
flagged; and we had time for carelessness because all seemed
safe'. Benson presented himself, wholly justifiably, as a man whose
energy would never flag. He would not rush at things, but what
had happened in the past 'teaches us to be practical; and the voice
of the past is "Organise the present".' Benson tirelessly set the
example. He crossed and re-crossed his huge and thinly populated
territory. Minnie used to get letters from the strangest places.
The personal worries of his last Lincoln year seemed forgotten.
'Penrose. 1st Sunday after Trinity, 1877. Dearest Life and Love,
I did wish you had been at Gunwalloe—a grassy slope towards
the land leaning up against quite awful black precipices, where
the great Spanish ship went to pieces and spilt doubloons which
every now and then roll up. Against the slope the quaintest,
neatest church, weather-beaten enough, but in perfect order,
which you ever beheld. A tower built away from the church into
the rock—and waves not so terrible as the day before, but of such
power—throwing themselves at the feet of Mullyon cliffs and
Halzephron (did you ever hear such names?) and sending foam-
flecks a quarter of a mile and more into the flowers and grass;
only one house in *sight* over all the rolling hills—and on Sundays
in summer nevertheless the church crowded till they sit on the
settles under the windows. . . .' He was having his effect.

At home at Lis Escop Minnie had a smaller family than once.
Martin by now was seventeen, and doing brilliantly at the top of
the school at Winchester; Arthur, eighteen months younger, was
at Eton. The girls, Nellie and Maggie, were going to somewhere
new, just founded by their father, the High School for Girls at
Truro. So only the six-year-old Hugh was constantly at home.
He, because of his four and a half years of separation in age from
the others, had to grow up much more alone. For the rest, they
all got on well enough together, except that, between the two

eldest boys, Martin and Arthur, there was never the closeness one might have expected. As for the two girls, Martin seemed an immensely grand figure to them both, adorable and without fault. Martin indeed was a paragon. He was brilliant and precocious. For Benson the schoolmaster he stood for all that a boy should be: quick to learn, obedient to his elders, yet in no way lacking in spirit. At his prep school (Temple Grove) he was top of the form in 1872 and was capable at the age of twelve of reading Carlyle's *French Revolution* right through and remaining undefeated. By fourteen he was clearly a favourite for a top award at a top place and Benson drove him relentlessly. 'What you seem to want intellectually is concentration of mind and body. For Listlessness of Attitude (want of smartness) springs from and then tends to reproduce Listlessness in Attention.' He scrutinized the boy's Latin proses with passionate attentiveness, and, although they were excellent, pounced on small mistakes and lamented and exhorted. 'Remember Accuracy is the very soul of a scholar.' Martin did not rebel; he was a willing, thoroughbred horse, and in September 1874 Winchester graciously accepted him. He wrote to his parents, with every appearance of delight, about his new hard life at William of Wykeham's Foundation. He told them about his duties, explained to them about the private language. 'Get up 6.15 and put up cold baths every 5 minutes, dressing in the meanwhile. 8.30, take my prefect's books through to Moberly Library. 12.00. Play football. 6.30. Wash up 3 cups and 3 saucers etc. 6.45. Swill mop. 6.50 Sweep up. (6.00 get Pref. books *from* Moberly.) 8.30 Wash tooth mugs and clean tablecloths. 8.45. Take letters to post. Only fancy I got 55 marks out of 60 for my Verse Task. Senior marks in the Div! I have been learning no end of slang (a brockster is a bully, to splice hollises is to throw stones) . . . I am going to the Deanery after Cathedral. Been, and oh horror a man has sat down on my cathedral, alias topper. . . .' To a modern comprehensive schoolboy, with his common-room and his counsellor and his conviction that the world owes him a living, this description of the life of a privileged and brilliant young person in 1874 would sound like a spell in a glasshouse. But Martin White Benson has no complaints; there are no entreaties that he should be taken home to be ministered to by Beth. He could be dreamy and inattentive at times, yet he could master abstractions without apparently any need for concentration. Long afterwards Fred Benson said of him: 'Mentally he was a boy of extraordinary brilliance. He had a gay passion for sheer learning which made its acquisition more of a pastime than a task.' The Bishop of Truro, whilst never slackening in his urgings of him upward and onward, saw much of himself in him and was proud.

Looking at that small, distant figure across the gap of more than a century, we may feel fairly sure, disregarding natural family prejudice, that Martin Benson was indeed what the dons call pure alpha. It is all the more clear that he must have been so because he had the ability, or at any rate outwardly seemed to have the ability, to shrug off all the tremendous pressures on him—the pressures which would so horrify a fashionable educationist of today—and still remain a spirited, unwarped youngster. He had the Benson fire and drive; he had as well the Sidgwick subtlety and fineness of intellect. In spite of the solemnities with which his young life was surrounded, in defiance of the exhortations aimed at him from all sides, he could apparently still keep his liveliness and play the fool—which is always so important. Once he went into school with four Japanese dolls tied to his shoelaces, and surely Dr. Ridding, the Winchester headmaster of his time and a man not frightened of innovation, would have been pleased with that.

Then, in February 1878, six months before his eighteenth birthday, whilst he was taking tea with a master, he found himself, suddenly and literally, struck dumb. They went in alarm for a doctor, and whilst they waited for the arrival of this member of the most fallible of Victorian professions, Martin signalled for a piece of paper, and wrote on it the one word: 'paralysis'. He was taken to the sanatorium, and for a while halting speech came back to him, but then, after only a few days, he became unconscious without ever again surfacing. He was buried in the Winchester cloister. The boy whom his father had striven to mould into the model of what a boy should be, the boy whom he saw as Edward White Benson transcendent, the dreamy boy whom in writing he had never hesitated to reprove ('. . . I am afraid you rather foster it [the dreaminess] than otherwise by reading novels. Novel-reading is a great cause of dreaminess. . . .'), the boy whom he adored much more than anybody else in the world, would not now, in this world, come to anything.

It had been brain-fever, the doctor said, and about brain-fever—

which we would call meningitis and which antibiotics would cure in a week—there was nothing at all to be done except apply cold compresses to the forehead and vainly hope. Of course the Victorians were inured to sudden death from causes which we would dismiss as scarcely more than trivial. The Prince Consort himself had been whisked away in the prime of life; the current Archbishop of Canterbury, Dr. Tait, had in 1856, when Dean of Carlisle, lost five young children from scarlet fever in the space of six weeks; Benson was used—they all were—to writing letters of condolence—he wrote a beautiful one to his friend Wickenden when Wickenden's sister died at the age of twenty-one; the literate amongst them wrote many hymns—'Days and moments quickly flying/Blend the living with the dead./Soon will you and I be lying,/Each within his narrow bed.'—and as they wrote the shadow was always standing behind their writing arm. The loss of children had to be accepted.

But Benson never accepted the loss of Martin. He told himself, as he was obliged to do, that this was the will of God. But telling himself availed nothing. Here Benson stuck. That Christian faith of his, confident, serene, unquestioning, armed at all points, received a wounding in that February of 1878 from which it never genuinely recovered. Of course he told himself, told others, that all was really well. He, limited in time and space, was in no position to question the workings of the Almighty in Whom he trusted. He assured himself that the firm edifice in which from earliest years he had chosen to take shelter and live, had not crumbled. But the fact was that it had. He wrote much in his Diary at this time; and notably he put this down: 'It [Martin's death] has changed all my views of God's work as it has to be done both in this world and the next, to be compelled to believe that *God's* plan for him really *has* run sweetly, and rightly for him and for all—and yet—he is dead. "One's views of life change very quickly," he said to me the last hour in which he spoke to me—my sweet boy, thou hast changed mine.'

This is a Benson unresigned, but fighting all along to reclaim lost ground. He went on all his life fighting to reclaim it. He told Wickenden: 'We are learning not to withhold him from God in our hearts, and my dear wife is the mother's example.' The first part of this is not more than self-persuasion. Benson had been teaching too long to be able to learn in a matter so grievous to him. Self-persuasion of the scruff-of-the-neck kind is all that he can manage. He never seems to have asked himself the questions which would immediately torment a father of today so struck; have I pressed Martin too hard? Have my formidable, proselytizing personality, my imperious certainties, my desire to dominate, direct and force a good but necessarily immature mind, been themselves enough to bring on this sudden mental collapse?

Minnie took it better. That much of what he told Wickenden was right. The brand of Christianity which Mrs. Mylne had taught her in Lincoln, whilst it could not make her impervious to sorrow, did curb mutiny, enabled her to accept. (Of course it has to be remembered that she had had long years of practice in learning to accept.) Minnie's strength throughout the tragedy made it finally clear to Benson that those long-held ideas of his about Minnie would have to be utterly scrapped; she was no longer his biddable little girl but a pillar to lean on—for them all to lean on. Another few lines from the diary of his anguish confirm this. 'His mother's bearing of all seems to me as perfect as anything can be. A few hours after [Martin's death] she knelt in our room and prayed aloud. "It is Thy will only that we will. He is thine, Thou hast a right to him." I cannot reach to this.'

Arthur, now the future head of the family, was sent for from Eton so that he could attend his brother's funeral. 'I shall never forget,' he says, 'the look on my father's white drawn face as the train drew up at Winchester, while he stood on the platform awaiting me.'

Benson returned to Truro determined to stamp under his feet the writhing little snakes of doubt that had suddenly sprung up round him. And there was much besides for him to do. He had to hunt back into the fold his dissenting Cornish flock who had strayed, a flock still strange to him, and, to his mind, stubborn, backward and disinclined to be cast into the Victorian mould. And he had a Cathedral to build. He still insisted on keeping his children very much apart and pressurizing them; they dwelt in his special Bensonian world, members of God's elect. He wrote, defiantly, to Wickenden in May: 'I sometimes used to wonder why we kept our Martin so much to ourselves—so that only two or three people besides knew what he was—and now I do not wonder at all.' He defies himself to believe that how he had behaved, what he had believed, could possibly be other than right. What, from then on, his faith lost in certainty he made up for in fierceness of protestation. Hugh, the youngest child, not old enough in 1878 to have much awareness of the tragedy of Martin's death, remembered the later years of tyranny and wrote of them when he was a man of thirty-five: 'My father's influence upon me was always so great that I despair of describing it. I do not think that he understood me very well; but his personality was so dominant and insistent that the lack of this understanding made very little difference; he formed and moulded my views on religious matters in such a manner that it would have seemed to me, while he lived, a kind of blasphemy to have held other opinions than his.'

For the new Cathedral—the first to be begun in England since the Middle Ages—he laboured hard. From ordinary Cornish folk he got a remarkable amount of support. He had discovered—the Lincoln days had taught him this—that he was better with the ordinary, unregarded people than he was with the high and the mighty. Perhaps his success at slumming was not altogether to his credit. His arrogant certainty of being right could and did irritate people of his own class and *a fortiori* the great ones. (The reader is reminded that Disraeli attended one meeting as member of the Governing Body of Wellington, and then attended no more.) Humble villagers listened, admired and obeyed. How in all respects right this was of them. And yet Benson was not a conceited man, never a self-important man. He simply knew he was right and was therefore pleased when people followed his leadership without all that arguing which tended only to hold up the progress of the good works he had in mind. Yet when F. W. Truscott, a Cornishman and Lord Mayor of London in the year of the laying of the Foundation Stone of Truro Cathedral, invited him up to the City to canvass support where support could so easily be lavish, Benson quite failed to magnetize the magnates. He wrote quite pettishly about it in his Diary (why, one is tempted to ask, should he have been surprised that Rothschild and his fellow-Jews should feel disinclined to put their hands in their pockets in order to support a new Anglican-Gothic pile in country far to the west beyond the Tamar?): '. . . this was not an expedition suited to its purpose. For our people's sake it was not fitting that I should say no to the proposal of this Lombard Street tour. But while I was more impressed than ever in my life with the existence, presence, activity and potentiality of "Money" as a living world power, our expedition was bound to fail. It was approaching the power from below, not from above. It was being a suitor to it; whereas those earth kings are intended to *bring* their glory and honour with them. So rather sick, determined to despond of nothing but to work no more in this fashion, I hurried off for Vespers at Westminster Abbey, full of the looks and words and pompous ways of the kings who would *not* help. . . .'

It is clear from this that Benson was not, would never be, a great political churchman. As Bishop of Truro he had no seat in the House of Lords, and perhaps it was just as well. He never liked 'Courts' and legalism. 'There be ways of settling differences,' he told his fifth Diocesan Conference in 1881, 'more apostolic and spiritual than the most spiritual of law-courts.' Archbishop Tait, a more worldly, much more political man than Benson, would never have dreamt of taking this sort of line in public; but he none the less greatly admired the immense energy and effectiveness which Benson brought to hard, initiating tasks between 1878 and 1882. These were years, in fact, when Tait began to think of him as his possible successor. He even set aside for him in Lambeth Palace a set of rooms in the Lollards' Tower where Benson could work and feel himself at home during his visits to London. He spoke his mind at Conferences other than that of 1881. Tact was never something he set much store by. He would on more than one occasion feel irritated that Tait should appear to sit comfortably through it all, apparently not greatly moved. No man, openly and categorically, schemed less, laid less deliberate plans for, the top job, the place of power. He went back to Cornwall and delighted in his work there. It was a place that suited him in everything except its humid, warmish climate. Two strong elements in his character found fulfilment there: his passionate love for things that were venerable and sanctified by tradition, and his genius for setting movements going, for action, for influencing people's minds and also for building and making in the purely material sense.

The poverty of his clergy was something he lamented but could do little about. Yet he visited them all and did what he could. Arthur, now his eldest son and at the top of the school at Eton, would be taken with him on long visiting expeditions either on foot or on horseback. The road to one vicarage led over the moors, bare except for the ruins of abandoned mines. Both vicarage and church were not venerable at all, but grim and cheap, built to serve a mining community whose work had ceased by now to exist. They found the vicar working in his garden when they arrived—'a tall, venerable man with a long beard, with something noble and pathetic in his face. His wife, the partner of his long life, was lately dead.' Arthur and Benson were taken into the house, the walls adorned by medical diplomas. The vicar told them he had begun life as a physician, but, feeling compelled to preach the gospel, had taken Orders. He had been assigned to his present living nearly thirty years before, and instructed by the ecclesiastical authorities then in charge, 'to fight with beasts'. The wastage of his congregation through unemployment had gone slowly on ever since. Now he was old and suffering from something for which there was no cure. Vast accumulations of useless literary labour lay about in his study—the second book of Kings (Arthur thought it was mainly) put into rhyming heroic couplets. The defeated man had had it printed, but not one single copy had ever been sold and so all copies had been sent back to him to clutter a cheerless house—an all-time record, one might think, in returned copies. Benson accepted a dusted copy, and offered consolation, but not even his dynamism could rouse his vicar to more than a shake of the head. Another ancient incumbent, far from a main road and quite cut off, sent to Benson for an assistant, saying he was ill. The assistant arrived on a Saturday afternoon, and found the old man very merry indeed, drinking brown sherry out of a tea-pot.

His cathedral was not completed till 1887, and by then Benson had been four years gone from Cornwall. During the whole of his episcopate he had to make do with a wooden substitute, but his talent for ceremonial dressed the place up and by making it warm, gave it impressiveness. It was he who first put together a short service (by Victorian standards) for Christmas Eve. He chose nine carols, most of them going back to medieval times, and interspersed them with nine lessons, all short and all related in some way to the Feast of the Nativity. This was the beginning of the Service of Nine Lessons and Carols, which now remains as one of the few bits of Christian ritual which the general public in the England of today still remains perfectly familiar with. All over

Cornwall he fought a hard, but losing, battle for sexual morality. His flock quoted chapter seven of First Corinthians at him to justify extra-marital fornication. He assured them that here lay no excuse for pre-nuptial sin. '. . . the knowledge that their parents had no kind of shame for themselves or their children . . . immensely affected . . . the morals of the young people. . . .'

After Martin's death he pulled his children even closer, if that was possible, around him. The Bensons became, more and more, a group apart; the children listened to his stories, absorbed his lessons, noted the wonders of the natural world which he eagerly pointed out to them on their regular walks, prayed when he laid it down that it was appropriate that they should pray—and yet in spite of all the care and all the genuine solicitude that he showed, they felt oppressed. Minnie's first words, when she saw that Martin was dead, were: 'Oh, Martin, how happy you are now.' Indeed as a convert she was a credit to Mrs. Mylne, and showed her husband up. But she made no attempt to modify the regime under which Edward thought it right to bring his children up. Indeed she never *fought* for her children, and it might be said that though she possessed in plenty affection and tenderness and sympathy and extremely high intelligence, she was not a woman endowed with that ultimate strength of motherliness which multitudes of simple, illiterate women could and can quite naturally turn to and conquer through.

He wrote to Minnie after preaching in St. Paul's: '. . . I had again a great congregation and the Judge; but my sermon was long and uneven, and not calculated to do anybody any good except the preacher by humiliating him. I hope that it may do its proper work. I can't get at the core. It is so because my life is behind my light.' What did he mean by the last two sentences here? It is evidence that the death of Martin was something too hard for his absolute, committed Christianity to digest. Benson kept remembering the boy; he returned to him constantly—would always do so. What sense was there, what infallibility of judgment, in a Divine Ordering that took away his Martin at seventeen and a half, not only from him, perhaps simply that he could have managed to bear, but from a world which would have so vastly benefited from his great gifts and manly (the beloved Arnoldian word) nature? How could he (Benson) get at any core while the shadow of Martin barred his way to it? 'My life is

behind my light'—a difficult phrase, but here too I think Benson
is saying that the uselessly dead Martin and his brilliance shine
constantly in front of him, and that this brightness, brushed off
the face of the earth and so unregarded, blocks his (Benson's)
onward, fruitful progress through life. If he were writing now,
Benson might have said that he was driving his car directly west-
ward into a dazzling winter setting sun, and was being forced to
stop because the immediate way ahead was blotted out for him.
He remembered the Cornwall walks and rides with this splendid
son of his—there had been so few they were easy to remember,
and he wrote achingly of one in his diary, probably taken in the
late summer of 1877: 'Our last walk was on the Piran sands with
John Wordsworth. We had driven there—and then walked to the
buried church—He [Martin] was very silent—and as we came
back, while we kept near the rocks (Arthur, J.W. and I) there
was "something prophetic" as J.W. has since written "in the way
in which he walked alone in the fading light along the margin of
the waves". Yes, you were already, dearest boy, on the edge of an
ocean greater than the Atlantic—You have crossed it alone—and
our light fades while we strain after you.' His sermons reflected
this vain effort. When his formidable sister Ada died in 1882, he
attempted consolation again, and again with Martin in his mind
more vividly than Ada whose personality Minnie always found
crushing. He wrote to his brother-in-law Christopher (the Wiesbaden Christopher): 'But of all the wonderful thoughts that crowd
round the door of the next world, none now impresses me more
than the consideration of the greatness of the instantaneous
bound in *knowledge* which, if they are happy at all, must at once
possess them that it *is* good for us as well as for them that they
should leave us to sorrow for the time.' Here a man practised in
writing lucidly, and perfectly capable of doing so, becomes ragged
and confused. He is doubtful about what he is saying and resorts
to desperate pleading. How he must have envied Minnie's new-
found, effortless, tranquil belief.

At that date, of course, there would have been countless thousands of others who, in a similar situation, would have been able
to say with her, substituting a different departed name, 'Oh,
Martin, how happy you are now.' A century on, only a few
hundred truly would; today christians and non-christians both
alike would find Minnie's attitude, and Benson's flailing attempts

to take a similar one, difficult to understand. Why? How to explain the vast gap that has opened up between us and a man like Benson who died within the lifetime of thousands of people still hobbling about today? All down the centuries until almost now the fact of sudden death has been so constantly recurrent that people *had* to have some consolation or else find themselves torn to tatters. The plagues, the diseases, the unaccountable whiskings away in the prime or at the beginnings of life virtually demanded some comfort of the kind which Benson sought. Then, from 1914 to 1918, we experienced a sudden, far nearer to total, destruction of human life which did not, this time, come 'from without', but which was clearly, and on a most colossal scale, the direct and demonstrable result of man's inhumanity to man. Did this fact bring about the fundamental change of attitude which so sets us apart from the Victorians? Of course down the centuries there had always been monstrous barbarities inflicted by men against men (the Ottoman conquests, the murderous slaughters of the Thirty Years' War, and so endlessly on); yet all these were on a small scale compared to the extinguishment of a generation, which was what happened between 1914 and 1918; furthermore, up to about the time of Benson's death, there was no immediate, full-scale detailed reporting of mayhem, so that suffering and death were, so to say, compartmentalized; individual losses and pains did not whizz round the world in twenty seconds. And this gave time, provided seclusion, so that each individual sufferer could spin round his particular irritant (to use too mild a term) his smooth, emollient pearl of faith. Might this explain the change which has occurred in our general attitude to suffering and loss, account for the swift motorcade, the sweep round into the crematorium during a momentary gap in the oncoming traffic, the quick quarter of an hour in the chapel in which tactfully vague words committing nobody to anything much are quickly muttered before the box slides on through doors opened by remote control, and the little handful who have dodged it for one more day shuffle out into the daylight and are at pains to look serious and decent but not embarrassingly moved? How deeply Benson would have been shocked by it all.

There can be no doubt that after one full year at Truro Benson had made for himself a name that people of importance had to take into account. He had already made a success of a testing job. He

took a genuine interest in the ordinary folk; he was a good
listener; his see was remote but he was never remote. Thanks to
his endless, exhausting peregrinations he had made himself
personally known to a degree few bishops have managed either
before or since. 'A fine man, Mr. Benson,' a tough North Cornwall farmer said of him. Working men would march into his
cathedral (the wooden one) to hear him lecture on his favourite
saint Cyprian. But what could St. Cyprian have meant to them?
Quite simply he meant Benson. 'A clever chap, he is,' one of them
said as he was leaving. And for him as for them all the cleverness
was not Cyprian's but Benson's.

He kept close hold on his children. By 1882 Arthur was twenty
and at Cambridge, but Benson was still watching them all like a
sheep-dog. He was taking it for granted that a son of Arthur's age
should share his father's enthusiasms unquestioningly. 'We will
have a talk about Sunday School work and the like. Few questions
are more vital to the Church life of the XIXth century in England
for the masses. How can it be otherwise? The seething future is
all quietly at school now,—like pools above the waterfall. Are we
to go on wasting and neglecting all the force, and watching it tear
its own rocks down?' Intent though he is for the most part on the
immediate thing to do, Benson shows an undeniable gift for
prophecy here; those quietly filling pools above the waterfall are
a wholly appropriate metaphor for the social situation of England
in 1882. Arthur, though, may not have responded with all the
enthusiasm his father would have liked. Arthur, not then nor ever,
could have been called a springy, up-and-doing man, but a
clouded, oppressed one, who worked tirelessly on through life,
whenever his nightmares allowed him, at projects his father would
have rated not very far above the trivial.

Not a few parents have, in the past anyway, striven to keep their
children unspotted from the world. Benson had a veritable
obsession about it. Percy Lubbock says of Arthur: 'His life was
entirely shaped for him, he had no opportunity to venture for
himself; he got no freedom until the lines on which he could use
it were fixed beyond changing.' Whilst at Cambridge he told his
father he had been invited to meet Henry Irving. At the time
Benson said nothing which might suggest opposition on his part,
but put some thoughts down in writing for his son that very day.
Might there not be dangers? Might it not in retrospect appear

distressing (to Arthur, of course, rather than to anybody else) that he had been drawn into a milieu, if only briefly, so worldly, so different from the one he had been brought up in, with its morning prayers and its compline? The Paternoster was not explicitly introduced into this caring communication, but at least the notion of 'Lead us not into temptation' was hinted at, and in the end Arthur decided that perhaps it would be wiser not to go.

The girls, Nellie and Maggie, were guarded like nuns. Maggie, it is true, went to Lady Margaret Hall, but had the feeling all the while that her father was watching her. The younger Hugh remembered that 'on Sunday afternoons in the country we would walk with him, rather slowly and recollectedly, for about an hour and a half; and during these expeditions one of us would usually read aloud, or sometimes my father himself would read aloud from some religious book. I do not think that these books were very well selected for a boy's point of view. The poems of George Herbert were frequently read on these occasions, and these very peculiar, scholarly, and ingenious meditations used to produce in me, occasionally, a sudden thrill of pleasure, but far more commonly a kind of despairing impatience. Or, occasionally, some interminable life of a saint or a volume of Church history would be read; or a book of Dean Stanley's on the Holy Land. . . .' After the walk they would troop into Benson's study for Bible-reading, or Greek Testament. They were all of them like stars, and dwelt apart. 'Rather a close little corporation' were words which Arthur used to describe this young, gifted, over-supervised family. He injects neither approval nor disapproval into his phrase —a suffocating mildness was the bane of his writing all through life, but he does admit 'we were rather unduly afraid of life'. Again Benson writes to Nellie (Mary Eleanor) in March 1882 to describe one of his endless journeyings hither and thither over the county, confirming people as he went. Was there ever such zest? '. . . I had such a drive across Cornwall yesterday—first from Launceston early to Altarnun . . . then a Confirmation in grand old church with great screen, and among some bits of stone I picked out basin and shaft of a Norman Piscina which the parson had never seen! But Church matters very feeble there. Then a long drive to Southill—and a Confirmation of 60 attentive people, old and young—and again a rapid drive over the Cornish highlands—out of sunshine up into a cold blind fog—and down again

into air as warm as milk—and home by 8 o'clock. Some holidays
or other you must go with me on one of my turns and read and
talk to me in the carriage between the Churches—I had rather have
you than the best of Rural Deans—good and kind as they be. . . .'
How strange, and unfeeling, of a father to think of his nineteen-
year-old daughter as an *ersatz*-Rural Dean. Nellie was at Lady
Margaret Hall at the time, and closely chaperoned. She was used
to receiving brisk sermons from Lis Escop. Did these pour out of
him mindlessly, or out of an intense effort to shore up his own
shakiness with Martin lying lost to him in Winchester cloister?
'. . . and you will yourself be wise in time to cast out *any* habit of
thought or feeling which has troubled your peace and stood in the
least between God and you. We must cut the Canaanite *quite* out of
our Heart-land. . . .'

Arthur, up at Trinity, was similarly watched over from afar.
An agnostic friend had invited Arthur to lunch one Sunday in
his first term. Benson flew to his pen. '. . . I am sorry, because
interruptions in Term time are very uncomfortable disjoining
things. You must be on your guard and be firm—for he is a *clever*
man—a man very regardless of others' feelings—not scrupulous
as to using a sarcasm or sneer where an argument fails—and, as
you know, very *opiniâtre* and *entêté*. Don't let him on any account
keep you from Services on Sunday. He is quite likely to try—after
he sees you strong he will begin to respect you. But if you were to
let your spiritual life go, or slumber, through fear of what he may
say or think, you know how, in such cases, we are soon left to
ourselves . . .' And Benson told them all—Arthur at Cambridge,
the two girls at Oxford, Fred at Marlborough—was careful to
tell them, with what entire seemliness young Hugh, still at home,
was taking to the spiritual life. He told them how they dedicated
a cathedral chapel on Hugh's birthday. '. . . Mama will send you a
programme. . . .' Benson first solemnly signed the licence, then
they had full choral Evening Prayer, and '. . . After that we
dedicated the Altar and all its appointments, Hugh bringing them
one by one from the credence and looking so reverent and simple
in his purple cassock and ephod like Samuel's. . . .' Hugh, like his
father, loved ceremonial, yet Hugh too was later to express some
doubts. '. . . to some degree, one's appreciation of morality was,
I think, dulled: since to forget an order, or to disregard it in a
moment of blinding excitement, was visited by my father with

what appeared to be as much anger as if it had been a deliberate moral fault. . . .'

Archbishop Tait died in December 1882. Benson was then, comparatively, young at fifty-three. He was stationed far away in a bishopric lowest in prestige and newest in age. He had been there barely seven years. And yet he may well have privately thought that the succession might land on him. Chance was on his side, as it was on Baldwin's in 1923. It would be wrong to suggest that Benson was ambitious except in the sense that any intelligent, forceful, energetic man is ambitious, but the idea of the Primacy could well have crossed his mind. Tait himself, as we have seen, had been at no pains to conceal how impressed he was by this immensely busy, markedly successful, more than usually handsome man; Thomson, at York, was ailing and would not do; Lightfoot had been Bishop of Durham for only three years; Richard Church, Dean of St. Paul's since 1871, was immensely distinguished, but from the Deanery at the top of Ludgate Hill to Lambeth Palace was still quite a step; Gladstone was Prime Minister and Benson, just before Tait's death, had made some show of going to Cambridge to give his vote for the Tory in the University seat, but Gladstone had noted how liberally Benson had spent his energies at Lincoln in the cause of the common man; Browne, Bishop of Winchester, had solid claims, but he was over seventy, and Gladstone, aged seventy-three, wrote in the kindliest way to tell him that the duties of the Primacy were 'too new and onerous to be undertaken by a man over 70'. And the Queen wanted him. Once the name of Browne was out of the way the Queen wanted him very much. Benson had been Albert's choice for Wellington, and how splendidly that had worked out. She had liked him when, as a young headmaster of thirty-four, he had visited her at Windsor on the anniversary of Albert's death.

And so, on 16 December 1882, a suitably scriptural letter went from 10 Downing Street to Lis Escop. 'I have to propose to your Lordship, with the sanction of Her Majesty, that you should accept the succession to the Archbishopric of Canterbury, now vacant through the lamented death of Archbishop Tait.

'This proposal is a grave one, but it is I can assure you made with a sense of its gravity, and in some degree proportional to it:

and it comes to you, not as offer of personal advancement, but as a request that, whereas you have heretofore been employing five talents in the service of the Church and Realm, you will hereafter employ ten with the same devotion in the same good and great cause. . . .' Benson, as was appropriate, said he wanted time to think. He wrote round to his friends in English sometimes, in Latin sometimes, asking for advice, asking them to pray for him; the Queen wrote from Osborne on 22 December to say she hoped earnestly that he would accept, and assuring him that she and her 'dear husband in byegone days' both thought highly of him. That clinched it. On the 23rd he wrote to Gladstone to signify his acceptance. He had Lambeth Palace to live in, and the magnificent country residence of Addington Park as solace for and retreat from his never shirked labours. He felt up to his job. What did his family feel? How did they all stand at the end of that triumphant year of 1882?

5

A Soldier's Death

MINNIE BY THIS TIME was just over forty, in her prime and conscious of her considerable powers; she could take her place amongst any number of notables without the slightest suggestion of stumbling or inadequacy. She could manage two great houses, and the high-powered entertaining—indeed would enjoy doing so, and did enjoy doing so. She was a Sidgwick after all, with the swift mind and swifter perceptions of a family not only allied to the Bensons but, taking them all round, far more gifted than they. She and Edward were now of the Queen's circle—if she can ever be said to have had such a thing, and Minnie beyond doubt enjoyed this more, was better at it, than Edward. She never became an inhabitant of the *beau monde*—her late-found, Mylnian type of religious conviction saw to that—but then, neither did the Queen. So long as it is borne in mind that life can never, for anybody, be a wholly enjoyable business, then it is true to say that Minnie enjoyed for nearly fourteen years being the wife of one of the five Most Elevated persons in the most powerful single country in the world.

She backed her Edward up devotedly. She knew by now that he needed her far more than she needed him. But her ideas about what was important in life differed from his, and never for one moment did she abandon those notions in deference to his. Edward accepted this. He had to accept this. Not to have accepted this might have meant losing her, and losing her was unimaginable. He liked campaigns, and aims and objects; he liked fine buildings, fine monuments. In a corridor which led from the

Guard-room to the drawing-room at Lambeth there stood, under a glass case, the shell of Archbishop Laud's tortoise; in the muniment room there were treasures—the bones of saints, relics that Cardinal Pole had handled; Edward treasured all this, delighted in it with passion, just as he did in that cathedral slowly building far away in Truro. Minnie would not have given a snap of the fingers for any of it. She kept remembering ruefully all those holidays abroad with him, the minute inspections of cathedral after cathedral, of shrine after shrine, which passionately excited him but which were so hard on the feet. Her religion was much simpler than his, and this led her to accept the hard knocks of life more readily than he. Her son Fred, a fluent, unbelieving man, cannot be taken as a reliable authority when he writes of religious matters, but he published a book about his mother in 1925 when she had only been seven years dead, and in it he has the sentence: 'She, to put it broadly, looked on God as a Father, he as an omnipotent King.' This establishes perceptively one of the central differences between them.

Her attitude to her children was also far from his. Edward was always for telling them what to do—and was swiftly inclined to become agitated and dictatorial if they did not do it. She accepted what they were, and went on loving them, but only in a placid way. Motherhood was never, I think, the primary passion of her life. If all her three surviving sons showed signs, marked or not so marked, of being homosexuals—well, that was how it was. Edward did not live long enough ever to suspect the Abominable in respect of any of his sons; if he had his sense of outrage would have been beyond even his power over words to express.

The social round had suddenly changed from entertaining depressed Cornish vicars and opening bring-and-buy sales in Penzance. Minnie was now the wife of one of the highest dignitaries in the land. She enjoyed it because she knew she was good at it. Under Minnie's supervision the elaborate and stately gormandizings at Lambeth Palace could take their place, with no feeling of inferiority, alongside those at the urban headquarters of a Lansdowne or a Rosebery. State receptions for foreign nabobs and home grandees delighted her. No shadow of apprehension that Mrs. Benson of Lis Escop—now where was that?— ever troubled her because she was conscious of intellectual strength in herself quite equal to any demand the Church might make. As for being a party to state secrets, as for being in the know about vast projects which must be secrets for the present because they were still only at the gestatory stage—this gave her an enjoyable little thrill. She would never blab about them in the wrong place at the wrong time. And this was probably because, deep down, she considered the whole gorgeous apparatus of power and might to be basically trivial. This is not at all to set her down as a superficial or flighty woman. She was immensely able and widely read. It was simply that she enjoyed all the grand tra-la-la, as it were, *en passant*. It was part of her duty as wife of the Archbishop of Canterbury, and if she was fully aware of the enjoyable side of her functions—well, why not?

It was part of her duty. This is not exactly a warm way of putting it, but it is probably the way that comes nearest to the truth. She knew that Edward depended on her to an extent that the admiring outside world never dreamt of; and she tried always to be there—to be depended upon. It was not a love relationship in the normal, two-way, give-and-take understanding of that phrase as it applies to a marriage in its later years. Her notion of what was meant by Christianity was one totally at variance with his. She knew that Christianity—his rigid, absolutist Christianity —lay at the centre of his being. She knew that to shake this, to attempt to alter by the tiniest degree a course so early set, would ruin him. She knew that his terrible moods of withdrawal and deepest melancholy might very well, if things went badly for him, swoop down and shut him off from the light, not for two or three hours or two or three days but for ever. She did not want this to happen; she was faithful to the role of guard-dog. He knew perfectly well that her religious ideas were quite at variance with his, but he knew too that in this dearest, most intimate case, he dare not assume the role of meddler or missioner which he was so good at; there would be the risk of losing her, and that was unthinkable. During the terrible time after Martin's death it was only Minnie's tranquil acceptance of it that saved him from losing the faith which he had consciously chosen as the central and irreplaceable supporting pillar of all his life and all his boundless activity.

Her family was his family. Her friends, for the most part but not wholly, were also his. But the quality of her human relationships differed utterly from his. And here also, as in the matter of

4

the emphasis of faith, Minnie was not prepared to step into his line. She was not prepared to see human beings as objects to be worked upon and to be influenced—even though this moulding process should be carried through, as with Edward it certainly was, from the kindest, most altruistic, most dedicated of motives.

This unbending assertion of difference on Minnie's part is best seen in the way he handled their children and in the way she did. Except with Nellie, who was outgoing, cheerful, less sensitive than the others to the subtle changes of mood which might take place in the people she was at that moment concerned with, Benson was not wholly at ease, wholly himself, with his children; the Master of Wellington kept pushing his nose in, as it were, and making it a threesome instead of the twosome which Maggie or Arthur or Fred or Hugh would far rather have been engaged in. Arthur, most circumspect and diplomatic of biographers, has little sentences here and there which betray his awareness of Benson's shortcomings as a father. 'I do not think he was an easy person to talk to.' 'He had not the art of eliciting information on subjects which were strange to him by questions, and was apt to deflect on to subjects which he knew. . . .' This inability to adjust, in a natural way, to the varying needs and differing viewpoints of others was as noticeable, Arthur thought, in the great world as it was in the family. '. . . Argument with him always engendered heat.' He '. . . expressed himself too vehemently to be agreeable; thus I think he did not, in later life, make many equal friends among men.' 'All his great friendships, especially of later years, have been with women; he was not really at home in an atmosphere of perfect equality; surround him with a certain deference and affection, and he was expansive, racy, humorous—but with men of like age, with views he imagined to differ widely from his own, he froze and became silent and severe. . . . He thought of the Church, or rather of religion, as *the* absorbing fact of life. People of diametrically opposite views he could not really tolerate. Cordiality with them was out of the question. And he would not really ever try to meet them or argue with them. Several times in the Education Bill he lost ground by not being able frankly to meet and discuss matters with certain leading Radicals, who would have been quite ready to meet him half way. . . . With certain politicians he had so little in common that he thought of them as dangerous and deadly enemies.' Neither Arthur nor Fred, at any period of their lives, ever found it possible to be in sympathy with any form of churchmanship; it is not difficult, having the father that Benson incurably was, to see why.

Hugh, the volatile, only twelve when they moved to the splendours of Lambeth and Addington, felt much as Arthur did. 'I do not think . . . that he made it easy to love God; but he did, undoubtedly, establish in my mind an ineradicable sense of a Moral Government in the universe. . . . He himself was wonderfully tender-hearted and loving, intensely desirous of my good, and, if I had but known it, touchingly covetous of my love and confidence; yet his very anxiety on my behalf to some degree obscured the fire of his love, or, rather, caused it to affect me as heat rather than as light.'

All the five children left to Edward and Minnie when Edward finally reached the eminence of Lambeth in 1883 could be judged as highly satisfactory so far, in their different ways. Nellie had done well and Maggie was doing well at Lady Margaret Hall. Arthur, physically the big one, was doing well at Cambridge, though he had strangely little to do with Minnie's family, the Sidgwicks. Henry Sidgwick, the most brilliant of them, was a man of the firmest moral principles, but not in any way sympathetic to Benson's absolutist Christian dogmatism. The young Arthur, still at this point submissive to his father's compelling imperiousness, may well have been told by him before setting out to a Cambridge swayed this way and that by strong winds of doctrine, that it would be wise to steer clear, in the politest way of course, of possible infections. Fred, sixteen years old, was at Marlborough but fairly shortly to follow his brother Arthur to King's College, Cambridge, and later on to write, amongst many other novels, one called *David of King's* which, if it is not a masterpiece, is still very revealing in a number of ways. Only Hugh, aged twelve, had still not quite reached adolescence. He was, though, even then, far less biddable than any of the others, but he already loved pomp and ceremony and, richly attired in processions, unaffectedly enjoyed holding a corner of his father's cope. Beth was of course there to see to his childish needs. Minnie was there to be written to and ready at all times to be responsive although never in the exclusive way which many mothers are prone to. The Benson family lived more thoroughly than most in close alliance, and, also more thoroughly than most, unspotted from the world. Only Martin was missing. Perhaps after five years his memory was beginning to fade. But for Benson himself Martin's memory could never fade. Martin's death was a blow aimed at him by the Almighty which Benson to the end of his days could never forget, and never satisfactorily explain. On his sixtieth birthday his diary records that the loss of Martin remained 'an inexplicable grief to me', and not long after, on 16 September 1889, in the quiet of Addington, he wrote a poem for the son by then long dead. Benson was not a poet and would never have wanted to lay claim to the title, but these verses are moving still.

> The Martins are back to cornice and eaves
> 　　Fresh from the glassy sea.
> The Martin of Martins my soul bereaves
> 　　Flying no more to me.
>
> One of them clung to the window-side,
> 　　And twittered a note to me.
> 'There's a Martin beyond or wind or tide
> 　　Whom you know better than we.
>
> 'His nest is hid in a clustered rose
> 　　On the Prince's own roof-tree,
> When the Prince incomes, when the Prince outgoes,
> 　　The Prince looks up to see.
>
> 'Calls him hither or sends him there,
> 　　To the Friends of the Holy Three,
> With a word of love, or a touch of care.
> 　　Why was he sent to thee?'
>
> Martin I know. And when he went home
> 　　He carried my heart from me.
> Half I remain. Ere Martinmas come
> 　　Go with this message from me.
>
> Say 'Thou Prince, he is wholly thine,
> 　　Sent once on a message to me.
> Yet suffer me soon, at morning-shine,
> 　　To see him on Thy roof-tree.'

'Half I remain.' This was true. The Archbishop, and the Bishop too for part of the time, had lost for ever the stout certainty that had characterized the Chancellor of Lincoln and the Master of Wellington.

Benson's tenure of the Primacy lasted for almost fourteen years, from the end of 1882 to October 1896—almost exactly the same length of time as his immediate predecessor, Tait. He therefore sustained the role of first peer of England for longer than most in the long roll.

We are not going to be concerned here with ecclesiastical history. No detailed account of Benson's primacy, of its triumphs, of its shortcomings, will be attempted. He was never a success in the House of Lords. He never learnt the rule about making one point over and over again, which is just as relevant in that House as anywhere else. He was too compressed. The large-scale proprietors of land and beeves were as slow at taking things in as the rest of the population. Benson, son of a small, failed Birmingham business man, could never accustom himself to this fact. He could be graceful, and say entirely the right things on social occasions, though he never enjoyed them in the unaffected way that Minnie did. As he got into his sixties he could become testy and overpowering, especially when the dark moods descended on him and took hold. In August 1890, riding with one of his daughters, he said: 'I came to look upon being angry merely as the quickest way of getting what I wanted.' And at an Oxbridge dinner once, the brother of the Master, a most trusting and holy man, suddenly irrupted into a polite and well-informed conversation with a startling new theme which required tactful handling all round. 'Mr Hawker of Morwenstow'—Benson came too late to see for himself the strange goings-on, the self-devised elaborate ritualizings which went on in the north Cornish parish of Morwenstow, but he would have heard many tales of this original man, devout and devoted, who wrote much fine poetry as well as 'And shall Trelawney die?' which may not be quite so fine but which is stirring. Hawker believed in God whilst never failing to take into account the operations of the evil eye which might— who knew?—be watching him, who took to opium in his later years, but who left a regenerated Morwenstow behind him— 'Mr. Hawker of Morwenstow', then, so said the Master's brother, 'told me angels had not wings;—it would impede their flight— but *I* saw one once, and it *had* wings—they were of gold.' Benson was a man impatient of eccentricity especially on public occasions. Verbal skylarkings such as this could put him seriously out of humour. And once he told Arthur, now of course fully of an age to accompany his father sometimes to the innumerable banquets and receptions which now became part of his almost daily routine: 'It is a great mistake to talk of your spiritual experiences in a mixed company.' This is the observation which singles out Benson for all times as the holy, undivided Anglican.

He kept a diary pretty faithfully during those last fourteen years—he could always find time for this, crowded though his days were, because he rarely slept for more than four to five hours out of the twenty-four. Perhaps it would be true to say that whilst at Lambeth his diary was a more constant confidant than Minnie. The diary indeed became a most vital necessity to him. Without it, the private man might well have disappeared utterly behind the grand façade of the public man.

He loved riding, and was not afraid of horses that pulled hard although he was never a safe seat and could be thrown more easily than an archbishop ought to be thrown. He was happiest probably at Addington, the magnificent country mansion now swallowed up by Croydon, which was then the country seat of those who sat on the throne of St. Augustine. Here he could indulge his passion for making improvements. Benson was a do-it-yourself man in an age which knew them not. On 9 August 1883, all new to the place and lusting to make alterations everywhere, he notes in his diary: 'Busily employed with workmen in "converting" the Chapel. It was hideous, with stalls on either side of the altar, and all other seats eastward. I have brought down Bp Juxon's rails, which I found in lumber room at Lambeth, which cannot be used in Chapel there, and some seat fronts which were made in imitation of Juxon's work, and were also in same limbo. With these I construct a screen which looks quite Belgian, and a reredos, and some side-pannelling, and turn the seats choir-wise. Nellie is to paint frescoes in red lines on walls, and Fred Wickenden gives us new glass and refits the old, which he gave us for our chapel at Lincoln, into the windows; I hope we shall obtain a quaint and grave effect, if not a very exquisite one; but we shall still see what colours and a little parquetry will effect. Nellie has drawn "Lazarus", Maggie "The New Jerusalem"; both good first attempts in this style.'

Arthur, twenty-one in 1883, duly collected his First from King's, and after that spent a while in Athens. He was thinking of becoming a schoolmaster, and Dr. Warre, due to become headmaster of Eton in 1884, would be sure to welcome on the staff an old boy with such distinguished antecedents. But Benson was not eager that he should be in a hurry about this. 'I hope,' he told him, 'you will not worry yourself about *scholastic* life, or make any change of plan with a view to it. It's very nice, but it's not all— and it makes me sad to think how many capable men, who might have added something to the "enrichment of the blood of the world", are by the temptations of schoolmastering so early quenched. Perfect your education on the best and highest lines, and the future will be cared for.' In the same letter Benson went on to say: 'Matthew Arnold is going to America to lecture. What a discipline, to grind for Philistines after he has mocked them with foxes and firebrands and all his riddles so long!' Benson was never very happy about Matthew's sad cynicism when contemplating the solid, middle-of-the-road Christianity of his famous father. Listening to him at dinner once, Benson somewhat testily reminded Matthew of a passage from Dr. Arnold's notable sermon on Christian education, and Arthur recalls the reply he got. 'Matthew smiled very affectionately at him, drooping his head sideways in his direction while he patted his shoulder, saying, "Very graceful and appropriate, my dear Benson,"—Matt, it must be remembered, was seven years Benson's senior—"but we must not take for Gospel everything that dear Dr. Arnold said." '

His new and enormously busy life went on. An Archbishop of Canterbury in 1886 was more central a figure in the affairs of the nation than any successor might possibly hope to be a century on. The moods of melancholy and depression, so total, so blanketing, so long-lasting of earlier days, became shorter in duration, more easily shaken off, but they still came, and he still needed Minnie's support and tact to help him through. His extreme susceptibility to (often imagined) injury or slight was enough to plunge him into a helpless despair. He examines one of these attacks with clinical objectivity in a diary-note of 1886. 'All day I have been in a cloud and out of heart because I thought quite early in the day that a mean slight was put on me by someone. If it is physical, it is very unpleasant and very closely tied up to the moral. If it is moral, it undoubtedly has a physical effect. My mere thoughts derange several organs at least slightly. My feeling moves particles of matter rapidly and not through any secondary exertion of muscle.'

He made few new close male friends once he had reached to the top. The ones who had been boys when he was a boy—Westcott, Lightfoot, Hort, and, until his death in February 1885, his 'dear friend and master' Bishop Wordsworth of Lincoln—were the ones he clung to. He interested himself in the feminist causes which women were by now beginning urgently to promote. He enjoyed their company too, but always in the properest and most strictly unemotional of ways. Adeline, Duchess of Bedford, was very close to him in this side of his activities. '. . . For some reason, not perhaps very definable, many thoughtful women were stirred in the years 1884–5'—as well they might have been—'with the desire to purify and elevate the moral tone of Society in London. . . . The Archbishop was approached . . . and . . . a course of addresses given by himself in Lambeth Palace Chapel . . . begun in the Spring of 1885, continued till his death. . . . The poetry of goodness was felt in his every word. . . . On the other hand, he never ignored the subtle attractions of evil to the lower nature. . . . Strenuous himself to the point of sternness, he could not tolerate an easy or sentimental pietism . . . he quoted with approval the saying of another that "few women are truly religious". A combination of piety with frivolity was necessarily distasteful to him, but, apprehensive of unreality in its subtler forms, he would sometimes say, when sure of his hearer, "take care not to fall into *religiousness*. . . ." '

Some might find the pejorative tone of Benson's use of the word 'religiousness' here a little surprising. 'Religiousness', or 'religiosity', which in meaning is only a millimetre away from his warning word might be used by many to describe the least admirable side of his own nature both as a priest and as a man.

He took a month off in the summer, spending it usually amongst the Alps which he always loved, but apart from that, few men in high public office can ever have laboured longer or more unceasingly. On 3 October 1887 for example he went to Wolverhampton for the Church Congress. 'The streets were filled with an enormous crowd, mostly working people. . . . The Chief Constable pointed out to me how the police had nothing to do—so great a growth, he said, in self-respect—even to keep the lines for the procession. In *these* ways England is gaining, and in 50 years more *either* the crowd will be all with us, or we shall have ceased to be able to move thus in public at all. . . .' Benson's gift for either/or prophecy shines out strongly here. The next day he addressed a crowd of nearly 3,000 in the Drill Hall and 'The Congress rose to its feet when I came forward'. From Wolverhampton after a whirlwind time he went to Cambridge to see his second son Fred, now aged twenty, installed in his rooms for the new term at King's College, Cambridge. By the 7th he is back at Lambeth, with time to note in his Dairy, 'I have just been reading Champion on Socialism. He contrasts the Lord's "Come unto me, all ye that travail and are heavy laden, and I will give you rest" with the "Primate's £15,000 a year and two palaces", and his recommending to the East End poor "the alleviation of spiritual consolations" . . .' Benson is not unjustifiably hurt at the jibe. '. . . if they only knew what a small fraction of either money or space goes for anything except to provide work and possibilities of work!' And he reassures himself that he at any rate works with furious concentration and stamina. '. . . I have been reading Oldcastle on the saintliness of Leo XIII, much exemplified in the fact that he rises at six and after a busy day "retires to his apartment at 9.30." About eight hours' rest, and may his sleep be sweet, sweet old man! But it is no particular saintliness to be called at 6.30, get up between that and seven, according to the hour the night before, and after a day of exceedingly hard work, with *ten* minutes' sleep sometime on most days, go to bed at a quarter to one a.m. This I have been obliged to do now for eleven months of the year for many years. . . .' Certainly Benson gave unstintingly of his energies and his time in return for his £15,000 a year (a vast sum, of course, in those days). He was not interested in what money might, in a personal sense, buy for him. He very rarely got more than five hours' sleep a night, and on that much he had to face a following day heavy with responsibilities and crammed with varying kinds of strenuousness.

By 1890 he was far from well in health, and when the time came for the month's break in Switzerland his depressions were moving in on him frequently again, like those weather ones that seep over the British islands from the west unremittingly through so many summers. Seeley, historian of British Imperialism and author also of that much-read book of unconventional Christianity which he called *Ecce Homo*, was staying in the same hotel—the Rieder Furca sited above the Aletsch Glacier—and Benson was very ready to talk to him, though not always of course to agree with him. All the Bensons were there—a great family cluster of them. (They were always great ones for family unity in spite of small internal wranglings.) Minnie was there, very much overweight by now but not outwardly at all bothered by this. She did not walk very much, but spent her energies keeping a close watch on Edward to see that he did not, as he always tended to do, over-exert himself. Arthur was there, a successful Eton master by now; Fred was there, finished with King's but undecided how best to employ his undoubted talents; Hugh was there, fresh from winning the First Prize poem at Eton in 1889 on the subject of 'Father Damien', living in London his always intense private life and interesting himself in Theosophy; Nellie was there, the most outgoing of the family (though she too could suffer from black moods). 'What shall we *do*?' she used to ask them, and then was always willing to fall in with the majority decision, or sense what the majority decision was likely to be, and speak up for it. She was the one, moreover, who stood least in awe of her father; later on, after she was dead, a novel of hers would be published called *At Sundry Times and in Divers Manners*, which is agreeable stuff and has its importance in that it demonstrates that not a single one of the Benson brood failed to get themselves into print. Maggie was there; she was taking pupils in logic, working at a book, and not as adventurous, in the mountaineering sense, as the rest.

Yes, they were all there, and Benson scrambled about energetically, in spite of Minnie, and noted things with his always sharp eye. 'Coming down from the slopes of the Bel Alp we met a great pig walking faithfully after a girl, like a dog, up the narrow stony path. He had socks tied on to save his feet. He had come from the Rieder Alp up and down the Furca and the steep descent through the forest over the moraine and the glaciers and with a most human expression of eye was still following the girl close. It must have taken them hours. He was toiling up to his death at the Bel Alp. (Nellie had seen Piggie lower down and mourned for his faithfulness—'we were much charmed afterwards to find it was not so tragic. They take the pig with them when they go from lower to higher pastures and back.')

And although he was energetic, and scrambled, and noted detail with an accurate eager eye in his diary, he still had time to add towards the end: 'Have read through the *Odyssey* since I came, all but a fragment which I shall finish on the road. Its teaching is so high that the occasional sins of the Gods are inexplicable to me. [That is a sentence very characteristic of Benson.] . . . Penelope . . . seems an argument for divorce writers. Whenever she comes in it is weeping, she cannot sit still except weeping, she weeps herself to sleep at the end of every story of her. . . .' How different from his Minnie, outwardly so placid and comforting and comfortable, to whom they all could, and did, run when life became grievous for them.

That Swiss holiday of August 1890 can be counted as the time just before life began again to be grievous for Benson in the way it had been at Truro after the death of Martin twelve and a half years earlier. When they got back to Addington there was talk of cases of diphtheria in the neighbourhood. It was a disease which, up to as late as forty years ago only, roved savagely amongst the young and killed those it attacked more often than not. By mid-October Nellie was showing symptoms of the illness, and on the 25th Benson wrote to one of his canons. '. . . Our dearest one is in a critical condition—they think that she is "not worse" today. Pray God her sweet and serviceable life may be granted us.'

But as it had been with Martin, God was not prepared to listen, and two days later Nellie died. She was just twenty-seven. Everyone missed Nellie. She was the family's diplomat. She had the gift, like her mother, of holding all their oddities together (except perhaps for Hugh who tended to go his way alone even from childhood) and enabling them to combine harmoniously. For her younger sister Maggie especially, who possessed a very powerful intellect but who was diffident, mistrustful of herself, and neurotic, the loss was a damaging one indeed. Now Maggie felt obliged to play Nellie's part as well as her own; she never shirked the burden, but it was to prove in the end too heavy for her. Benson himself was not shattered by her death to the extent he had been by Martin's; his grief was genuine enough, but Christian consolation was this time perhaps just adequate to its task. '. . . she was to me really,' he said, 'such an unobtrusive instance of a little saintly spirit using *all* its capabilities to help others and to love us with the utmost daughterly dearness. A piece of self seems gone from this world, for no one *can* be what *she* was. I remember her startling me when she was but eight years old, when I said to her something about the poor, by answering, "I do not think so much about the poor—they *suffer* so. . . ." '

And although Benson does not italicise 'think', it needs italics just as much as 'suffer', if Nellie's meaning is to be fully conveyed. As for Minnie, it can be said with fair certainty that she was closer to her daughters than she was to her sons, but for all that it may also be said that she accepted the loss of her elder daughter in her middle twenties as she accepted all the blows of life; with no lapse into a mood of the worst kind of rebelliousness—the kind which can serve no purpose which is not harmful to and destructive of whatever good that may be left to be derived from the situation giving rise to it.

But that autumn of 1890 is a time when no one, however alive to his very real faults, can fail to be sorry for Benson. He was, just at that very time, approaching the most difficult single decision of his whole reign as Primate of the Anglican Church. He had, that November of 1890, to pronounce judgment, after hearings which had been going on since August 1888, in what was known as the 'Lincoln Trial'.

The private affairs and embroilments of the Church of England do not now preoccupy the nation as a whole with the intensity which was felt a hundred years ago. Indeed in Benson's own time —and he was well aware of and worried by it—massive support for the church throughout the land—actual churchgoing—was already beginning to dwindle. For the nonconformist *British Weekly* in 1886 Robertson Nicoll took a count of Sunday presence in all places of worship in the area controlled by the LCC. Mudie-Smith made another, much more elaborate, survey for the *Daily News* at the end of 1902. These two enquiries showed that, in the interval period of fourteen years, Sunday attendance in the Church of England had dropped by almost 140,000—although, of course, the population of the LCC area had vastly increased in that time. The downward slide had begun, and it was due, in the main, to the vast growth in town population, to the consequent depopulation of the country parishes, and it was also due to the decline in intellectual quality of the parsonry as a whole.

But all the same, in 1888 doctrinal conflicts within the Church could arouse high excitement and intense partisanship. By now the old antagonisms between 'High Church', 'Broad Church' and 'Low Church' have largely subsided—although even today an interested visitor to London might profitably visit All Souls, Langham Place, on one Sunday morning, and All Saints, Margaret

Street, on the next—Jack Nicklaus could comfortably drive a golf ball from one church door to the other—and find himself, within the space of a week, in two quite different worlds. By now, indeed, it is probable that the great majority of the population of these islands has ceased to have any knowledge of, or interest in, the word 'church' at all, let alone the nice particularities of 'high' and 'broad' and 'low'. But in Benson's time church politics and policy still mattered extremely, and so, after much anguished consultation, Benson held judicial court in Lambeth Palace to try Edward King, Bishop of Lincoln, on a charge of 'Ritualism'. Benson began all this in a mood of the greatest distress and reluctance, but, as he put it to the Dean of Windsor in February 1889 just before the opening of proceedings, 'When a horse bolts downhill it's safer to guide than to stop him. Especially by getting in front of him. Would it had never begun! But that is such a different thing!'

Of the whole business Arthur, who during the whole of his maturity, never accepted membership of and adherence to any church, Anglican or other, wrote: 'The points at issue seem, it is true, to those who are . . . not in connection with the electrical circuit of ecclesiastical sympathy, to be almost pitifully unimportant.' And what were the points at issue? When it came to the trial before Benson at Lambeth, he had sitting with him the Bishops of London, Oxford, Rochester, Salisbury and Hereford as Assessors, and heard no fewer than six Counsel. Three of these represented the Church Association, the 'Low Church' organization who were making all this fuss about what the saintly Edward King had been up to away there in Lincoln; and three made the case for the Ritualists. When the moment of trial finally came on 4 February 1890, the 'charges', so to call them, amounted to seven: 1. Mixing water with the sacramental wine during the service and subsequently consecrating the Mixed Cup; 2. Standing in the 'Eastward position' (i.e. with the celebrant having his back to the congregation) during the first part of the Communion service; 3. Standing during the Prayer of Consecration on the West side of the altar, in such a manner that the congregation could not see the manual acts performed; 4. Causing the hymn *Agnus Dei* to be sung after the Consecration Prayer; 5. Pouring water and wine into the paten and chalice after the service and afterwards drinking such water and wine before the congregation; 6. The use of lighted candles on the Communion Table or on the retable behind, during the Communion Service, when not needed for the purpose of giving light; 7. During the Absolution and Benediction making the sign of the Cross with upraised hand facing the congregation.

Well, it seems a great deal of hullabaloo over very little. But it needs to be remembered that the Church of England already at that point had three hundred years of history behind it, that the Reformation had happened and that for a multitude of reasons it was still important, that Cromwell had waded through blood and slaughter over matters not dissimilar to these, and that the Lutheran Bismarck, addressing the Reichstag not twenty years before the date of King's trial, had told them: 'To Canossa we will not go, neither in the flesh nor in the spirit.'

Benson himself, although a Ritualist by inclination, certainly thought it a great to-do over what were, by then, really minimal matters. But he listened carefully to the six barristers although already before setting out he knew much, much more about the business than the sum of the knowledge of all six barristers put together. The hearing lasted three weeks, closing on 25 February, and after it Benson announced that he would reserve judgment. The gestation-time for his judgment was nine months, and was delivered on 21 November. 'It has been grievously penible to write,' he said, 'because the topics are so infinitesimal in comparison to others which ought to be uppermost in the minds of churchmen', and, much later on, when the Swiss holiday at the Rieder Furca was over, 'It is agonising to be working at candles and ends with my Nelly so ill overhead.'

Benson had to bury his daughter, and so the Judgment had to be postponed until 21 November. Then, 'serene and dignified', he gave it in the great library at Lambeth. All the bishops sat in a semicircle with Benson on a raised seat in the middle in full ecclesiastical panoply; Sir James Parker Deane, vicar-general, with his scarlet and his full-bottomed wig, supplied yet more colour to the gathering. No single extra person could have been crowded into the huge room. A great occasion was about to be enacted. Benson went calmly through it all in the greatest detail. The Judgment, with its accompanying appendices, occupied ninety-nine pages of the Law Reports of 1891. Benson found for Edward King, Bishop of Lincoln, on five points, for the Church Association on two. There were squawks and protests and resignations of course, but generally it was felt that justice had been done and had indeed been seen to be done. Not in any minute particular had Benson dodged his responsibilities.

It was, of course, a victory for the Ritualists in the main, that is, it was a victory for the clergy as against the laity, because undoubtedly the Church Association's bulk support came from the laity; and perhaps we might say, with slums and prostitution and direst need swirling around them as they sat in Lambeth on that dark November day, the bishops could have found better things to spend their time on—Benson himself, as we have seen, had no doubt about where the priorities lay. But ritual was and is important in human life. The lack of formalized, naturally accepted ritual in the common life we lead today is causing restlessness—as well as destructive searchings for something which may serve as a substitute. Perhaps Benson was justified in wearing himself out in the task of coming at an equitable reconciliation of fruitless divisions. The Attorney-General, Sir Richard Webster, later, as Lord Alverstone, to be Lord Chief Justice, wrote to Benson: 'It is not only masterly, and to a fair-minded man conclusive, but the spirit of peace and Christian toleration which has been infused into its [the Judgment's] whole tone, cannot but have a vast influence for good in our Church.' Minnie's brother Henry Sidgwick, not a religious man in Benson's sense of the adjective, was favourably impressed by his brother-in-law's performance, but thought that when it came to Appeal—as of course the Church Association saw that it did—the law lords would make short work of Benson's reasons for flying in the face of legal decisions. 'Your father,' Sidgwick told Arthur, 'still seemed confident as to the result; but I thought him unduly optimistic. Well, as you know—to quote the *Law Quarterly* again—"the Church's logic prevailed" and the Judicial Committee submitted to "eat its own words and say that it was taking in new light".'

Benson spent Christmas at Addington. But he was tired, and not physically fit enough to take the exercise he always enjoyed—and in a sense needed. This depressed him. On New Year's Day 1891 he wrote in his diary: 'When I looked out as an augur on the earliest weather of the year a hanging mist clothed the tree-tops and all above them—the earth was iron-bound in frozen snows. There was a thin island of blue in the north-west and in it half a *moon* shining palely. I looked away and the moon was gone

when I looked again. In the middle of the day the *sun* shone warm.
. . . The tobogganing went on gloriously from the top of Fir
Mount right over the path to the garden. And the Soul which
would have been the soul of all their enjoyment is somehow not
far from us and knows she is not forgotten a moment.' The 'Soul',
of course was Mary Eleanor Benson. Her father's 'somehow'
sounds a bit desperate; but he was quite right in thinking of her
as the one capable of holding together over a long spell in open-
eyed jollity a talented, close-knit, neurotic company. Benson, at
sixty-one no longer capable of the vigorous physical exercise he
enjoyed, fretfully fought off melancholy—'Tomorrow will be
the seventh week since I have been able to ride,' he noted on
13 January—and busied himself, while public affairs were slowly
coming to life again after Christmas, with his life of St. Cyprian.
This biography of his is the basso continuo of all his days. He
worked at it all his mature life, and finished it just before his
death in 1896. Crowded into boxes, the ancient volumes, the
countless papers he needed for his task, accompanied him on his
journeys. In Switzerland, in the Lake District, at Addington,
Cyprian was always there, to be turned to, if only briefly, as a
relief from a too busy life. He admired the Carthaginian Father of
the Church primarily perhaps because Cyprian was a man of
action, a scorner of indolence, so that his temperament chimed
with his own. And when he became Primate of the Anglican
Church, he must have admired him because Cyprian was prepared
to maintain, even to the utmost limit of martyrdom, that the
Bishop of Rome could not be accepted as holding supreme juris-
diction over all the other bishops of all the other places scattered
over the Christian world. Benson's work is not much read nowa-
days, but it does have that fluency which he passed on to all his
literary children. He contrives to make it sound like the work of,
perhaps, two hard years, instead of the laborious work of a lifetime which it was. In the last fourteen laborious years of his life
The Life of St Cyprian became more and more a kind of refuge.
From the meetings and addresses, from the conferences and the
minutes of the last meeting, from the endless Victorian dinners
which were so bad for his digestion, from the ritualist bickerings
of the Lincoln Judgment as from the patience-testing ramifica-
tions of the Tranby Croft scandal—from all these he could run for
cover, now and then, to Cyprian's third century A.D. Carthage,

and study strains and stresses out of which, over the passage of fifteen hundred years, all the heat had drained. 'I am in want of rest,' he wrote in 1895, 'but here I cannot get rid of an hour of work. . . . It is really necessary to do something distracting if any head is to be left on me.' Not many would think of the martyred St. Cyprian as a distraction. But Benson did.

The Tranby Croft scandal broke in 1891, not long after the beginning of Benson's labours on the Lincoln Judgment. But whereas in settling wrangles between Ritualists and Evangelicals, Benson was, at any rate, on ground he thoroughly knew, here he had to feel his way over unfamiliar ground. Of the Affair it might be said that, if every age enjoys, or suffers from (according to the angle from which it is observed), its own particular brand of scandal, then surely the Tranby Croft affair belongs inescapably to its own 1890s.

The Prince of Wales, now fiftyish and having suffered through long years from not having enough responsibility, went up to Yorkshire for the 1890 St. Leger meeting. He stayed at Tranby Croft, guest of Arthur Wilson. A wealthy, *crème de la crème* gathering had assembled at Tranby Croft, and in the evenings they played baccarat and doubtless other games as well.

On the first evening the son of the house saw, or thought he saw, somebody cheating. And surprisingly this cad, if he was a cad, was Sir William Gordon-Cumming, a lieutenant-colonel in the Scots Guards. Young Wilson told a subaltern in Cumming's regiment who was sitting beside him, one Berkeley Levett, what he had seen going on. So thereafter Levett too kept a close eye on the changes and chances of the baccarat game, and, having done so, agreed that yes, Sir William was up to no good. Whereupon young Wilson—why do I find myself disliking this young man?—spread the news. He told his mother; he told his brother-in-law whose name was Lycett Green; and Lycett Green told Mrs. Lycett Green. The quintet decided to watch together again the following evening.

Round Two of the affair duly began, and this time, as before, the Prince of Wales was banker. By the end of the evening's activities all five self-appointed invigilators were convinced that Sir William was guilty of the gruesomest crime in their calendar— cheating at cards. Surreptitiously he was adding to his stake once he knew that his hand was a strong one, and quietly reducing his stake once he knew that the cards he held were likely to make him a loser.

On Day Three the findings of the five were laid before Lord Coventry and General Williams. So now they were seven, and all in a state of shock. They decided to tackle the suspect, and also to tell the Prince of Wales. Cumming was sent for, and told, in the Prince's presence that he must sign a written statement promising never to play at cards for money again. Cumming said he had never done anything so ultimately caddish. Very well, if he would not sign, then sixteen extremely upper-class lips would no longer consider themselves bound to secrecy. Cumming signed; the document was handed to the Prince of Wales, who put the paper in his archives. But, as is the way of cover-ups, this one refused to stay covered up. Someone leaked the story, and Cumming brought an action for defamation of character. He singled out the five originators, and cited the Prince of Wales to appear as witness.

Sir Edward Clarke, for the plaintiff, vigorously stirred mud. He put the Prince of Wales up; he was not in the dock, of course, but even the witness-box could not be said to be a pleasant or appropriate place for the Heir Apparent to be standing in. After all, one of the self-appointed judges of Sir William had broken his word and leaked the business to a grateful press; and there can be no doubt that the Prince of Wales disliked the situation he found himself in very much indeed.

Still surely Sir William must have done what his examiners said he had done—because if he had not, and was innocent, what conceivable motive could there have been for his having signed the note which he had signed? To this question Sir William stoutly replied that it had been his wish, at whatever personal sacrifice, to keep the Prince's name out of the unsavoury business. Sir Edward Clarke got the utmost he could out of this. Indeed he went further. If the Prince of Wales had for one moment suspected that Cumming was guilty would he not have felt obliged to communicate this to the Service chiefs? Yet the War Office had not been brought into the business at all. Therefore, Sir Edward argued, the Prince of Wales could not at any time have considered Cumming guilty. At this point one brave juryman popped up and put the obvious question to the Prince of Wales: did he, or did he not, think Cumming guilty? To this the Prince replied—and it was an answer which did him no good at all—that he had felt obliged

to concur in the majority verdict. The jury found for the defence;
Sir William lost his case. And the British moral conscience,
luxuriating in a sense of outrage, got up on its hind legs and
roared. And the rest of Europe joined in. Overnight the playing
of baccarat became the sin against the Holy Ghost.

And the man singled out for the fusillades, the sitting target for
a thousand brickbats and ten thousand arrows erratically aimed by
journalists with eyes fixed on daily or weekly circulation figures,
was of course the Prince of Wales. The Prince, they said, was a com-
pulsive gambler; the Prince, on his visits to many-tiered mansions,
forced his hosts to turn their gorgeous palaces into gambling halls.
Editors of obscure local papers delighted in expressing their sense
of disgust. W. T. Stead of the *Review of Reviews* asked why such a
man should be prayed for every Sunday by priests of the Church
of England? It did not seem to occur to W. T. Stead, that humour-
less man, that if all the nonsense that was being printed was true,
then what candidate for supplication could the Church of England
more suitably pick? *The Times* itself printed a leader at the conclusion of the trial, and in the 1890s *The Times* spoke with the
voice of Moses and judged over everything and everybody. Of
the Prince of Wales, *The Times* chose to speak reprovingly: would
it not have been a good thing if he too, like the erring Sir William,
had signed a note abjuring baccarat from that moment on? The
Prince, on account of his position, had to keep silent. But a day
came when he decided that he had had enough. He acted. He sent
for Benson.

Benson's domestic pleasures were reading aloud and writing
Latin verses. It is quite reasonably possible that he did not so
much as know how many cards constitute a pack. He did know
though—who could not?—all about the Tranby Croft affair;
and he knew also that the Prince of Wales was in no small fury at
what ecclesiastical opinion had been putting about concerning
him and his reprehensible pleasures. He knew too that *The Times*,
the Thunderer itself, powerful as a moulder of opinion to a degree
in those days which no newspaper now could conceivably aspire
to—he knew that *The Times* had delivered judgment on the play-
boys of Tranby Croft on its leader page; and amongst other
rumblings had candidly expressed its sorrow that when Sir
William Gordon-Cumming had put it in writing that never,
never would he play cards again, the Prince of Wales had thought

it neither necessary nor appropriate that he too should sign along the same dotted line.

Benson went to Marlborough House and was carpeted—for an ex-headmaster a new and almost too bracing experience. The Prince told him that he was being hounded as a disreputable gambler; he said further that he considered Benson to be the founder and begetter of this campaign of insult and defamation. And so now he, the Prince, had sent for him so that he could listen to any attempt at self-justification the Archbishop might wish to make.

But Benson had been in positions of power and authority for far too long to be shaken by explosions of wrath, royal or otherwise. He stood his ground. Neither verbally nor in writing had he ever, even by insinuation, commented on the scandal which was the topic of conversation everywhere. This did not mean, Benson went on, advancing into enemy territory with purposeful, headmasterly tread, that he did not have his private opinions on the Prince's goings-on, and if the Prince wanted these he could have them, either now face to face, or later in a letter.

The Prince took this well. Queen Victoria's first-born was an intelligent man and like all intelligent men enjoyed being stood up to. Immediately they began to talk as friends. The relaxed atmosphere so beloved of modern communiqués became for once something genuine and not a form of words. The Prince agreed that he enjoyed a small flutter but was no gambler in the serious death-or-glory sense. Benson said that gambling was wrong because it involved putting at risk, even in a small way, something that belonged not to the gambler but to God. The Prince informed Benson that one of the first men he had ever played cards with had been Bishop Wilberforce—Soapy Sam in person.

Perhaps at that point Benson said 'Touché'. At all events both men spoke their minds; both emerged from the encounter with respect for each other enhanced; there was a cordial and sensible exchange of letters afterwards. And the Queen, who was no come-what-may supporter of the Heir Apparent, wrote Benson a charming letter in December 1891. There was no open mention of Tranby Croft, but she contrived to make it clear that she thoroughly approved of her Archbishop for not turning and running when under fire from heavy guns.

For Benson though life was exhausting. He slept little and ill, but insisted in carrying out to the last detail the innumerable calls upon his time and attention. Disestablishment, foreign missions— he toiled away at problems and policies which quickly grew large and multiplied like mushrooms over the space of a warm September night. His face—handsomest of faces—grew more lined and venerable. Now and then he took a holiday—to Switzerland, to North Africa, and he would go back to Winchester as often as he could, because his dead Martin was never for long out of his mind. He was there in February 1894. 'Yesterday my wife, Lucy and I [Lucy was Lucy Tait, daughter of his predecessor as Primate, Archbishop Tait, a lady about whom there will shortly be more to say] . . . went down to visit our dear grave in the Cloisters at Winchester. All sweet, still and beautiful. There was never a sweeter rest for a sweeter creature. But His removal of such a bright intellect and such a stedfast will is one of those fearful riddles which most help one to realise that there is a living Providence. No fate or chance could have directed such an arrow. It is marvellous and happy to think of him with Nellie, and it would be more marvellous to imagine they are not together and not praying for us'. Here again, after sixteen years, you have the feeling of a man trying very hard to convince himself, and not really succeeding.

Through it all Minnie supported him. She had her private life, her private thoughts; she had her special sort of religion which was not his, and Edward of course knew all about this. Undoubtedly he grieved about it, but knew too that not even his enormous energy and masterfulness could force a way through to the inaccessible regions. He was obliged to accept this isolationism, because he knew that without her, without her strength and loyalty, he would have been lost. Intense activity seemed on the whole to help ward off his melancholia. It visited him still, but it was now neither so fierce nor so frequent. He had chest pains, and during those holidays, briefly relieved of strain, weakness and exhaustion crept alarmingly over him. Minnie's anxiety about him became obsessive. She had forebodings which, she told herself, were irrational. 'I don't really at bottom think there is anything radically wrong, but I fear. . . .' She had always been fond of her food; now her concern for him led her into sometimes spectacular over-eating; the vast and variously enticing Victorian banquets she had to give, or eat in others' houses meant that temptation was always at hand. She got fat. She vowed she would diet. She did diet. And then, disgracefully, resolve would weaken. 'Scarcely any loss of weight,' she noted. 'I AM going to be rigid this week.' In September 1896 he was due to embark on a long and arduous tour of Anglican churches in Ireland. His doctor, Douglas Powell, examined him before he went. Powell, and a colleague, considered that his heart was 'weak in power', but neither of them felt that a giving up of his visitation, nor even an abridgement, could be considered necessary. It was in this way, as Minnie perhaps alone knew, that Edward's will and forcefulness could mislead even when he was seriously failing.

Arthur went back to Eton for the new half—he had established himself as a most successful master since 1885, and 'Benson's' was by now a house much sought after—and on the day, Arthur remembered, he 'came out to see me off, waving his handkerchief as his custom was till the carriage had surmounted the brow of the hill'. Then, not many days later, Edward and Minnie themselves set out from Addington.

He was in high spirits, and tireless. He talked well. He preached well. He impressed. After a sermon in Kildare Cathedral he walked with Minnie to the Deanery for lunch. A squally shower broke, and as he had no umbrella, Minnie opened hers and tried to shelter him. 'You may put out my eye, dearest, but don't spoil my new hat.' He finished his tour in Belfast on 9 October, and spoke fierily to 2,000 people. Then they set out for home. Minnie noted it. 'We drove to the station and ran down the lovely little bit of line to Larne—as we went I said to him, "You've spoken beautifully all through, and this was the best of all"—and he just smiled.' They got to Carlisle by noon. 10 October was a day of rain and tempest, and as the train took them down to Chester Edward wrote busily away. 'We had some agitating moments at Chester station,' Minnie wrote, 'where a despatch box went wrong . . . but all was serene when we arrived at Hawarden. He was looking forward immensely to the visit—we had constantly been asked, but never able to go. Mr. Gladstone received him with the greatest warmth and deference—just as his manner always was—and they settled down at 5 o'clock to talk about all the business of the Pope's Bull which had come out whilst we were in Ireland. . . .' They talked and dined and talked. 'When your father came upstairs at night,' Minnie told Arthur, 'he was very bright and full of talk; he and I went on talking on every subject till 12 o'clock—I never saw him better, more active, serener.' Snow fell in the night, but they were both up for Early Service, and then, after breakfast, more writing. The household was gathered to go off to Mattins, but Edward kept them waiting, and Minnie was obliged to go up and hurry him. Minnie drove to church with Mrs. Gladstone; Edward walked with Mrs. Drew and they talked about Mr. Gladstone and Mr. Balfour. Mrs. Drew noticed that he stopped a lot on the way, and got out of breath.

As they all knelt to confess their sins a frightened Minnie heard his death-rattle. They clustered round; the saying of the Lord's Prayer began, but, with no time for a parting word, Edward was dead. They laid him in state in the library of Hawarden Rectory, and Gladstone said to Mary Benson: 'It was a soldier's death—a noble end to a noble life.' Perhaps she was comforted. She was comparatively young, after all, and resilient. She was to live until 1918.

6

Tremans

SUDDENLY MARY BENSON WAS NOTHING. She had watched over Edward, hastened to supply his needs—needs sometimes that he was himself scarcely conscious of. Her active, outward life had been his totally. Of her six children two were dead, the other four all grown up. Hugh, youngest and most wilful, was twenty-five. He was the only one of all of them with a religious vocation—and even so, it was not of the kind wholly to satisfy his father. Still, in the Advent ordinations of 1894, he had been ordained by his father, who wrote: 'I had the wonderful happiness of laying hands on my Hugh.' Maggie was thirty-one. After her First she had lived at home, been lady-like, and to some extent had indulged her aloofness which kept her from taking as busy a part as her elder sister Nellie in the smaller duties and sociabilities of life either at Lambeth or Addington. She painted a good deal, especially animal-painting—she was always fond of animals; she wrote an unfrivolous book called *Capital, Labour, Trade and the Outlook*; she visited friends; she had scarlet fever in Switzerland, was moved to an unfrequented part of the hotel which was curtained off by carbolic sheets, and was nursed back to health by her sister. In 1888 she arranged with the Headmistress of Croydon High School to teach logic to the senior pupils. The Headmistress, Maggie told her brother Arthur in a letter, 'appears to have a great theory of "everybody doing some work in the world" so she is intensely amiable to me—so amiable that I am beginning to have fearful misgivings.'

In 1890 she wrote her mother a mysterious letter. 'My Dearest

Mother, There is something I want very much to write about. I had a long talk with B the other day about the principle of her not talking to me about certain things because I was young in my mind—she *feels* strongly against it, as you know, and as you do, but couldn't defend it much, and the ultimate point was that you didn't wish it—and had said so to her.

'Once I did think so too, but now I don't—you know that I don't wish to know things for the mere sake of knowing them— but it does seem to me that I have reached a point'—it was a girl of twenty-five who was writing—'at which knowing so little as I do does really separate me from other people—B couldn't ulti- mately deny this though she did at first. Her argument was that it was much better for me not to—that it would only disgust me— I'm sure I hope so—but at the same time I do feel that with her for instance I come to a deadlock now, since this cuts off from me the possibility of knowing in any thorough sort of way the prob- lems that she (as other people) has to deal with. In so many ways we have come to a stop too. The things that are problems to me are out of her line altogether. With all this I daresay there is very little that she could tell me—would care to I mean—and as far as that goes I have nothing to do with it—and certain instincts in her which are against it I don't want to interfere with—only I should like her to feel free about it, and you see she is so particularly careful.

'I fear you will feel about this as you did about Nellie and C. As you know, I don't want it for its own sake, only when you are brought near to the alternative of knowing things you don't like, or not really knowing people you do like, I don't see how it's possible to choose the latter. Of course I'm very vague as to what I want to know, and it is just that I am not able to understand the questions that touch her in their real bearings that bothers me.

'My writing is getting on more or less. I am just getting to Immortality, which pleases me. I am going to cut Martineau out. Please give my love to everybody and Beth. Your lovingest daughter, Margaret Benson.'

Could any young woman of twenty-five in the late 1970s believe that I had not made this letter up? That a young woman of first-class intelligence, beautiful, eager and spirited, should have to write, in hesitant, shamefaced tone, to her mother to ask her if it might now be possible for her to be given just a tiny, tactful bit of information about the facts of life, about the differences between the male and female sex, about copulation, the act, its preliminaries and its consequences—that such total ignorance of the essentials of her life, of anybody's life, seems to us incredible. And why had not Mary told her? Perhaps it was because Mary herself, all ignorant, had been brought into sharp collision with these facts at the age of (just) eighteen, and that her sexuality had been warped in consequence; perhaps it was that in 1890—and for many long years after that, it was considered normal, right and proper that young women of the upper classes—the generality of them anyway—should be hemmed in by a conspiracy of silence on such matters. Yet to Mary Benson, herself so subtly intelligent and perceptive, the second explanation is hardly likely to apply. It was the shock of what had happened to her that caused her to shy away from explaining to her daughters what, in any reasonably ordered society, ought properly to await them. Did the pathos of 'Of course I am very vague as to what I want to know' affect her mother? Perhaps she felt unable to cope with it. She was a loving and sympathetic mother, yet with her there was never the intensity of involvement that there is with many mothers. Fred, on coming down from Cambridge, did some archaeological work on Chester's north wall, and was, in consequence, invited to Hawarden in 1888 or 1889. He tells how at lunch there was talk of clever women and of how there was agreement that his mother was the cleverest woman in England. Gladstone, who apparently had retired into private meditation while this chatter flowed, was stirred at this to return instantly to the present. 'No, you're wrong,' he said, 'she's the cleverest woman in Europe.' Even so, her younger daughter Margaret felt obliged to write to her in terms such as this when she was twenty-five.

Gladstone might well have been right, but for all that the sudden plucking of Edward out of Minnie's life was a shock which she found it difficult to adjust to. She had subjected herself to his will and ways for nearly forty years. The cleverest woman in Europe had deliberately made herself a reflection. All the entertaining, all the high-powered sociability which she had beautifully coped with and enjoyed suddenly ceased. At one moment on an inhospitable Sunday morning she was the mistress of two vast houses and one of the first ladies in the land; at the next she was nothing, with not even anywhere to live. Her secret, long-held dread for Edward and his life was proved to have substance between the ending of the general Confession and the beginning of the Lord's Prayer. As it had been at the time of the loss of Martin, and at the time of the loss of Nellie, she took it well. There was no frenzy, no hysteria, no rush for support to her three grown-up sons. Lambeth and Addington had to be left in the shortest time possible—if only because their maintenance, with no archi-episcopal income at her back, was frighteningly costly. And Frederick Temple, the heir apparent, although without the slightest wish to hound a widow woman, would naturally need to take up residence as quickly as possible. Mary Benson did all the necessary things; but Edward had held no private house in reserve. So where was she to go?

She solved the problem by putting it off. After Nellie's death in the autumn of 1890, Maggie had dutifully sustained the role of only daughter in a very large, and endlessly busy household. But although she was immensely able, she was not outgoing and practical in quite Nellie's way; social duties were something of a burden to her. At the same time she kept up her intellectual interests. She worked at her philosophical-religious book *A Venture of Rational Faith*; she took a holiday in Egypt and thereafter worked at Arabic, hieroglyphics and the whole complicated discipline of Egyptology. But it all gradually became too much for her health. She became arthritic. It became necessary for her to spend stretches of the winter out of England. Accompanied often by her brother Fred, she spent time at Aix-les-Bains, Florence, Athens and finally Egypt. In that autumn of 1896 it already seemed likely that Maggie again would have to follow the swallows southwards. The young Hugh, working at that time as a priest at the Eton Mission in London, also suffered an attack of rheumatism. It was decided therefore that Mary should accompany Maggie and Hugh to Egypt for the winter once the urgent matters had been settled. Lucy Tait of course accompanied them. There is a good deal to be said about Lucy Tait, but for the moment the insertion of 'of course' into a simple statement will have to do. Arthur had his house at Eton to attend to, and Fred was left behind, in a half-dismantled Lambeth Palace—Temple was at all times a model of kindness, consideration and efficiency—in order to supervise, with the assistance of Mr. Alexis Larpent, the proofs of the *Life and Times of St. Cyprian*,

Archbishop of Carthage, which his father had worked on for some thirty years and which he had finished just before his death. Fred brought to this duty a tempered enthusiasm. '. . . night after December night he [Larpent] and I used to sit . . . at Lambeth, while Mr Larpent explained to me why he proposed to omit a reference to Plotinus or insert a passage from St Augustine. Of all these things I knew nothing whatsoever, but I had to give my decision whether or no this should be done or the other left undone, and often I felt myself casting a glance of deprecating apology towards the image of my father at the idea of my correcting his Cyprian for him.' Fred was the frivolous one of the family, and not the man, in the ordinary way, to concern himself zestfully with the lives of the early fathers of the Church.

The winter expedition to Egypt proved calamitous; Fred caught up with the party later, at Luxor. Maggie was an experienced Egyptologist by this time, and proposed to continue her excavations at Karnak. Mary and Lucy Tait were greenhorns, and Maggie had to protect them from beggars and importunate salesmen of fraudulent antiques. Mary was the more easily tempted of the two and needed more looking after. This was the beginning of an extraordinary exchange of roles between mother and daughter which lasted for some years until readjustments were finally made. Maggie, from being the dutiful, questioning, somewhat invalidish young woman, suddenly became, after the death of her father, much more dominating and decided. Feeling better in health, Maggie now saw the need, so far as her mother was concerned, to take over where her father had left off and be the mistress who took command. This led quickly to a complicated and uneasy relationship between them because Mary, given at times to a surface friskiness and larkiness, was an immensely able and determined woman, and not a person, once her Edward had been taken from her, to renounce for one moment the commanding family role she rightly considered to be hers. And there was another element in the situation which made for difficulty between the two of them. This was Lucy Tait. She was a middle-aged woman by now, comfortably off, a survivor. In a few weeks, between March and April 1856, when Tait was Dean of Carlisle, he lost five of his children from scarlet fever. Lucy, and three other girls, did not succumb. One of these, Edith, married Randall Davidson, himself Archbishop of Canterbury from 1903 (succeeding Temple) until 1928 and one of the longest-lasting holders of the office ever. Lucy therefore retained throughout life strong links with the highest luminaries of the Church of England. After her father's death in 1882 she stayed on at Lambeth and became part of the Benson family. The friendship between her and Mary Benson became close and even intense. For Mary, indeed she became the successor of Mrs. Mylne and others. Fred held it to be a Lesbian relationship, and said so, not in so many words but all the same fairly openly. 'My mother's intimacies and emotional friendships had always been with women; no man, except my father, had ever counted in her life, and this long love between her and Lucy was the greatest of all these attachments; it is impossible to think of them apart.' He may well have been right. Mary and Lucy slept in the same double bed in which, long ago, Mary had borne six children; but now she was not Minnie any more, but Ben, because Lucy called her Ben, and so Ben she shall be in this book from now on.

Maggie resented the considerable role of Lucy Tait. She put up with it, but now, necessarily older, better in health, and seeing herself, almost obsessively as taking control in family affairs in the manner of her father, she was finding forbearance increasingly difficult to sustain. And of course here in Egypt, which she was beginning by now to know well, Maggie found the issuing of strict instructions easier than she had back in England. She employed Egyptians to do the spade-work for her, paid them a sufficient and regular wage, and stood no nonsense. There was also Mohammed, her personal attendant, so skilful with the fly-whisk. In all this Ben, though delighting in all the strangeness, was at a disadvantage.

Still, for a while, they enjoyed themselves, especially after Fred arrived. Maggie grubbed out treasures from the tomb of Akhnaton. Hugh went out with a gun in pursuit of anything that was wild, and ran, or flew. Fred hired a canoe, paddled out to a Nile sandbank, and swam and sunbathed. Ben and Lucy boned up on their guide-books and listened to Mohammed's fanciful tales. In the evenings they swapped poems, or drew each other while Lucy, not particularly good at drawing-room cleverness, nodded off. Already all the younger ones were writing—for sheer literary fluency there has surely never been a single family to equal the young Bensons—and it was Ben's duty and pleasure to listen to and comment on what was being produced. Then Hugh left them, after getting the better of a touch of fever, in order to return to England by way of Palestine. Ben and Lucy went off up river by themselves to visit Aswan, and Maggie, left alone with Fred, fell ill with fever too. But her fever was violent and developed into pleurisy. Ben and Lucy came hurrying back from Aswan and a worried doctor visited Maggie three times a day. After a day or two he drew off fluid from Maggie's lung, and this for a while gave her relief. Then, on a Sunday morning, her face and hands went blue and she suffered a heart attack. For a few minutes it looked as if she was about to follow where her father had so recently gone, but then her colour came back, and slowly she began to mend. She was carried down to the Nile steamer on her bed, and the party stayed at Helwan near Cairo for a week to give her a little time for recuperation. But before they set off it became Fred's turn to feel very queer indeed. He was not going to Helwan, but straight on to Cairo by a faster boat, but on the way became delirious. Doctor Page May examined him at Cairo, diagnosed typhoid, and took him, in an ambulance with two nurses, to Helwan. Ben, Lucy, and Maggie, accompanied by only one nurse, arrived there shortly afterwards. Lucy Tait thereupon began to feel shivery, went to bed, and was found to have typhoid as well. Helwan began to look like Scutari on a bad day. Only Ben remained unscathed. She took control, for sixteen weeks remained outwardly cheerful while anguish gnawed at her and the three of them slowly recovered. She had no time even for her diary, but when it was clear that they were all going to be all right she did make an entry: 'The visitations of God bear fruit in the soul. But the soul must dwell in peace, and let the fruit ripen.' Nowhere in the diary is Ben's gospel of acceptance more plainly stated.

Eventually the party returned to Europe, Maggie to Aix for a while, Fred to Athens and then Capri, the two older women to England, where Edith, Lucy's sister, and her husband, Randall Davidson, Bishop of Winchester, received them at Farnham Castle.

They were glad to be back, and Ben, looking round, thought Winchester might do as a place to settle in. She soon found a Georgian house in St. Thomas's Street which was roomy and handsome with a plenteous garden, along the bottom of which

ran the ancient wall of the cathedral close. Although the house
was large, Ben and her children possessed more than enough to
fill it. Crammed pantechnicons lined up along St. Thomas's
Street on a hot August day in 1897; the draught horses munched
from their feed-bags; removal-men sweated because the movables
were almost immovable by virtue of their weight. Cavernous,
innumerable wardrobes, Edward Benson's library which contained multitudes sufficient today to provide ballast for an oil-
tanker, a billiard-table, a two-manual organ, a grand piano, all
Maggie's booty from Egypt which included a granite seated
statue of Rameses the Great—slowly and laboriously the heavy-
weights were edged in. Used to migrations from palaces to
palaces, Ben supervised. She had a home again, and this, even
though it was a home in disarray, was reassuring. At Christmas
the whole family reassembled for a brief while in that Winchester
house, but already Ben was beginning to feel dissatisfied. Her
occupation was gone. It was Edward she had served rather than
the Archbishop. Once Edward was dead his ecclesiastical plans and
purposes meant nothing to her. She felt *désoeuvrée* and listless.
Arthur was being a great success as an Eton schoolmaster and was
also busy writing, with all the ferocious speed and facility which
all the second generation Bensons possessed once they held a pen
in hand, the official two-volume biography of his father. (Arthur,
had he felt drawn to the subject, would have polished off a life of
St. Cyprian in six months; his father took most of a lifetime over
it.) Hugh was at the service, as curate, of the wealthy, high-church
incumbent of Kemsing parish church. This vicar visited his flock
in a shining landau, kept up a style befitting a Renaissance Prince of
the Church, and was charming to Hugh. But Hugh was beginning
to think of joining Charles Gore's Community of the Resurrection
at Mirfield as a first step on his road to popery. The passionate
Anglicanism of his father was not going to satisfy him for long.
Fred abandoned for a time a lightweight historical book he was
engaged on in order to go out to Athens. Here he was to help in
relief work on behalf of those Greeks from Thessalonia whose
homes had been overrun by the Turks. He spent two months on
the move, and saw grim sights as he gradually used up the relieving
cash he had been in charge of. Then he returned home by way of
Capri, an island which enchanted him and which was to play
a considerable part in his life from then on. He was back in

Winchester by July 1898. The three women left behind found the
Winchester winter rough. Maggie worked on her philosophical
book, and became very withdrawn except on the single day of the
week when Lucy Tait went up to town to do her district visiting
in Lambeth. Ben suffered the pains of uselessness and empty days.
Winchester, after all, was a dump, with nothing much going on
that she, accustomed to whirlwind high life in London, could
count as exciting. She had *le cafard*. Maggie's bouts of depression
began to resemble her father's in an alarming way. Indeed from
Ben's point of view they were really worse. Edward had always
accepted and relied upon her attempts at consolation and homely
therapy; Maggie on the other hand resisted all sympathetic over-
tures. She very much turned her back on Winchester, shut herself
up, wrote busily, made occasional visits round about, and cultivated an intense friendship with Nettie Gourlay. This had begun
some while back. Nettie had accompanied her on some of her
earlier Egyptian expeditions, and wrote an account of these in a
book called *The Temple of Mut in Asher*, in which Maggie had a
share. Nettie drifted into invalidishness after the sad fashion of so
many Victorian spinsters, and doted upon her little nephew Cecil,
who fell ill in December 1897. Maggie wrote: 'My dearest. . . . I
have prayed and go on praying . . . that whatever may come, he
may not suffer, and yet God knows so much better than we how
little and tender he is, and also what he can and should bear. And,
dearest, even if in spite of our prayers, suffering of some degree
should come, do try to remember how thankful one can be for
suffering—though it would be so far worse for you to see it than
to suffer it. Yet it may be part of the birthright of that sweet little
soul. . . . Good-bye, my darling—you'll feel me near you.' Is this
routine, mawkish stoicism characteristic of the time—a protective
screen of words to be put up yet one more time round something
nasty? It would be a mistake to think so. Maggie was strong, clear-
sighted, swift and sure in judgment and able to frame that judgment in phrases as brief as they were telling. She could be intoler-
ant of slow thinkers; she could dominate and could enjoy
dominating. She was a bracing woman to be with. Wanting to
share in the anguish of her beloved Nettie, she wrote in the way
she did because her generation, confronted with suffering,
especially childhood suffering, on a scale which it is difficult for us
to conceive of, came to terms with it in a manner which present-day

humanists may titter at, but which may still, for all that, be as effective a method as any of achieving calmness of spirit in a world as full as it ever was of bother and suffering and agony. As for the 'dearests' and the 'darlings' and the constant whiffs of strong emotionalism which rise up from that letter—it simply has to be said that Maggie's strong emotions always boiled and curled like an angry sea round members of her own sex. This was how she was. It was something natural and inescapable. It was something, no doubt, which she got from her mother—the mother whom, over those brief Winchester months at any rate, she kept always at rigid arms' length.

By the time Fred got back from Thessalonia it was clear that the spirits of all three women had dropped so low that a drastic change of course would have to be made. All that mighty furniture would have to be heaved out of the St. Thomas's Street house, and set on the road again. But where to? Ben decided that a provincial town would never do, and was unshakeable. If she had put her own inclinations first she would probably have decided for London. But the problem still was an unco-operative Maggie. Ben's good sense told her that so much cloistered bookishness could scarcely be good for a woman still young; Maggie loved animals, and gardening, and country matters. Ben thought that space and quiet, and wild creatures at the bottom of the garden— badgers perhaps—would be good for her. A country house must be sought and found. Property advertisements in the upper-class, spacious range were looked at, and the accompanying photographs scrutinized. There was one near Horsted Keynes in Sussex which looked as if it might do. Ben sent Lucy Tait out on reconnaissance. Lucy returned full of excitement and pleasure. This was a place that would certainly do. Ben took Lucy's word for it. She was not herself really interested in houses in the deep country—and in 1898 there was still plenty of deep country left even in the south of Britain—but if Lucy was fully satisfied, then Ben was prepared to accept her judgment without demur. They moved.

The house was called Tremans, and it became the headquarters of all the Bensons for the next twenty years. Ben lived in it till the end of her life. The younger generation came and went, but, in the earlier years at any rate, mostly came. Fred, most *mondain* of the family, could work himself up into a state of swooning ecstasy

5

over it. He described first the estate, with its yew hedge, its bowling green, its pergola, its fragrant, crowded flower-beds and orchards, and then took you on to the house itself: 'Embowered thus stood the serene old house, low-ceilinged, with panelled parlours, and broad oak staircases and spacious lobbies. Girt with the green freshness of its lawns, it was cool always in any stress of summer, and in the winter it had its open fireplaces, each with its bellows for the brisker burning of the logs, and (be it whispered) central heating to reinforce their flames. Of ancient oak was its woodwork, panels and floors and staircases, so seasoned that never a creak or a crack betrayed an insolidity, and here and there in third-storey rooms and passages the beams of its construction were grey between the spaces of lath and plaster. It was always faintly fragrant with the smell of woodsmoke (for in winter the fires never died down on the hearths), even when through the windows in summer there flowed the scent of wall-flowers, or when the lilacs were in bloom. . . .' Ben settled to watch and wait till the time when, she hoped, Maggie should come round. There was room to spare for her three sons, all unmarried and to remain so, whenever they chose to visit. In one sense her life was over, but in another it was simply renewing itself with fresh cares and fresh delights; and those three sons, who adored her more even than she adored them—she had time now, in the reposefulness to think back over what they had so far achieved. As for what might come to them—well, for a great deal of their time at any rate, she would be there to see.

7

Eton and Magdalene

In 1864, when Arthur was two, Wellington College received that visit from the Queen. Both he, Martin, his elder by two years, and the baby Nellie received a kiss. Her Majesty hoped that they would be good boys; Nellie was not yet of an age to benefit from good wishes, even of the most elementary kind. Martin certainly, in the brief span granted to him, fulfilled all expectations, royal or otherwise. Arthur too, if in not quite so orthodox a fashion, gave the fullest satisfaction. He became, incidentally, much closer to the Queen than any other member of his family—and that in spite of the fact that his father was for nearly fourteen years Archbishop of Canterbury. His education was of the strictly upper-class, traditional kind. When he was nine he was sent to a very good prep school—Temple Grove, at East Sheen. His headmaster was Waterfield, who stood among the leaders of this very specialized branch of his profession.

In 1886 Arthur published a book he called *The Memoirs of Arthur Hamilton*. On the surface it is fiction, because he alters dates and places and names. Yet it is, for all that, if not in any way a notable literary achievement, quite closely autobiographical. He was ten when his father moved to the Chancellery at Lincoln, and this was, of all the houses of his childhood and youth, the one which he loved most and which had the greatest influence on him. It was here, in the extensive grounds, that he acquired his great love for nature, though he never had, as Wordsworth did, any sense of spiritual kinship. 'In moments of grief and despair, I do not, as some do, crouch back to the bosom of the great Mother; she has, it seems, no heart for me when I am sorry, though she smiles with me when I am glad.' Still speaking of this substitute Arthur Hamilton, he wrote 'He was very sensitive to rebuke,' adding: ' "I am not so sensitive as I am always supposed to be", he said to me once. "I am one of those people who cry when they are spoken to, and do it again." ' Arthur Hamilton-Benson further roundly states: 'He disliked his father, and feared him. The tall, handsome gentleman, accustomed to be obeyed, in reality passionately fond of his children, dismayed him. He once wrote on a piece of paper the words, "I hate papa," and buried it in the garden.'

Arthur was clever, like all the rest of them, and good at concealing what he was really feeling and thinking—as is common with children of an imperious father. His deepest and sincerest love was probably felt, not for his mother, but for the old nurse, Beth. She was simple, and naturally affectionate, easily taken in by Arthur's complicated attempts to arouse sympathy. To the all-pervasive religious feelings of the household into which he was born, Arthur reacted in the way the offspring, if they are clever, often do. He had no religion, in any convinced, unquestioning sense, either as a boy or as a man.

He became a Colleger at Eton, in the Election of 1874. If 'Arthur Hamilton' is anything to go by, and he almost certainly is, he had the usual emotional experiences. 'A sixth-form boy took a fancy to me, and let me sit in his room, and helped me in my work. The night before he left the school I was sitting there, and just before I went away, being rather overcome with regretful sentiments, he caught hold of me by the arm and said, among other things, "And now that I am going away, and shall probably never see you again, I don't believe you care one bit." I don't know how I came to do it . . . because I was never demonstrative; but I bent down and kissed him on the cheek, and then blushed up to my ears. He let me go at once; he was very much astonished, and I think not a little pleased; but it was certainly a curious incident.'

It would be wrong to conclude from this that Arthur, either then or at any other period of his life, was a homosexual in any busy, practising sense. Adolescent sexuality, especially if it is reined in as tightly as it was in Arthur's generation, will obviously tend to make shy sorties in all sorts of directions. But Arthur's sexuality, whether as a Colleger at Eton, or at any time in his busy, haunted life, was sluggish. As boy and man he was one who liked to be busy, but hated to be storm-tossed, whether by passion or anything else. He enjoyed a cosy, ordered life; he shunned transports of any kind because these would probably lead to awkwardnesses, disruption and the destruction—temporary or even perhaps permanent—of a settled routine. All three of these were, in Arthur's view, to be classed as calamities, and the commonest, likeliest method of bringing them down on your head was, as any intelligent person could see by looking round— and Arthur was a very intelligent person indeed—to enter into a neck-or-nothing love-affair with a member of the opposite sex. A friendship with a member of his own sex—Herbert Tatham, say, who was of his Election at Eton—had that beautiful element of stability, was so much less likely to become troublesome. In the summer of 1913 he wrote in his enormous diary: 'I have a quiet spirit in some ways. . . . My own real feeling is that I have never been in vital touch with anyone—never either fought anyone or kissed anyone!' This, coming from a man of fifty-one, seems almost incredible. His carnal desires were never more than fitful little flickers, never remotely strong enough to plague him. He walked a lot, even delighted in it, but Tarquin's ravishing stride was something entirely unknown to him. This was comfortable ignorance, and he took pleasure in it. In Sixth Form Passage at Eton he and his fellow Collegers—Tatham, Boyle, Childers, Wood—talked busily of books, of funny incidents in the daily round of school, of the diverse characters of the masters, but randy fantasies seem to have been barred.

Having lived long enough, an Eton Colleger of the 1870s could transfer almost automatically to King's College, Cambridge, if that was his wish and that of his parents. Arthur duly went up to King's in October 1881. It was a case of the same atmosphere, the same faces, but a much grander chapel to worship in, whether you wanted to worship or not. The set of rooms had once been those of William Johnson, who changed his name to Cory, who was still an Eton master and famous for his translation, 'They told me, Heraclitus, they told me you were dead . . .' J. K. Stephen, only three years older than Arthur, had not long since occupied the set below—on the staircase nearest to the chapel. As an undergradutate he was a bit of a lounger. Of 'Arthur Hamilton', who is himself, Arthur says: 'He never let anyone into the secret of his motives; he never confessed to any plans for the future, or to taking any interest in one line of life more than another.' He dabbled at playing games; he wrote quite frequently for the *Cambridge Review*; he was a member of the Pitt Club, which was, and is, aristocratic; he never spoke at the Union; he enjoyed music, and used to drop into King's chapel not so much for devotions as to listen to the choral singing; he read a lot but not purposefully—an ordinary sort of undergraduate life, in fact. But he duly got his First in the Classical Tripos, and tried unsuccessfully for a fellowship by submitting a study of Archbishop Laud, which was published three years later in 1887.

He was sociable, good at attracting friends, and good at keeping them. Nevertheless, in his last year at Cambridge, if *Arthur Hamilton* is to be believed and almost certainly it is, he found himself face to face with some sort of personal crisis. He lost his easy friendliness. He was, as the book says, 'no longer young'. This other Arthur had formed a passionate friendship at school. His partner had come on to Cambridge, but had, without Arthur's first suspecting it, fallen in 'with a thoroughly bad set there'. At first the close friendship continued, but then 'disclosures were made. . . . What passed I cannot say. I can hardly picture to myself the agony, disgust and rage [his words and feelings about sensuality of any kind were strangely keen and bitter], loyalty fighting with the sense of repulsion, pity struggling with honour, which must have convulsed him when he discovered that his friend was not only yielding, but deliberately impure.'

Of course this may all be fiction. 'Arthur Hamilton' may not, in this instance, be Arthur Benson. Arthur had, beyond doubt, a facile inventiveness as later novels were to show. It may be that what Arthur is describing here is the first of those attacks of prostrating melancholia which were to become much fiercer and more long-lasting in his later life. It may be that all he is doing here is reaching out in his imagination for an explanation of a bout of *accidie* which might pass muster. He was always good at finding words for feelings which were vaguer than he made them seem. But still, when reading this account (carefully imprecise) of a betrayed affair of the heart, the temptation to substitute for 'Arthur Hamilton' the name 'Arthur Benson' is strong indeed.

It is typical that he should find it difficult to know what to do with himself after failing to get his fellowship. Few people of course can ever have had an upbringing more thoroughly soaked in churchiness than Arthur, and in spite of his unbelief the forms and rites of Anglicanism remained powerful in him to the end of his life. Undoubtedly his father, with Martin gone, wanted him for the priesthood. But the maturing Arthur did not see it like this. He had no vocation. Indeed, apart from enjoying writing and finding that the business of stringing words together came easily to him, Arthur had no vocation in any direction whatsoever. Certainly schoolmastering did not constitute an intrusive temptation, as the Archbishop seemed to think.

But then from Edmund Warre, who had just become head-master of Eton, came the offer of a mastership there to begin in January 1885, and Arthur accepted. Probably he accepted, not because it was a case of 'And gladly wholde he lerne, and gladly teche', but rather because the offer meant a swift return to a familiar place and a mode of life he was thoroughly accustomed to. Arthur always liked to be comfortable. He was not, at any time in his life, a venturesome man. At all events he took to his duties with easy competence. After a year or so it was clear that Arthur was going to be an outstanding success as a schoolmaster. He lived in Edward Lyttelton's house, Baldwin's Shore, and his pupil-room was quickly full. Herbert Tatham had gone back too as a master, and the friendship between the two of them was close and constant for twenty years. Together, in spare hours, they walked the country round about—so quiet then, and, in M. R. James's words (he and Arthur were born in the same year): '. . . the boy who in his Sunday questions illustrated the friend-ship of David and Jonathan by that of Mr Tatham and Mr Benson was right.' In 1892 he became a house master, and 'Benson's' quickly became, and always remained throughout his time there, a house of note in a very special sort of way. The Lytteltons, Leo Myers, Percy Lubbock were some of his boys—they all thought well of him, remembered him in later life, and Lubbock of course became a close friend and edited an abstract of his four-million-word diary.

Why one man makes a successful schoolmaster and another, perhaps equally or more able, does not, is a question difficult to answer. To begin with, of course, he must be able to keep order, and Arthur, tall, burly and of good presence, could certainly do that. To a superficial onlooker it might appear that boys enjoy being taught by someone who lets them do as they like. Secretly though they despise him. This is a fact which is called in question today but which is nevertheless still just as certainly a fact as it was in Arthur's day. Arthur could keep order, but at the same time he strove always for a relaxed atmosphere. He never aspired to ferocity—would have hated trying for it. 'A new division,' he noted in his diary in 1897, 'sitting like mice, all demure; they seem amiable and serious . . . I hardly ever raise my voice above a conversational tone, and very rarely set a punishment. But it's a precarious trade, and depends much on calm nerves.' This is true. The ease of an authority which is never strenuously insisted upon —Arthur, with his great gifts, fine bearing, and his background of high culture, always possessed the trick of this; it is a trick that lies at the heart of successful schoolmastering. The hundreds of Etonians who came under his influence—Maurice Baring, Edward Cadogan, the Lytteltons, the Sturgises—all to a man approved of him, found him stimulating and good to work for. 'Benson's' was a good house. He did not, of course, exactly fit into the strict mould of Eton masters of those days. He took little interest in athletics for instance. If the house won a cup for something, well, that was nice; if it did not—well, that was nice too. Although possessing his first in the classical Tripos, he did not believe that the grand old fortifying classical curriculum— virtually universal in the British public schools of his time— should count as the beginning, middle and end of the education of young gentlemen. The fact that tradition was too strong to allow him to break out of this mould irked him all through his schoolmastering days. In 1897 he has a diary-entry: 'Today I sit for an hour and a half rewriting a copy of Latin Alcaics by C—. . . . They are quite worthless. . . . The work racks my brain . . . and it is poor enough when done, because the subject is impossible. Meanwhile to do this I scamp my history paper . . . and C. does not know what it means, and Warre probably does not look it over; but this form of work is what is called the Eton system— to crush the master under mechanical and useless work, give him no scope for stimulating work with his pupils, knock him up with exhaustion, and for two or three boys who don't read what is written and don't know whether it is good or bad. This will be *incredible* fifty years hence.' He did what he could to break out of the narrowness. In talk he wandered wide. On Sunday evenings in winter he used to tell a story to any in the house who cared to listen. 'Exactly at the appointed moment,' E. H. Ryle says, ' "my Tutor" would emerge from his little privy writing-room, which was rather a mystery to us. . . . He would turn up the light in a green-shaded reading-lamp on a little table, bury himself in his great, deep leathern arm-chair . . . frown prodigiously at his hands clasped before his face, and from out of a deathly stillness inquire, "Where had we got to?" Nobody ever replied, and after a short pause he would briefly indicate the point at which we had arrived the preceding Sunday, and then steadily, but not monotonously, and in a low conversational tone of voice, with never a check, he would narrate . . . an absorbing tale. . . . Shortly after its publication in 1903, I started to read *The Luck of the Vails*, by E. F. Benson, "my Tutor's" brother. I wondered why it seemed familiar, and then it flashed upon me that the story . . . had been spun out to us on the ten or eleven evenings of (I think) the winter half of 1899–1900. I imagine that A C B, after realising the pleasure it had given to a youthful audience, passed on the outline of the plot to E F B. . . .' This was one of the ways in which Arthur sought to counteract 'the Eton system'. But it was little enough. Schoolmastering in his time, Arthur felt, was not the job it could and should have been. Was he there, with his large and comfortable success, on false pretences? Was it right to be toiling at an occupation which was so much more fruitless than he considered it had any right to be? This was a question he pondered much. Although he was getting on into his middle years, he still could not admit to being launched into something permanent.

There was always that 'little privy writing-room' of his which Ryle and all his other pupils knew about, but into which neither they nor even his co-evals like Tatham or Arthur Ainger were admitted. Here he wrote, and wrote with a facility which amazed and still amazes. Words like an ever-rolling stream bore all his cares away—or some of them at any rate. 'I wrote two sonnets in the evening before dinner,' he notes in his diary. 'I find myself much slower at writing poetry and much less disposed to do it than two years ago. . . . I have a certain facility in language, and now and then a gleam of artistic excitement. But this is not enough.' Two sonnets between the end of school and dinner—and he reproaches himself for getting slower at it! The Queen,

5*

just across the way in Windsor, found nothing at all amiss in this miraculous fluency. Little Alfred Austin became Poet Laureate in 1896, and after that disastrous appointment she turned quite often to Arthur when she felt the need of something public and poetic. And later on he was to write the words accompanying Elgar's 'Pomp and Circumstance' march, *Land of Hope and Glory*. Up to 1945 these were, of all measured words, the ones most widely known by the English-speaking people. Now perhaps they are becoming less familiar, though they are still roared out, ecstatically if inappropriately, on the last night of the Proms each year, and still have a wide currency through that alone.

Arthur then can be said to have led a double life. He was a divided man. First there was the public man, the one known best by schoolboys, in college common rooms, in cathedral closes, in the Athenaeum. This man was endlessly entertaining, the very best of company. His talk was shrewd, sharp, wide-ranging and amusing. Authority, not asserted but still quite strongly there and prepared at need to exercise itself, radiated from him. He was not exactly the son of his father—he lacked the tenseness, the dynamism; yet here, certainly, was a presence, and sometimes an overpoweringly vigorous one. On the other hand there was the man-in-the-writing-room, the man nobody ever saw. This was someone uncertain of himself to a degree bordering on neurosis, a self-examining, self-questioning person. This was a man plagued by bad and fearfully vivid dreams, engaged in fighting off a numbing and prostrating melancholy which was always there, lurking at the edge of consciousness and ready, the moment there was any sign of a relaxation of the defensive posture, to march in and take full possession of the mind's territory. This second man was a figure out of tragedy, but he is to be admired too—perhaps more wholeheartedly than the first, companionable, successful one. Arthur, in his second role, fought hard and gallantly against an enemy who was very strong as well as being desperately elusive —the Benson enemy, his father's enemy, Maggie's enemy, the enemy capable of destroying great gifts and wrecking opportunities which in their brilliance were outside the scope of all but a few. He understood, just as well as Kipling, that there were 'two sides to his head'. As he put it in his diary: 'In my books I am solemn, sweet and refined; in real life I am rather vehement, sharp, contemptuous, and a busy mocker.'

The long holidays were of course something. They gave him
relief from his discontents. Unlike Fred and Maggie he took no
great delight in going abroad. He liked walking and bicycling
round about. He enjoyed the wide sky-sweep of the fens. He was
not home much while his father was alive; the Egyptian catas-
trophes of the rest of them passed him by; St. Thomas's Street,
Winchester, he scarcely got to know. But once Ben was settled in
Tremans, though the tensions and religiosity of that household,
which will become more apparent later, made life there sometimes
uncomfortable to him, he made it a second home. Involvement
in emotional tensions he tried always to avoid. Howard Sturgis
and Alfred Ainger shared a holiday house at Tan-yr-Allt in North
Wales, and he went there a great deal. Stuart Donaldson, another
Eton master, had one at Dunskey, in Scotland, and there too at
holiday times Arthur was often seen and always welcome. In 1898
a tart spinster named Miss Browne was there as well. 'I discussed
marriage with Miss Browne,' he writes. 'We decided that the old
maid was much happier than the old bachelor, because she
generally had a circle and home ties—no selfish ineffective loneliness as the old bachelor. True, I think. I wish I saw my way out
. . . but I don't think it is good to marry after forty [he was thirty-
six]. Still I can believe that it is wisely withheld from me, partly as
a *lenis castigatio* for my many infirmities and partly because I am
not loyal-hearted.' This is a revealing entry. Marriage is waved
good-bye to without the slightest sign of heartbreak. And he
was not *loyal-hearted.* How well he understood himself. Arthur
was agreeable, a deft and ready conversationalist—but there was
always that sanctuary, that inner writing-room. His instinct was
always to back away from other people's troubles, even the
troubles of close friends.

In 1899 he moved to somewhere more spacious, Godolphin
House, at Eton. This was a sign of his success as an Eton house-
master. But he still could not accept Eton and its life as something
permanent for him. In May 1901 Warre sent for him. '. . . he
wished me to take orders. He then went on to say that he could
not be headmaster for long—three or four years—and he hoped
that I should succeed him. It needed an Eton man and a wise man,
who would make wise changes and not fear popular clamour or
the newspapers. . . . He should do all in his power to secure it. . . .'

Arthur liked Warre. And to be headmaster of Eton, after all,

was to be quite something. He refused, however, to become at all
excited. 'But really,' he goes on, 'I hardly agree with him at all. I
cannot take orders of course. . . . Prominent position and great
work are so bound up in my mind with *gêne* and odious publicities
and bonds of all kinds that I do not desire them. . . . Of course
orders would give me a share of such pickings as there are, but I
don't want loaves and fishes at that price. I should be afflicted with
permanent moral asthma. . . .'

In August 1901 he went back to King's, just on a visit. It was
thirteen years since he had been back in Cambridge, but the place
was still as idyllic as ever. 'At Cambridge station a high grain
elevator and mill in buff brick—hideous but impressive. Drove
down to King's. . . . Everyone, porters, dons, bedmakers, were
extraordinarily welcoming—chid me for my absence, over-
whelmed me with kindness. I felt like coming home. . . .' Of
course it was not quite the same. Dons now could marry. '. . . the
little tutors hurry off to small, new, red-brick houses on the
Trumpington road. The men, too, seem gentler and more
decorous than of old; but I suppose only the mildest are up just
now. . . .' Perhaps a note of regret is sounded here. 'Tonight a
pleasing concert, sung by solid and sober-looking young men. . . .
We lounged in silence, and smoked, the behaviour perfect. Lionel
Ford sang my song, "Twenty Years Ago". I sate [Arthur always
used the old spelling] in a kind of happy dream, not regretting
the old, pleasant, sociable days. . . .' He made something of a name
for himself as a writer of words to music. Indeed he had just come
on to Cambridge from London, where, in company with Fred he
had heard a performance of his *Ode to Music*, set by Hubert Parry.
All the time though he was feeling that Eton was stealing away
from him time better spent in writing. Should he give up schoolmastering? Although he was so successful at it, although, if he
was prepared to make concessions such as the taking of holy
orders he could be considered as first favourite for the headmastership when Warre retired as he soon would—yet he knew,
privately, that he was less than wholehearted as a schoolmaster.
He was even something of a sham. 'Here is my dilemma,' he
wrote, communing with himself, 'on the one hand a useful life,
which bores me—on the other hand a life which is not useful, and
which would probably bore me still more, but which I love. And
still I hesitate; and what makes me despise myself still more is

that even my hesitation is not noble-minded—not fearing to sacrifice usefulness, but mere timidity and habituation: the monkey in the kettle. . . . I say I write less—and yet I have written 20,000 words in this diary, 100 small octavo printed pages, in a month.' Five thousand words a week, in fact—and that at the busy end-of-the-half time when Eton was, if anything, more demanding than at any other time. When writing is something that comes so easily can it be something that you, in the fullest sense, deeply love? This was a question which he did not put to himself.

The visit to King's helped to move him in the direction of formal resignation, but still he did nothing in a hurry. Commissioned literary work was coming in. He was asked to write a shortish book on Gabriel Rossetti for Macmillan's 'English Men of Letters' series, which had by then gained for itself some fame and much success. In 1899 he had brought out his two-volume life of his father, which is an adequate compilation even if it does not glow with filial affection; he had published a volume of stories called *The Hill of Trouble*; and he had made a beginning on what was to become by far his most profitable literary line; meditative-melancholy-reflective books with little bits of narrative artfully interspersed—mild, gracious, soothing, undisturbing stuff, which the readers of those unhurried days, when even a Mr. Pooter, with a well-polished, well-worn boot a long way down the ladder, could afford a capped and aproned maid to answer the bell-pull, lapped up and actually bought in quantities which would make the lips of a thoroughly established and successful novelist of the late 1970s purse with envy.

Still without finally committing himself, he bought a house in Cambridge. That was in the summer of 1902. By then he was forty, and it was time, he felt, that somewhere he should have a house that was properly his own—and where more suitably than Cambridge? The house was called the Old Granary and was close to Silver Street Bridge.

He lingered on at Eton for one more year. Then, in July 1903, he got a telegram from Viscount Esher, who was very close indeed to the new King, Edward VII. Would Arthur come over at once to see him at his house, Orchard Lea? It was an invitation, Esher said, made at the king's own command. Arthur of course went, and as the distance was not so great, he took his beloved bicycle.

He failed to find the front door, but, propping his machine up against a side-entrance, knocked. Esher was reading in his summer-house, and took Arthur walking in his large well-tended garden which was coming to its peak. He was empowered to make him an offer. Would Arthur, in collaboration with himself, edit the correspondence of Queen Victoria for the years 1837–61? To his diary Arthur confided: 'Of course I had no real doubt, and yet with no motive to go at any particular minute. Suddenly in the middle of all my discontent and irritability a door is silently and swiftly opened to me. In the middle of this quiet sunny garden, full of sweet scents and roses, I am suddenly offered the task of writing and editing one of the most interesting books of the day—of the century. I have waited long for some indication—and was there ever a clearer leading? He told me many details. . . . I asked for a little time, decorously to decide; but all the time my heart told me I had decided already. . . . I had a bad night—and no wonder; shirked chapel, and then wrote two letters, one to Warre, resigning as simply as I could, and one to Esher, accepting.'

After the decision Eton, no doubt of it, was in dismay. Arthur was genuinely treasured. He had bad dreams—all through life his dreams were vivid, intense, and sometimes frightening. One of his dreams though at this crisis was funny—even if he himself did not seem to find it so. 'A dreadful night of dreams—voyages on wide blue waters, interspersed with many interviews with the Prince Consort. In one of these we were by a tea-table—we two alone. He helped himself liberally to tea, cake, etc.; then he turned to me, and said, "You observe that I offer you no tea, Mr Benson." I said, "Yes, sir." "The reason is that I am forbidden by etiquette to do so, and would to God I could alter this!" He was overcome with emotion, but finished his tea, after which a grave man came and served me with some ceremony.'

Arthur did not of course pack his bags and leave Eton then and there. As with the Prince Consort's dream tea-party some ceremony had to be observed. Also the bulk of the work on the royal correspondence would need to be done by someone living in, or close to, Windsor. He formally finished schoolmastering in December 1903. 'God bless Eton,' he wrote on 16 December 1903, 'and the dear boys, and my old comrades here—and never mind me! I think I do care more that things should go well here, and that the boys should be pure-minded and public-spirited, than anything else. I wish they could learn something too. . . .' School-masters do not, in the general way, get much fame. They are the launching-pads and not the rockets. And as this century wears on their influence seems to be steadily decreasing. How careful Aubrey is, even though his lives of notables are generally so brief, to tell us, if he can, who the schoolmaster concerned was in most of the cases. Of John Milton, 'He went to Schoole to old Mr Gill, at Paules Schoole'. Now we would say that he went to St. Paul's, but old Mr. Gill would not rate a mention. Benson came towards the end of the time when the art of pedagogy still counted for something, and, although he was to live for another twenty-one years, and although he was to be endlessly industrious right to the end, apart from some blank times which were not of his choosing, it is probable that his greatest and most enduring achievement was as a schoolmaster—stimulating, authoritative without ever countenancing the petty tyrannies of the martinet, eager not to destroy the classical curriculum but at least to loosen its strangle-hold.

After Christmas he shared his time between Eton, where he lodged with Arthur Ainger, who had retired from his mastership, and the Old Granary. At Cambridge he was not of course the established and regarded figure that he was at Eton; but Stuart Donaldson had also left Eton at just about that time in order to become Master of Magdalene College. They used to go bicycling round the Cambridgeshire countryside together—such admirably flat spaces for bicycling on provided the wind is not blowing sharply from the east. And one day in the early summer of 1904, as they were pedalling, Donaldson told him that Magdalene had to elect a fellow, but that there were difficulties because the financial position of the college—a small one—was not at that date at all good. The salary of one more fellow would have to be provided by the sad means of lopping a little off the salaries of all the existing fellows so that the newcomer should not at any rate starve. Donaldson went on: 'I wish we could find somebody who could afford to accept a Fellowship without income.' Did he fly his kite in the knowledge that Arthur was a man of fairly sub-stantial means? Had he not produced no fewer than three books in the previous year, *The House of Quiet*, *The Hill of Trouble*, and something on Tennyson, and had not the first two at least been read and bought eagerly by very large numbers of people? Doubtless these were thoughts that had floated, or were at that moment floating through the Master's mind. Even so, the swiftness of Arthur's jump at the bait may have caused his front wheel to wobble. 'Well, what about me?' were Arthur's immediate words; and this putting of himself forward on terms so advantageous to the college naturally delighted Donaldson himself and the fellowship as a whole. At the beginning of the Michaelmas term 1904 he was formally admitted as fellow of Magdalene College, Cambridge. It was to be a lifelong partnership, and one from which the college was to benefit enormously.

Even at that late stage, though, his decision to make a break got still another testing. When he had left Eton in December 1903 he had noted in his diary: '. . . it struck very chill on my heart, I confess, to see my hall and stairs all dismantled—the cases in the dining-room—the old life all breaking up and going . . . most of all I thank God for giving a very timid, feeble and weak-minded person the chance of doing a little useful work. . . .' One wonders whether he meant this. Well, weakness, feebleness, timidity *were* part of him, but not by any means the whole of this complicated man. He was physically big, could dominate well enough on occasion, and yet, yes, perhaps this disparagement of himself is nearer the mark than he himself in his heart thought it to be. The attack on his resolution came with Warre's definitive resignation. He knew, as we have seen, that Warre wanted him as heir apparent. He knew there was strong support for him at Eton in general. He knew too that there was an opposition party, that there were those with the strongest distaste for his reformist, curriculum-widening views. Characteristically he decided not to put in for the appointment but instead to wait to be asked. All that summer and autumn the question was niggling at him. He worked hard at the Queen's correspondence and did some travelling about—in the United Kingdom as usual. He examined himself intently. 'I am not tired, but a little bored and stale with this hot weather—and with an odd desirous yearning of the heart to the very thing I have turned my back on all these years. One *ought* to be married, no doubt; but it is too late now—and I think I love my liberty better.' He went round York Minster again and was not satisfied. '. . . the spirit which built it is all gone, I think. Religion—by which I mean services and dogmas—what is it? I

1a Archbishop Benson
   Radio Times Hulton
b Mrs. Benson
c Nellie and Maggie, 1876
   Photo R. Slingsby, Lincoln

2a The Archbishop's birthplace, 72 Lombard Street, Birmingham *From a drawing by Henry Tuite*

b Truro Cathedral *Photo Argall, Truro*

3a Maggie, aged twenty-eight
    Photo J. Thomson
b Tremans, Horsted Keynes

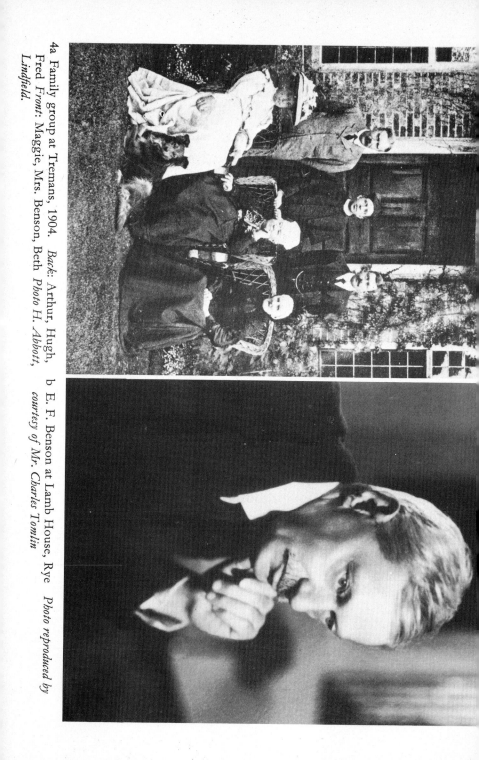

4a Family group at Tremans, 1904. *Back:* Arthur, Hugh, Fred *Front:* Maggie, Mrs. Benson, Beth *Photo H. Abbott, Lindfield.*

b E. F. Benson at Lamb House, Rye *Photo reproduced by courtesy of Mr. Charles Tomlin*

sometimes think it is like tobacco, chewed by hungry men to stay the famished stomach. And perhaps the real food for which we starve is death.' And still the question: who should succeed Warre at Eton was being debated. And still he managed to cling to his original position: he would not apply, but if he was asked he would consider. 'Fancy papa sending in his name for the Archbishopric!'

But the Governing Body, although they would have liked him, refused to turn themselves into suppliants. If Arthur could be mulish they could be mulish too—and in any event there was the possibility that too much change too quickly introduced might be bad for Eton. Dr. Edward Lyttelton was appointed, and Arthur, because he was a very human man, felt hurt. Could not his supporters have, perhaps, urged him more strongly? Well, 'I like my stall at Magdalene better,' he consoled himself, and on the last day of 1904 he wrote the whole thing off in his diary. He was at Tremans, the home, of all the parental homes, which, apart perhaps from the childhood one at Lincoln, he liked the best and visited most frequently. 'Now let me say a few words about 1904, which has been indeed a blessed and happy year to me. I have had *lots* of little worries, but the great strain is gone—the tension that pulled at one's heart, like a dog tugging at its chain, and drew the blood away, whenever one allowed oneself to think of it. The thought of the old slavery, the fussy, fretting days—the running hither and thither, the scramble, the weariness, and what made it far worse the *purposelessness* of so much; that was what knocked the bottom out of the Eton life for me. To feel that for nine tenths of one's furiously busy hours one was teaching boys what they had better not learn, and what could do them no good; drumming in the letter, and leaving the spirit to take care of itself. It is sickening to reflect about. Well, all that is gone.'

These are strong words, and derive perhaps in part from pique rather than from carefully thought out conviction. Arthur was not really very good at carefully thought out conviction. Just as papa had been asked to be Archbishop of Canterbury so Arthur would have liked to be asked to be headmaster of Eton. He was right of course to be impatient about Eton and its perpetual classics; but the superficiality which was his bane is apparent in his condemnation. 'Drumming in the classics,' 'leaving the spirit to take care of itself'—it was sheer intellectual inadequacy on his

part to say that the day-in-day-out sniffing around over the car-
casses of two dead languages was irremediably uneducative. The
fact is—and Arthur fails utterly here to take this into account—
that a good schoolmaster can be educative whatever the subject
he happens to be teaching; the bad schoolmaster will be uneducative whether he is talking about Shakespeare or the law of
diminishing returns or about how to plane a piece of wood so
that you don't end up with a pile of shavings. This refusal to be
clear-headed is apparent in the slackly meditative books which
were now gushing out of him as smoothly and swiftly as water
out of a hole in a mountainside. *The Hill of Trouble, The House of
Quiet, The Isles of Sunset, The Upton Letters*—there was no end to
them—and no satisfying the publishers' appetite for more.
Edmund Gosse, with whom he had become friendly—Gosse
was thirteen years older than Arthur and could assume the role
of mentor quite appropriately—thought little of them and told
him so. 'While lunch was preparing, G. and I walked arm-in-
arm up and down the little gravelled garden. He spoke to me
very kindly and frankly. . . . He says my energy is restless and
sub-divided, and wants one channel. But my channel is now
literature, with a slight "hem" of academical duties. (What a
metaphor!) He did not like my *Isles of Sunset*—thought it should
have been written in verse; thought I was doing too much, and
ought to be silent for a bit. . . .' People of discernment—and he
passed his days amongst people of discernment—were always,
tactfully or less tactfully, telling him this; but this strange man,
with a good mind, was not to be put off. He stuck to his slop. He
had an answer for Gosse. 'I pointed out that I did my best, that
my work was not hurried nor particularly slipshod; that one must
follow one's bent in the fruitful years; that he wrote much more
than I did. . . .'

*　　*　　*

By this time, when Arthur had finally turned his back on the
work which, for all his talk of 'following his bent', was probably
the most useful and durable he ever achieved in his life, Tremans
and its occupants had settled into a permanent routine. Ben had
been there over five years. Beth was eighty-seven and frail, but
still acted out her chosen role of being mother to them all.
Maggie's health improved swiftly. She supervised the extensive

grounds; she looked after the livestock both indoors and out. (She was a great animal-lover, and even, in 1901, published a book of short pieces, with animals for theme, called *The Soul of a Cat*, and other stories, which are agreeably full of exact observation.) She worked over her father's papers and came to think of herself, in a strange way, as heiress of his imperiousness. This led to tensions. She could not be unaware, even if imprecisely, of her mother's relations with Lucy Tait. This closest of friendships had been going on for so long, was still going on, and would continue to go on—if for no other reason than that Lucy made a far from negligible contribution to the upkeep of Tremans, a place built and designed in a fairly grand manner and even in those days costly to run. Lucy took a small house in Barton Street, West-minster, which she used as a *pied à terre* when in London on her charitable works, but Tremans was her permanent home, and that, Maggie or no Maggie, was how Ben wanted it to be. As a counter-weight to Lucy, Maggie brought in Nettie Gourlay, her Egyp-tologist friend whose widower father had married a second time a girl younger than Nettie herself. It was not a ménage where Nettie could feel thoroughly at home; and so, although accom-panied by Maggie she made frequent visits there, Tremans was her refuge for a great part of the time. Ben took note of the situation; four women cooped up together—well, not cooped up, perhaps—Tremans was roomy enough for three times that number—but at any rate in close proximity to each other, and three of the four—never Ben herself—with their claws just slightly protruding in a most ladylike way. They were four very able women, and only one had ever had relations with a man. It was natural that there should be strains and magnifications of grievances. Ben, who had much the greatest natural ability of the four, easily recognized this. In particular the new vigour and aggressiveness which Maggie was showing at once pleased her, amused her and saddened her. Probably amusement was the strongest element of the three. For over forty years she had coped with the desires and difficulties of a family. For over fourteen of those years she had presided with superb aplomb over the crowded comings and going of a great London house. She was quite content to drop the reins and give Maggie her head for a while, but she did not want Maggie to be hurt. Ben wrote, with that lightness of touch which was characteristic of her handling of affairs at this time: 'Maggie was very good at using help. When she was writing the *Venture of Rational Faith*, she could keep several people employed—it was like the Japanese plate trick—as many as seven volunteers could be kept going, and each revived with a smart touch when flagging.'

Of course Ben was far from having her daughter permanently at home. As long as Maggie was well she was busy. She founded, and ran most competently, a movement she called the 'St. Paul Association for Biblical Study'. This was something for women only. It was appropriate that Maggie, with her outstanding abilities, should take some share in the slowly strengthening movement for the liberation of women which established itself in Great Britain as one of the primary public issues of the 1890s and 1900s. She arranged monthly meetings in London, got lecturers to lecture, initiated and steered the ensuing discussions. 'She *was* the St. Paul Association,' somebody said. 'All the life went out of it when she could no longer be there. At the end of the set paper, she was almost always the first to speak, and fill the horrid pause with suggestion or criticism. I remember her saying, "I am always left to make a fool of myself, while Nettie and Gladys [This was Gladys Bevan, who had a London house, which was convenient, and was another close friend] are convincing each other of some important point in whispers at the other end of the room".' She also started a Vacation Term for biblical study either at Oxford or Cambridge which was an extension of the London activities. Undismayed by the dire sufferings inflicted on her during her last Egyptian visit, she went there again in the winter of 1900–01, accompanied as usual by Nettie Gourlay and also this time by her aunt Henry Sidgwick. This time she suffered no illness, and got a proposal, not of marriage but exciting all the same in its unfleshly way. 'Mr Newberry has been planning to write a history of Egypt—a big history and a standard one—to be more complete, but especially more literary than Petrie's. It appears that he approves of my literary (!) powers, and he has asked me to help him. . . .' This was how she put it in a letter to her mother, and she went on to note objections. 'I can't feel that Egyptology is the thing most worth doing in the world, though I feel that about most other things while I'm doing them. Such a lot of times in my life I've been driven this way and that—things stopped just when I thought I was getting to them, or like

Egyptology, opened just when I could do nothing else; or perfectly clear and without any question, like Papa's books. . . .'
As soon as she was away from home, her father's 'perfectly clear and without any question' attitude to life and people dropped away from her; she became childlike and confiding towards her mother. '. . . anyhow I don't think, but *know* that you are the most wonderful person in the world,—as you say, "What a Mama I've got." ' Her aunt Ada Benson, wife of Andrew McDowall, had died young in 1882. The infant Stewart had always provided the opportunity for the exercise of Maggie's thwarted maternal side. By now he was old enough to be thinking of a career, and the career was to be holy orders. Maggie took him through the doubts and the difficulties with a perspicuity which showed the range of her first-class mind. Her letters to him on the subject are vivid and fresh, and constitute a sizeable little volume of Christian apologetics. 'If the scientist says deliberately, "It's all I have," meaning "I'm not going behind phenomena and physical causation,"— well, if he insists on taking that agnostic position, he must. If he confesses that limitation *after* a study of philosophy and religion, it is probably a real limitation of his own mind. But if it is *before* such study, it is a limitation of an ignorance with which he hasn't set himself to contend. It can no more be called *honest doubt*, than it would be honest doubt in me to disbelieve in the truth of the Differential Calculus.' Maggie must have been a great concentrator of her cousin Stewart's mind—and the minds of many other people as well. This was in 1903, when she was a brilliant, masterful woman in her late thirties. Ben watched over her anxiously—and yet amusedly. Her health, her lungs especially, could still, even in these good years, have been solider. The winters had to be guarded against. There were visits here and there, with friend or with family, to places where it was likely to be mild—to Mullion, in Cornwall especially. There of course all the Bensons were still welcome, and highly regarded, figures. And so far as creature comforts were concerned, and freedom to do what you wanted when you wanted, and the perfect feasibility of staying in bed for two or three days at the onset of the tiniest physical threat—a snuffle or two, a sneeze now and then— Maggie was made free of all these delights, if delights is quite the word for them. At Tremans there were personal maids, and housemaids, and underlings to bang the gong for meals, and gardeners

to keep nature tidy, and grooms and coachmen to take care of mobility—it was, in some ways, a wonderful world, and one now deservedly forgotten. In her sadly circumscribed way Maggie thrived on it—till the summer of 1907, when hideous things began to happen.

8

A House of Women

MEANWHILE WHAT OF MAGGIE'S THREE BROTHERS?
Arthur we have already seen settling, pretty comfortably, to his
second career. He found Tremans on the whole an agreeable
place, and was there more frequently, and for longer periods than
had been his custom since his first leaving home to become an
undergraduate in 1881. It was a place where he entertained his
many friends of his own sex. Fred (Edward Frederick), born in
1867 and at the beginning of his thirties when the move to
Tremans was made, has so far only been seen as a sharer in
Egyptian troubles. Hugh (Robert Hugh), born in 1871, the
baby of the family, the wayward one really even though he was
the only one to follow his father's footsteps into the priesthood,
has still to be given a character. Arthur had little patience with
him. 'Petulant, wilful, full of originality, fitful, independent' were
adjectives he applied to him. As indicators of character they were
none of them—not even 'independent'—likely to draw a warm
response from Arthur. He was a man always in deadly earnest, yet
always somehow, without quite meaning to be, something of a
comic turn. Fred, the suavest of them all, had little use for Hugh
either. 'He never set much store on human relationships,' he
wrote of him. Hugh, at any rate, was fairly easy to diagnose. Fred,
by contrast, although by far the most worldly of them all, the most
conformist to his class, was oddly, in spite of this, by far the most
enigmatic. As a writer he was, like his two brothers, hugely
prolific. To count up the total tally of words of Arthur and Fred
to see who came out the winner would be a vast and, even by

biographers' standards, fruitless undertaking. If the whole of Arthur's diary were put into the computer undoubtedly Arthur would finish well in the lead. But the diary remains and in all probability always will remain, in some part unpublished; and Fred's score of published words would put him into the first position if only because he lived longer than any of them— from 1867 to 1940, and he delivered his last manuscript to his publisher only ten days before he died in the February of that most fateful of years. Both of them wrote much about the family. Arthur's two-volume official biography of his father was the weighty foundation-stone of a sizeable Benson memorial.

Fred, besides writing countless novels and fairly lightweight biographies, also turned in much upon himself and his family for the raw material of his authorship. He wrote a book called *Mother*, which has much about Ben in it certainly, but also much about the others; he wrote another called *Our Family Affairs*; he wrote *As We Were*, and *As We Are*, which are amusingly anecdotal—and also very Bensonian; he subtitled *Final Edition* 'an informal autobiography'. But although he can be very candid on some points—his mother's lesbianism, for instance, his own qualified dislike of his father, his own distaste for women as sexual partners—there is, none the less, about himself and his doings a marked lack of candour. His manner is utterly different from Arthur's. Arthur—big, overweight Arthur getting perhaps a little testy as the years flow by—gazes intently at himself, puzzles and worries over himself, acknowledges defiantly that there are 'two sides to his head'. Here is a man trying his best at the hardest task of all—being honest about yourself. Fred is much, much more slippery. He likes to present himself to an audience. He wants to entertain, and he succeeds beyond question in being entertaining. He comes on to the stage and at the beginning everything is neat and beautifully executed; but as the audience's excitement increases, as it is made aware that the nub, the essential bit is coming nearer, Fred slips behind the curtains—or suddenly remembers a lovely anecdote about Tennyson in his baronial years which he will proceed to unfold in that smooth, adroit way of his which skirts flippancy but never falls into it.

Born in 1867 at a public school where his father reigned as the most absolute of absolute monarchs, living out his childhood and youth in closes, cathedrals, episcopal and archi-episcopal palaces, he was an unbeliever like Arthur—but without ever sounding Arthur's note of regretful apology. What Fred liked best was mockery—mockery decorated here and there with a thin, delicate, never, never over-emphatic coating of sentiment. As a child at Lincoln, he, with his sister Maggie usually because they were the two closest in age, often visited Bishop Wordsworth's palace called Riseholme. Here they enjoyed playing in the grounds which were, he says—with that characteristic penchant of his for the not too unfamiliar phrase—'an earthly paradise'. Bishop Wordsworth was kind and at the same time formidable. To a youngster of nine or so he must have seemed much, much older than Mr. Gladstone himself. But, so far as the poetic muse went, Christopher had inherited only the more fallible aspects of his distinguished relative's talent. Christopher liked writing hymns, and, when the mood was on him, was capable of stuff like

> What the Holy Prophet meant
> In the Ancient Testament,
> Thou revealest to our view,
> Lord, for ever, in the New.

Or else an opening such as

> Let us emulate the names
> Of St. Philip and St. James.

It is characteristic of Fred that he should exult in episcopal infelicity and, in a book of reminiscence—one of the many he wrote—parade it before us when he himself had reached an age not far short of the Bishop's at the time of his writing about him.

Like his brother Arthur, Fred wrote a very great deal about the Benson clan. But he differed from him in that he had no passion for self-scrutiny. The millions of words of intensive indecisive inner debate with which Arthur indulged himself were not at all in Fred's line. He could be candid—quite startlingly so sometimes, especially when the generation he belonged to and the family background he grew up in are borne in mind. But he remains more elusive than the others. Writing about his father, Arthur says: 'He said to me once that he had been late in discovering that one cannot alter the decided bent of a character, and the interest he took in my brother Fred's writings was an instance of this. He did not care for fiction, still less for fashionable fiction; but he read my brother's books with a candid admiration for their *élan*, their vigour, though with a kind of mystification as to whence these qualities were inherited; and he was intensely amused to hear a report that he himself had read *Dodo* "with tears streaming down his cheeks".'

Fred went to Marlborough, and not to Eton like his two brothers. Marlborough was, if anything, more athletically minded than Eton, but Fred took quite kindly to this. He had something of Arthur's build, but was leaner and not quite as tall. He enjoyed games and was good at them. He enjoyed them all his life. He did not allow the world to trouble him in the way Arthur or Maggie did. He was the practical one. 'Fred has been a great stand-by,' Arthur wrote in 1924, and it was always so. Yet they had little in common. 'Our ways of life,' Fred wrote when Arthur had long been dead, 'our diversions had little in common, and never, since we were boys, had we spoken of things that intimately concerned us as we spoke of them to our friends. Close blood-relationship certainly implies dutiful instincts. A man who does not stick up for his kin nor is ready and eager to help if they are in trouble is wanting in normal decency, but it does not imply any warmth of friendship. His death left me with no relations nearer than cousins whom I scarcely knew.' There is a certain coldness about this—something which he shared with his mother. Ben cared for her children devotedly, was always fond of them and welcoming to them. But total self-abandonment, save where Edward was concerned, did not come easily to her. When Martin died just as life was opening to him, his father's grief was overwhelming; his mother took it differently: not, most certainly, with indifference, but none the less with a serene sense that life was still there to be lived.

As with Arthur, Fred's sexual tendencies were satisfied through associations with men. But unlike his brother he knows much more decisively where he stands. Arthur's muffled, half-hearted ponderings—should he get married? Ought he to? Would it perhaps be pleasant if he were?—these do not have any place in published self-examinations on Fred's part. When he spoke of himself, and he did so frequently, it was in a much more objective way. Fred Benson is, as it were, a character in one of his own novels: you see bits of him—the bits necessary to keep alive and credible the situation or the anecdote he is dealing with. And if you ask: what about the whole person, what about Fred complete? Then Fred turns his back smartly on you and tells you, without for a moment ever losing his good manners, to mind your own business.

He can write mawkish scenes in which a passionate attachment between two sixth-form boys, soon to part in order to plunge into the wider life of the university, are described with much more elaborateness than such commonplace matters deserve. But too much should not be read into these. They are in the fashion of the middle 1880s, and Fred all his life through was one who liked to be in the fashion. He put his Marlborough life into a highly successful novel which he called *David Blaize*. When he was old, and healthily self-critical of what he had achieved in his writing, he was still prepared to defend some of his early work, and *David Blaize* was one of the titles he would not apologize for. Into it, he said, 'I had put emotional imagination.' This is ambiguous of course, but it might be taken as a statement of his sexual preferences throughout life. His father visited Marlborough at the end of Fred's last term there—July 1887. He preached in chapel in the morning, and then, as he notes, 'Afternoon wife and Maggie and I walked with Fred in Savernake—marvellous heat. He read us some of Geo. Herbert with much appreciation, so that this is the third generation of us that have delighted in him. Fred is a very manful and sweet boy. He is head of all athletics here and has just got the English poem. Pollock [then an assistant master at Marlborough] says he should take a first at Cambridge.' 'Manful' is the Archbishop's word. 'Manly' is the one more favoured by the late Victorian age. But they both mean the same thing— masculine, muscular, decent (in the sense that normal human passions exist, of course, but are on no account to be made apparent), and deferential to age and authority. By now all this has become a matter for hilarity—perhaps in some respects too much a matter for hilarity.

Fred duly took his first in part one as well as in part two of the classical Tripos at Cambridge. He achieved in fact precisely what his brother had achieved five years earlier, and achieved it as a member of the same college, King's. He wrote a continuation of *David Blaize*, and called it *David of King's*. Do the two books between them offer a reliable account of Fred's schooldays and his time at the university? It would be unwise to be too trusting on this point. When the young Fred wrote novels he was writing to win attention, to be a success, to be popular. He was obedient to market forces. When you read *David Blaize* it is difficult indeed to be persuaded that here, under another name, is Fred the outward-looking, the easy mixer, the good comic actor, the singer of comic songs, the lad among the lads. Consider the story. Young David is sent to the prep school Holmsworth. The picture of it is fairly generalized, but it probably resembles in quite a fair measure the place Fred himself was familiar with. (He had a great gift for recalling his past, but it is difficult to be certain about how much touching up he indulges in, even in those later books where he purports to be writing personal or family memoirs.) A master called Dutton is caught by the headmaster reading Maupassant under the cover of the Bible whilst supervising his charges. The head takes over, and takes over the boys himself which is so much better in every way. He rips the disgusting Frenchman up—strong action to symbolize his contempt for such stuff. David himself is represented as lovable and as being unaffectedly interested in whatsoever things are of good report. Cricket matches are described at great length. During one important match in particular David feels 'beastly'. This is because his father, an archdeacon, arrives for the occasion. He is dressed oddly, so David's teammates think, in his full ecclesiastical rig. This slight divergence on his father's part from good form quite puts the boy off his game which in the ordinary way is dashing and brilliant. . . . Then David goes on to his public school which is called not Marlborough but Marchester—a distinction without a difference. Here he meets Frank Maddox, three years his senior and already a great hero. David becomes Maddox's fag and unqualified admirer. Still the cricket matches go on, and still David shines. He and Maddox are very close indeed. By the time David enters the sixth Maddox is off to Cambridge, and now we are nearing the climax. At the end of the summer term, David heroically stops a runaway horse, but is himself very seriously injured in the process. He is put to bed, and his chances of living are not thought good. But Maddox, hearing of the mishap hurries from higher things to comfort and tranquillize at the bedside. He does this to such effect that David drops off into a long sleep, out of which he climbs a saved young man. *David of King's* continues in much the same vein though by now of course David is more mature. The atmosphere is sweet—too sweet; there is a warmth that can become unpleasantly sticky; emotional thunderclouds march across the sky without ever being menacing in any significant sense. How did an intelligent and gifted man come to write such stuff? It is the same question as the one posed by Arthur's *The Upton Letters*, *The Thread of Gold*, *Thy Rod and thy Staff* and the too, too numerous others. Arthur, the competent, authoritative man, shrewd, incisive and amusing in talk, was quite aware from the outset that what he was producing amounted to no more than flimsy extemporizations. Percy Lubbock, his friend, used to worry about it. 'This one,' he says (meaning himself), 'since leaving him a couple of hours ago, had muddled and scratched away at a few sentences; while he in his study, sitting comfortably by the shrubbery-screened window, had produced as many pages as the headlong pencil could cover in the time. What were they about? "Oh, the usual twaddle—you know my style!" and he would heap up a derisive account, extravagantly picturesque, of his books as they were viewed, or supposed to be viewed, by his icily fastidious friend. They were mocked and travestied with rich enjoyment, exploding into irresistible laughter.' Fred, basically a stronger, more creative writer than his brother but afflicted like him with a too easy copiousness, took longer to come to see that his strings of volumes lacked for the most part the quality that would give them permanence. But when he was old he had the courage to look back on the productions of his early and middle years with perceptive ruthlessness. 'For a quantity of years I . . . earned the admiration of many readers and indeed of critics, but such as it was, it had certainly been fading. Imperceptibly to myself, I had long ago reached the point at which, unless I could observe more keenly and feel more deeply, I had come to the end of anything worth saying. My interest and pleasure in writing were unblunted, and though nobody can write to any purpose unless he enjoys it, such enjoyment in itself is no hall mark of value. I knew (and maintain) that I could express myself lucidly and agreeably, but I had been learning nothing. I had not been delving into myself or others, only turning over and over the patch of ground I had already prepared, and setting in it cuttings from my old plants. I observed with a certain acuteness, but not with insight. I made my people bustle about, indulge in what may be called "stock" experiences, talk with a rather brilliant plausibility, but, as a depressed perusal of some of my own volumes convinced me, they lacked the red corpuscle. I found other faults in these books, the chief of which was that I had often tried to conceal my own lack of emotion in situations that were intended to be moving, by daubing them over with sentimentality. I despised sentimentality in other writers. I looked upon it as a deliberate fake yet whenever I got in a difficulty I used it unblushingly myself. . . .'

This is acute and courageous self-analysis. Does he offer excuse? Well, he begins with something that is important—and perhaps self-justificatory. 'Thirty years ago,' he says, '. . . I had scored without any effort beyond that of amusing myself a very big popular success. My first book—it was called *Dodo*—had sold enormously, it had furnished a theme for discussion in alert circles for many weeks, it had aroused serious as well as amused attention. Edmund Gosse—I never dared to remind him of it later—had told me that I had produced a work of high moral beauty, and that if I would work, work and live, I should set my mark on English fiction.'

Fred worked on *Dodo* immediately after coming down from Cambridge and at the beginning of his spell of working for the British School of Archaeology in Athens (1892 to 1895). His criticism of it at the end of his goodish stretch of life, when the Second War was either threatening or about to begin, is clear-sighted and unsparing of himself. That concealment of 'my own lack of emotion in situations that were intended to be moving' points at the weakness that was to bedevil all his novel-writing. In *Dodo* he talks of the *beau monde* of the 1890s. The action moves from London in the season, when coachmen wait all night outside the doors of great houses to trot their masters and mistresses home in the dawn ('Decidedly somebody washes the world every night,' remarks the Marchioness of Chesterford—'Dodo'—after spending the night dancing with a Satanic and masterful Austrian Prince Waldenach: the sort of apt phrase that Fred can catch so easily out of the air, and with it nudge the reader, as he constantly does, into realizing that whoever does the washing, it will most certainly not be Dodo), moves on to country houses where hunting and shooting diversify the mornings, where clusters of footmen scurry at the sound of bells, where in the evenings perhaps there will be Edith Staines's music to be listened to (Edith Staines is Dame Ethel Smyth—Fred knew from the outset how readily the smart set of his time would be attracted by the *roman à clef*), and languid merrymakers, primed with Wildean witticisms, consume vast breakfasts of kidneys, kedgeree, bacon, sausages, eggs, ignorant about cholesterol and quite uninterested in the fact that perhaps at that very moment (1892) James Keir Hardie was taking his seat in the House of Commons as member for West Ham South.

As for his work for the British School of Archaeology at Athens, Fred seems to have treated it pretty well as a young upper-class Englishman's excuse for not doing anything at all. Maggie, flying with her weak chest from English winters, was with him much, and he had all the time in the world to look after her. 'I went with her several times to Egypt' (multiple typhoid and cardiac arrest were still some four years away), he writes, 'to Athens, to Florence, and stayed with her more than once at Aix. . . . At Athens we got up a farce, *The Duchess of Bayswater*, nominally to amuse English Governesses and residents. Then the British-Mediterranean fleet came into Piraeus, and we said the sailors might come, if they would supply half the entertainment. This was done, and the first half consisted of hornpipes and songs. Then the Royal Family announced their intention of being present, and the audience consisted of Kings and Queens, governesses and sailors. The play in question is a roaring farce, and Maggie acted the Duchess. Next day the Queen of Greece sent for her, and asked if the English aristocracy really behaved like that. . . .'

Maggie as a stage comic Duchess is hard to imagine, but she was only twenty-eight after all, and her *Venture of Rational Faith* could not have been expected to fill her young life entirely. Fred, who was always the frivolous one of the family—though 'frivolous' isn't quite the word to apply even to him—would have encouraged her, and delighted in the antics without *arrière pensée*. *Dodo* by now was out and a big popular success already a reality. He knew furthermore that he could turn out successors to *Dodo* with all the facility which was the blessing as well as the bane of all the male Bensons. Is he thinking of himself when he writes of Jack Broxton in *Dodo*? 'Jack's life at this time was absolutely aimless. Before he had gone abroad he had been at the Bar, and had been called, but his chambers now knew him no more. He had no home duties, being, as Dodo expressed it, "a poor little orphan of six feet two", and he had enough money for an idle bachelor life. . . .' Fred was never of course a barrister, and he was not aimless—he had produced around one hundred books by the time he died—but he did enter with some enthusiasm into the activities of what the French called 'le high life' of those days, and Dodo herself, it was commonly said, was modelled on Margot Tennant, later to become Asquith's second wife. (She, in her *Autobiography* of 1920, denied this, but a woman is not upon oath in her autobiography.)

It is certainly true at any rate that the great success of his first book did, as he came to see, do him harm as a writer. 1893 turned out to be not the glorious dawn but the opening fanfare preluding long years of repetitiousness. Throughout however he was the man of affairs of the family. After his father's sudden death it was Fred, not Arthur, who took command of the situation. It was Fred who sorted out his father's affairs. It was Fred who looked after them all through the hail of Egyptian illnesses which floored them in the first half of 1897—even though he too in the end fell a victim. It was he who stuck it out at Tremans until 1899, when he was thirty-two, because he had promised, at the time of his father's death, that he would live with his mother. Fred's life never had the 'absolute aimlessness' with which he credits Jack Broxton's life in *Dodo*.

His relief work in Thessalonia had happened before 1899, and has already been mentioned. His return home by way of Capri has also been touched on, but that Capri visit was important and needs to be returned to. Fred adored the place, and, gregarious as he was to a degree exceeding Arthur's and much exceeding Hugh's, he enjoyed the émigré company of Capri, which was talented and queer and which Norman Douglas and Compton Mackenzie—Mackenzie with by far the greater brilliance— described in books such as, respectively, *South Wind* and *Vestal Fire*. Fred formed here a relationship—whether it was a homo- sexual relationship in any warm-blooded sense it is impossible to say, Fred was on the whole a cold-blooded man—with one John Ellingham Brooks, a very wealthy literary dabbler who made his primary object in life the rendering into English of the sonnets of Hérédia who wrote pieces as static and as highly polished as a dead cavalryman's riding-boots. Fred was much too intelligent not to recognize the emptiness of such devotion, but none the less Brooks amused him, as did Axel Munthe, and Kate and Sadie Carter, and Mr. Coleman the American artist whose dedication far exceeded his talent, and the English vice-consul (the Freddie Parker of *South Wind*), and Count Fersen, and all the other gilded lilies (some past their best and due for dead-heading) of the island. Fred was to return there many times, for long periods, in the ensuing years.

But he did remain faithful to his promise to support his mother with his presence, and kept Tremans as his headquarters till 1904. By then he was a fashionable writing success of the first magnitude and his novel-output was well into double figures. By then also he was thirty-two and was acutely uncomfortable in a house of women—even though that house was beautiful and welcoming and presided over by the most understanding of mothers. He watched the triangular tensions building up between Ben and Maggie and Lucy, felt his own helplessness in the matter, and, what was worse, was certain that if he stayed much longer an estrangement between himself and his adored mother would be the result. Arthur, grumbling and dissatisfied at Eton, would surely not stay there much longer, and, once parted from the place, would be free to spend a much larger part of his time at Tremans —a house which he approved of just as much as Fred. Ben, seeing his uneasiness, took the first move as was characteristic of her. She spared him the anguish of having to tell her that he was obliged to live his own life in his own place in town. She wanted to set him free from his promise, she told him; and joyfully he fixed himself up in a small flat in Oxford Street. Tremans became a place to be visited, and for that reason a place to be enjoyed with none of the reservations which had niggled at him up till then. Fred was never a lover of women, either singly or in concentrations. Except of course for Ben—and for Beth who was for all of them not so much a woman as an institution, changeless and immortal.

*   *   *

But what of Hugh? Where did he stand in the family? Could he not bring a masculine presence to Tremans? The answers here have to be hesitant; with Hugh you could never be quite sure of

6

anything. Youngest of them all, he arrived when Martin had only seven years left to live. And so it was that the young boy was never steam-rollered by his father in the way all the others had been. Benson accepted that, in his desire that Martin should be the immaculate model of industry, virtue, and righteous success, he had perhaps driven the boy too hard, had even in some indirect way been responsible for his tragic collapse—it was better that he should shoulder the blame for it, rightly or wrongly, than that he should turn in rage against his Almighty, Ever-living, Ever-loving God for snatching his first-born paragon away from him. Hugh skipped about like a young lamb, watched by indulgent eyes. Arthur and Fred were rebellious all their lives about the rites and ceremonies of ecclesiasticism. Hugh by contrast, perhaps because in his case there was never the same compulsion, delighted in them. When the solemnities of the laying of the foundation-stone of Truro Cathedral were being prepared, nine-year-old Hugh delighted in being a small acolyte in the thick of the celebrations—the founding of the first English Cathedral since the Reformation. Hugh though was not dedicated to Godliness from his earliest years. He was an ordinary, playful boy, a great lover of animals which became a bond between him and his much older sister Maggie; his prep school was Walton House, Clevedon —a straggling, modern, unexciting sort of place. Hugh, in ordinary human affairs anyway, was never a conformist. He enjoyed being busy with his own small private concerns—not, in fact, the type to derive pleasure or to earn approbation as a member of a prep school. He did well enough however to be one of the Eton Election of 1885, and so became a Colleger in the same year as his elder brother Arthur became a master. He was elected in due time to Pop, so he must have found favour with his co-evals, but was not academically distinguished after the manner of Arthur and Fred at Marlborough, nor, surprisingly, did he then show any particular interest in religion. Lyttelton prepared him for Confirmation—a rite which Hugh had expressly asked should in his case be deferred—and wrote: 'I can recall the exact spot in a huge armchair where he sat and I was preparing him for Confirmation. I don't think he understood much, and was not the sort of boy to feel very deeply the sense of sin.'

In his last year he bestirred himself and got into the 'First

Hundred', but still had not acquired that smooth academic con-
formity which would ensure his painless transit to King's. Hugh
decided instead that he would like, of all things, to try for the
Indian Civil Service, and so, with the Hervey Prize Poem as his
only Eton trophy, was enrolled at Wren's the crammers in the
summer of 1889. His father was disappointed, but acquiesced. On
his last night at Eton Hugh wrote, quite chirpily taking all things
into account: 'My feelings on leaving are:—Excitement. Fore-
boding of Wren's and fellows there. Sorrow at leaving Eton.
Pride at being an old Etonian. Certain pleasure in leaving for many
trivial matters. Feeling of importance. Frightful longing for India.
Homesickness. DEAR ME!' This is typical Hugh. The (by now)
Archbishop must have found it difficult sometimes to have
patience with him. Ben of course took what she must have looked
upon as Hugh's switch to the slow line placidly and without
complaint. Maggie, from Athens, wrote a letter which showed
how much she loved him. Above all, she did not want to preach
at him. Dutifulness was not the first of virtues, she thought. She
wanted to read with him, but did not think of this as in any way
'a covert way of improving you—only I would rather read with
you than with anyone—you like poetry, I know—besides—well—
you are you—I wonder whether you know how much I have felt
that, from the time when I used to teach you out of "Reading
without Tears"—right up to now—when our relation is an *equal*
one. . . . I have been considering you as *well* over eighteen for
some time past. . . . I've been thinking that when someone edits
your Life and letters, they will be puzzled over "Brer Rabbit"
[Maggie's name for him], and will rightly conjecture that "Brer"
means brother, and make a brilliant suggestion that "Rabbit" is
really a misreading for "Robert". Don't you think so? *Good-bye.*'
All through life there was a sense in which "Brer Rabbit" was
exactly right for him.

At Wren's Hugh read J. H. Shorthouse's still occasionally read
novel *John Inglesant*, which had been published in 1881. Written
by a middle-aged chemist from Birmingham, *John Inglesant*
crucially influenced Hugh's life. This romance of the seventeenth
century, about Platonism and Nicholas Ferrar and Little Gidding
and Inglesant's coming to see that Christianity and Platonism
between them fused the world itself, with all its materialism, into
a sort of sacrament—this stirred Hugh into a permanent and

passionate set of convictions. The book itself is patchy, has dull
moments, can be sententious, but it has exalted moments too and
these went straight to the heart of Hugh's mind and consciousness. The Indian Civil Service was quite forgotten. Hugh had his
vocation. Hugh would be a priest. He went up to Trinity in
October 1890. He was back on the Bensonian main line again. He
would be no solitary stranger, learning his way about with
difficulty. Fred, with his First, was still a great name at King's.
He began to write for the *Cambridge Review*. Having read Fred's
Dodo in manuscript he was obliged to report on it to senior
members like Walter Headlam, J. K. Stephen and Monty James.
'Well,' Hugh told them, 'it's very wo-wo-worldly!' (Hugh always
had an attractive, not disabling, stammer.) He was small, coxed
the Third Trinity boat all through his time. He played golf not at
all badly. Dab-handedness at ball games was a streak which, with
the Bensons, kept popping up from time to time. Fred of course
was a very good games player indeed. He shared Arthur's love
of grand-scale walking. One winter during his undergraduate
time he and Arthur went up to Yorkshire to investigate their
Benson ancestors. It was very cold, the water in the ewers of
their inn-bedrooms froze, they whiled away the ten-mile stretches
of their tramp by improvising a long story, odd chapters to one,
even chapters to another. It was like the kind of thing Arthur did
with his house on Sunday nights at Eton, but Hugh was good at
it too; he had the effortless narrative inventiveness which
characterized them all. Henry James's *Turn of the Screw* owes
much to Hugh and Fred Benson's talents for narrative spooking.
He set out to walk with Bosanquet from Cambridge to London
in a day, and was not defeated till he stumbled exhausted into a
stopping train at Ponders End. He lived an active, enquiring life
—Swedenborg and mesmerism much interested him—but though
endlessly busy, did not canalize his energy with that purposefulness which culminates in a first-class honours degree. He loved
music, especially organ-playing, and his father allowed him a
summer visit to Bayreuth. He delighted in it all, especially the
Grail motif from *Parsifal*, though the heat and the food were both
oppressive. '. . . many bibbings of iced liquor and large meals
under awnings—at all hours of the day. We stayed at Ratisbon
on Sunday last and went to the Cathedral there—gorgeous
Gregorian services and ceremonies. . . .' Hugh never tired of

ritual. But there was never a trace of ninetyish languor about him. He was a tough, hard little chap—and the hardness needs to be emphasized. He was never one for repining—that was his mother coming out in him—and he never suffered from the brooding— even diseased—depressive melancholy which was the Archbishop's curse, and Arthur's, and, most tragically of all, Maggie's. He got a Third, which dinted his father's pride—or self-pride? But now, at any rate, he was going to be ordained, and that Edward Benson would be performing the rite with his third and youngest son was a fact which rejoiced the Palace of Lambeth and more than made up for Hugh's fallibility in the Tripos. He went for pre-paration to Dean Vaughan of Llandaff. Vaughan, a Rugbeian under Arnold, never found himself obliged to question faith but maintained his Evangelicalism throughout life. He married a sister of Dean Stanley—a brilliant and in some ways wayward woman. They got along, but it is open to doubt whether Vaughan was ever really the marrying sort. In spite of the Evangelicalism, Hugh appears to have enjoyed himself. One of Hugh's most attractive characteristics was his ability to enjoy himself whole-heartedly. The Dean, like so many Victorians, took to his bed frequently with illnesses severe and not so severe. During one of these lie-ins, Mrs. Vaughan went into the sickroom anxious to have a ruling on some question connected with the Higher Criticism. Ought not some troublesome passage from the Old Testament be discussed—and forthwith? The Dean said firmly that he was not in the mood, and Mrs. Vaughan came down-stairs, her Bible unopened, to find someone waiting below who had called to find out how the Dean was getting on. 'I have just come from him,' she said, 'and it is naturally a melancholy thought, but he seems to have entirely lost his faith. He would not let me read the Bible with him; he practically said that he had no further interest in the Bible!' Hugh enjoyed publicizing this kind of story. *John Inglesant* still strongly occupied his mind. Would it not be most agreeable to found a community house on the lines of Nicholas Ferrar's at Little Gidding? He would prefer a gathering of individualists to one of conformists, of course; but without doubt an idea worth following up. Perhaps Dean Vaughan dismissed all this as simply a young man's dreaming. If he did, he was failing to comprehend his pupil. Hugh, soon to be like his brothers a prosperous writer, had a way of turning dreams into startling reality—and of doing this with quite startling suddenness. That a youngster of twenty-one should be thinking at all along these lines shows that, like his brothers again, no thought of bedding down with a woman and adapting himself to domesticity ever occurred to him.

His father ordained him in Croydon parish church, the nearest to Addington, and then came the Eton Mission in Hackney, the Kemsing curacy under the moneyed Skarrat, his narrow escape from bacilli-attacks during the Egyptian family sortie of 1896–97, and his decision, in 1898, to go as a probationer to Charles Gore's Community of the Resurrection at Mirfield. Before becoming professed in 1901 Gore asked him whether he was in any danger of lapsing to Rome. This surprised him; he answered No; and in July Ben came up to the industrial north to see him installed. But Rome beckoned; papal infallibility was a stumbling block; but the disinclination on the part of the majority of Anglicans to accept unquestioningly the need for Authority nagged more and more urgently at his mind. In 1902 he began to write a book of stories which he called *The Light Invisible*, and the work he did on these seemed to help in the crystallizing of his notions. On the Good Friday of 1903 he preached the 'Three Hours' in a south of England Anglican church, descended from the pulpit exhausted, and knew then that he would have to turn his back on the Reformation—and on his father which was more difficult. Once, when they were riding back from Birdcage Walk to Lambeth, Hugh had suddenly asked his father how he was to understand the creed's 'I believe in the Holy Catholic Church.' 'For instance,' said Hugh, 'are the Roman Catholics a part of the Church of Christ?' The Archbishop had been slow to answer this one, but then ventured, 'Perhaps the Roman Catholics have so far erred in their doctrinal beliefs as to have forfeited their place in the Body of Christ.' At the time, Hugh says, this had satisfied him as an answer. Six weeks after his father's death he spent travelling in Europe and then eastwards as far as Palestine. It was during this journey, he says, that he realized 'what a very small and unimportant affair the Anglican communion really was'. He had lived out his life up till then formally identifying himself with the official side of the Church of England. 'Now I looked at things through more professional eyes, and behold! we were nowhere.' After that it was really only a matter of time. Ben would not have dreamt of making any attempt at influencing his course of thought on such matters.

And so, in the autumn of 1903, Hugh went out to the College of San Sivestro in Rome, having been received into the Roman Church in the September of that year. He was ordained—or re-ordained—nine months later.

* * *

And so it was that by the beginning of 1904 the males of the Benson family had scattered. Arthur was at The Old Granary in Cambridge and was to become a fellow of Magdalene that year; Fred had his London flat, went through the antics of the London season, stayed with grandees in August, notably with the Batterseas at Overstrand in Norfolk. Lord Battersea had been Cyril Flower and had been Liberal Whip in the House of Commons. Then he had married the enormously wealthy Constance Rothschild, daughter of Sir Anthony Rothschild of Aston Clinton in Bucks. He had a good brain and delighted in splendour. He was made a peer, kept a grand place called Surrey House at the corner of Edgware Road opposite Marble Arch. Then he bought two semi-detached villas at Overstrand, called the combination 'The Pleasance', and set busily to work to turn this embryo into something palatial: arches, libraries, loggias, pavilions, extensions— the place became a wonder, and Fred, in common with many others—Meredith was a frequent and welcome visitor there— enjoyed himself. After August would come travel abroad with somewhere suitable for skating a few months on, because Fred was a skater of outstanding ability.

Tremans became a house of women. The brothers visited of course, and visited frequently. Arthur particularly visited for long spells. Cambridge life offered more leisure than life at Eton. He brought his friends there for graciously long Edwardian escapes from comparative bustle. Ben, critical sometimes but always accommodating, welcomed them all—or almost all. Although she lived at Tremans for twenty years, she never became a country woman. She loved always crowds and bustle. When Hugh came back to Tremans in the summer of 1904 from Rome, now a committed Roman, he spent some time there, putting the finishing touches to *By What Authority*. He saw quite clearly how his mother felt, as is to be seen in a letter he wrote at this time. 'The world is divided into two classes—those who like people, and those who like things. It has come to us as a good classification at home. My mother yearns continually for town, and loves eleven hundred people; and all the rest of us love the country, and cocks and hens, and small events on the lawn like the dog digging a hole, and discuss them as if they were the pivots on which the world moved.' That is lightly said. Yet how Ben must have chafed, and suffered.

Arthur and Hugh and Fred could come and go as the mood took them. Pampered repose in gracious surroundings was an agreeable prospect to hold in reserve, as it were. Ben on the other hand was more or less bound. There were occasional visits up to town to stay, together with Lucy, in Lucy's small Westminster house, but for the bulk of the year Ben was stuck with Tremans— and her grown-up children, with strong and separate personalities had to be kept harmoniously together. Arthur for example had by now acquired authoritative bachelor ways that could be trying indeed. Tremans life ticked slowly by punctuated by religious observances. This was a pattern which Ben insisted upon—first because it was only right that Edward's passionate convictions and beliefs should be respected and remembered, and second because of that quite private and personal religiousness which she herself had acquired in early middle age. Therefore at 10 p.m., whatever was going on, the housemaid would knock and enter and announce prayers. And there would be a quavering hymn too, accompanied by the organ which Ben had had lugged all the way from Lambeth to Winchester and thence through dusty lanes to the deep rusticity of Sussex in early Edwardian days. In addition to this there would, on Sundays, be Compline. 'Compline', Arthur confided to his diary, 'which I detest with every fibre of my being—the discomfort, the silly, idiotic responses, the false sociability of it all.' When Arthur arrived for the Long Vacation therefore, Ben, for peace's sake, scrapped family prayers. But on Compline she would not budge. If Arthur had chugged all the way down from Cambridge in his newfangled motor-car—his books were prospering enormously by now—then he must be prepared to take Compline with the smooth. After all, Arthur could be lordly and perhaps take for granted what had cost her time and trouble and tact. He would bring down troops of friends after just a casual enquiry on whether this would be all right.

And of course it always was. George Mallory, a charming young undergraduate, later to be for ever lost somewhere near the top of Everest, would be invited. Luxmoore, an old Eton colleague, a bit dandified, with histrionic tastes, who enjoyed reading aloud to an appreciative audience, would be another of his guests. Edmund Gosse would spend a couple of nights, bringing, perhaps prudently, his own wines. Percy Lubbock would often be there, not yet sufficiently prepared to tell us all about the craft of fiction. Ben enjoyed these fresh faces—fresh at any rate until time began to drag on and turn them into familiars. Arthur, though, was so tiresomely fond of organizing them. Arthur's walks were always important to him, and if they were important to him, why not to others as well? His new motor would be brought into use. It would take them carefully up to some centre on the South Downs. Then Arthur and his guests, and his brothers if they happened to be at home, and poor Lucy would be set down and they would push off towards some agreed destination where the motor, still carrying Ben and Maggie—who though comparatively strong and active now, was not thought capable of long-distance tramps—would scoop them up and take them home for five o'clock tea. The timing was important. Arthur had to be back by then because the hours up to dinner time were the ones when he flung himself into his second character part. Through the day Arthur was the busy, autocratic, arranging man. Maggie, who supervised the huge garden, would be told how she might supervise it better. His correspondence was enormous and had to be attended to. Business connected with the City Livery Company he later belonged to—the Fishmongers'—occupied him. But during the early evening hours Arthur became the A. C. Benson who, through the medium of the printed page, dispensed sweetness and tenderness and light to hundreds of thousands of eager readers. The big, bustling man of affairs, with the sharp, incisive tongue and the keen eye for human frailties—this man, whose company large numbers of very intelligent people enjoyed, would be put firmly to one side. He stretched a board across the arms of his chair, placed his sheets of white paper before him—and wrote. He wrote with staggering ease. The words flowed, and they were the right words; of that he was sure. He covered page one and dropped it into a basket; page two was begun without a pause, so was page three, and on and on till the dinner-bell sounded. He

6*

did not read it through. He did not correct—what possible need could there be for correction? The next morning the typist would gather up the output and tap it out all ready for his publishers who were eager for all they could get, because Arthur sold abundantly.

His intellectual friends—and Arthur, make no mistake, could talk on equal terms with any of his intellectual friends—worried themselves about all this mellifluous claptrap. Percy Lubbock expressed his anxiety with as much candour as was consonant with a close and genuine friendship. 'He gave himself away with both hands, cheerful and careless. He fell upon the time-honoured riddles of life and death, art and philosophy, faith and morals, as irresponsibly as though no one had given them a thought before him; new every morning, fresh for debate, was the perplexity of the freedom of the will, the meaning of evil, the way of all flesh. How can a man, with these fascinating mysteries ever before him, exhaust his wonder and leave speculation to the pundits? He could not, for one; to him they remained as enticing as ever they have seemed to curious candid youth. And as with the daring of youth he delivered his thought on these high matters, so with unaging quickness of eye and humour he watched the world about him, near at hand—a world of a well-marked horizon, not large, but it was more than enough to gratify his appetite for amusing detail . . . he did not ask for wonders and rarities, he preferred the shelter of the life he had made for himself, and the sober landscape of his choice. . . . He thrived too on the impatient irritations and vexations of the day; they did their part to sharpen the zest with which, in the good unshadowed times, he devoured the hour. No doubt he lived and thought and worked too fast—too fast for safety. . . . But if he paid heavily for the years of enjoyment, at least he enjoyed them. . . .'

This is two-edged stuff. But it is shrewd and just. Arthur was delightful company, a popular man, a contradiction. He wrote *Thy Rod and thy Staff* for the public—and he kept a rod in pickle for his intimates. He saw no insincerity in the mingling of roles. Ben, during those long vacations at Tremans, tended to see the crusty side more often than the tenderly reflective; but she did not mind. She delighted in her children, was wonderfully patient with them, always withheld a central, secret part of herself from them, was pleased at the astonishing success they achieved, but was far too intelligent not to know perfectly well that none of the countless books of her three author-sons had that quality of in-built durability—except, perhaps, just now and then, for a few of Fred's. And these came at the end of his life, in his sixties, when Ben had gone to join her Edward.

But of course, although Ben delighted for the most part in her children's friends, and in the entertaining of them in what must have been one of the most delicious houses in all England, she was very far indeed from being simply the resident hotel-keeper, supervising the making up of beds for the next arrivals. Lucy was always there, or almost always there, to talk to, and her relation-ship with Lucy was stronger than with anyone else—had been so even in the later days of her marriage to Edward. Lucy and Ben complemented each other. . . . Lucy had a good mind, though not a first-class one, as Ben undoubtedly had. But she had a firmer grip on practical affairs. Ben, in spite of her deep religiousness, her love of prayer at all times, possessed what can only be called a sort of paradoxical flightiness—a love of letting things rip, and laugh-ing at them. She loved her food, for example, grew far too fat, wrote reams in her diaries about this problem, how she must exercise restraint, how she must knock off the puddings—and yet the all-conquering second helping never ceased to beckon. And she notes it all down, and as you read the words three-quarters of a century on you hear the laughter in them and relish the tang of self-mockery. Ben relied on Lucy to 'keep her straight'. Arthur, Fred, Hugh—well, they were all men. And a female-male relationship, in its fullest sense, had never, since that monstrous declaration to her made by Edward when she was a child of eleven, been possible for her. Arthur was gruff-and-grum on occasions but splendidly good company on others; Fred was dashing and amusing and frivolous and she adored his devotion to her; Hugh, as her youngest, was charming but seemed to her never properly to grow up. As for her relations with Maggie, these by 1904 were easing. The awkward combination in her daughter of feminine frailty and Edward's driving will to domineer—this had slowly softened at Tremans. The garden and the animals gave her practical interests which balanced the intellectual ones; and then she too, like her mother, had her passionate female relationships—with Nettie Gourlay and Gladys Bevan as chief votaries—and with the help of these was working towards an uneasy harmony. At the end of 1905 she wrote to

Gladys Bevan: 'I want to write more about your letter, but I have had such an absurd morning that I can't. This was the order or disorder of it—8.30. Mother came in, before going to London with Lucy for the day. 9. Beth, conversation about shortcomings of the cook, especially what was done with some sausages. 10.15. While I had my hair done, my mother's maid came in much gloom about the Stool-ball club's entertainment. 10.30. Coachman. Acute crisis about new horse. Then to cook with tactful and leading questions and suggestions. 11. To Arthur and my aunt, when there came a stream of telegrams so that the boy who brought one carried away four, and another arrived directly after. 11.45. Began my book; fire, sofa and bedroom. 11.50. Nurse for an interview, in the middle of which came Arthur about a book. Back to my room and book. 12.15. Midday letters. Horse crisis more acute; up to Arthur about the other book, and back to my room. 12.30. My aunt to say one telegram hadn't gone, consequent rush downstairs. Back to book and room. 12.45. Stool-ball crisis more acute. Back to book. Then a message from the cook. 1. Beth to say she wouldn't interrupt me. Back to book till 1.20—and there's the gong for lunch. And since then another telegram; and the blacksmith's daughter on the Stool-ball crisis. I fear I do rather waste time in small ways!' This letter, from a magnificently gifted woman of thirty-nine, has a deep pathos. It is full of self-contempt. She is nursed and coddled and comfortable; but she lacks any understanding of her emotions, and the drive and self-confidence which might have enabled her to harness these emotions in the service of a career which might, so easily, have become a career of note. How much happier and more effective Maggie's life might have proved if only she had had the damn-your-eyes determination of Ethel Smyth, who was a frequent visitor at the house, and a great admirer of Ben.

Because Ben of course had her visitors as well as the menfolk of the family. There was the severe Mrs. Creighton, widow of Mandell Creighton, Bishop of London, who took it upon herself to tell Ben that her rule at Tremans was altogether too indulgent and negligent: Why should all these grown men be allowed to amble down to breakfast at any hour they pleased? There was the very gifted Mrs. Henry Sidgwick, a sister-in-law, and sister of A. J. Balfour who was, at that very moment, 1904, Prime Minister and First Lord of the Treasury. There was Eton's Mrs. Cornish who was always such fun; there was Mary Cholmondeley, a novelist of much ability who wrote *Red Pottage*, a great success in its day and well worth returning to now; and there were the two sisters, Isabel Lady Henry Somerset, and Adeline, Duchess of Bedford. Lady Henry, the elder, was separated from her husband. No grandee ever worked more ferociously than he to earn the right to be separated from, but Isabel did not allow her wrongs to dim her sparkle. Her principles disallowed divorce, but not, in her view, the right to make public the reasons why she had left him. In this way a great scandal arose because the Victorian rule was that grand ladies should never, even under the grossest provocation, reveal how disgracefully their titled husbands had behaved. So Isabel's entry to the great houses was barred. She took this on the chin, devoted herself to good works, fought the good fight against the demon gin, established a home for alcoholic women at Duxhurst, and never lost her capacity to enjoy, and make, good jokes. Adeline was more starchy and conventional. To live life in the grand style, the Bedford style, which was upheld and made possible by the lucky possession of countless acres of London slums, did not strike her in any way as inappropriate. But both Lady Henry and Duchess Adeline were religious. Ben, either as the wife or the relict of the primate, was someone round whom they both could gather on, as it were, safe and neutral territory. And gather they did.

Sociability was what Ben enjoyed. Tremans and its country beauties did not really interest her at all. She took Tremans because she thought the place would be good for Maggie—and indeed it is true that Maggie spent her happiest years there— even though these years were brief enough. She spent much time in prayer and devotion; she wrote a vast quantity of letters; she kept her diary in which she remonstrated with herself; she did not mind, even enjoyed, being interrupted when members of her family, or one or other of the endless visitors, came in for consolation, advice, rational discussion on a high plane, or just gossip. She raised no objection when Hugh came back from Rome, a fledged Roman Catholic priest, in the summer of 1904, although he immediately started causing her a great deal of trouble. Tremans had a top room which the Bishop of Chichester had licensed as a place where the (Anglican) holy communion could be celebrated. It was after all only proper that in a house as country-buried as Tremans, the widow of the Archbishop of Canterbury should be enabled to carry out her religious duties without the necessity of getting wet. But when Hugh arrived, all enthusiastic, he wanted a chapel too, a chapel all to himself. What was more, he had a licence from the Holy Father himself for just such a place—and what other place than the top room? Well, why not? Ben was not a woman to be frightened by a word like oecumenicalism. The top room became a meeting-place for mighty opposites. . . . Hugh smartened up the subfusc Anglican plainness of everything; a plaster cast of the Virgin, some pictures on the walls, and of course a bell to wake people up for high moments like the Elevation—all this Ben accepted, though it was a great nuisance, and even agreed to ordering mass wafers from a biscuit firm. Hugh was delighted when they arrived, tasted a few at breakfast, pronounced them good, and passed them round for guests to have a nibble and find out for themselves.

9

A Basket of Scorpions

ONE OF HUGH'S EARLY GUESTS though did test to the limit
Ben's readiness to make her family's friends welcome. In the
summer of 1904, soon after his return from Rome, Hugh discovered a book called *Hadrian VII*, the author of which, as set out
on the title-page ,was Fr. Rolfe (Frederic Baron Corvo). The story
is reasonably well known: A young Englishman has been rejected
for the Roman priesthood. The various Monsignore responsible
for this rejection have behaved dishonestly and unfairly towards
him because no young man could ever possibly have been more
suitable in every way for admittance to Holy Orders. . . . All this
is in the past at the book's beginning in which this reject gets a
visit from no less than a Cardinal, and a Cardinal, furthermore,
prepared to eat humble pie. The young man has been monstrously
abused. *Of course* he is wonderfully suited to the priesthood and
he, the Cardinal, will admit him without more ado. After this
official back-tracking the young man goes to Rome, where, as it
happens, the citizens are all eagerly watching for smoke-signals
of the right colour to puff out of the chimney to announce, visually
that 'habemus Papam'. By a singular combination of circumstances
the young man is himself, against all the odds, elected Pope. He
takes the title Hadrian VII, and Rolfe then goes on to describe for
us the remarkable, unconventional, and wholly beneficial happenings of his Papacy. . . .

The book is a fantasy, written by a man with a certain limited
writing talent who was never, at any time of his tragi-comic-
disreputable life, quite right in the head. But Hugh, full of the

multi-coloured splendours of his new faith—Rolfe was good at
describing multi-coloured splendours hazily viewed through
good thick stupefying incense-smoke—took a huge fancy to
Hadrian VII. In one of the unluckiest moments of his life, he
wrote a letter to Rolfe to tell him so. He wrote it in February
1905, from Llandaff House in Cambridge. Perhaps, if he had
dashed it off a bit earlier, while he was still at Tremans, and if he
had shown it to his mother as he might quite probably have done,
Ben would have managed, in the tactfullest way, to talk him out
of it. . . . But, as it was, the letter was sent. How grateful he was.
. . . He had read Hadrian three times finding it more brilliant with
each reading. . . . Rolfe had taught him the value of loneliness,
Hugh said—but could Hugh, brought up in princely comfort,
have had any notion of what Rolfe, eleven years older than Hugh,
meant by loneliness? Could he have known how Rolfe, in 1893,
had asked the House Surgeon at Aberdeen Royal Infirmary to
certify him as insane so that he might gain admittance to, and
hence free board and lodging in, the local asylum? No, Hugh
knew nothing of all that—and so he dangerously added a final
paragraph to his letter: 'I believe you are in Italy now; I wonder
if I can be of the slightest service to you here in England? I am
fairly often in London; and should be delighted to do anything
for which I was competent. . . .'

A letter from a son of the late Archbishop but one, from a son
moreover who was now not merely a convert to the true faith but
a priest? Rolfe naturally snapped at the invitation with the swiftness—and ultimate destructiveness—of Joey, Ben's beloved
parrot so disliked by all other members of the family because of
his lightning pounces on unguarded thumbs. Could he come?
Hugh put the question to his mother merely as a formality. He
knew perfectly well that she never said No to anybody because it
was her nature always to look for, even expect, the best from
everybody whilst at the same time being far too intelligent and
perceptive not to be aware, more quickly than most, of the almost
universal fallibility of human beings in general. Fr. Rolfe, Baron
Corvo, proved however more of a trial than most. Fr. Rolfe's
talent for picking a quarrel amounted almost to genius. . . .

Rolfe's story has of course been told, and very well told, before.
People know about him. He is even at the present moment enjoying a small vogue. The reverberations of his endlessly long

drawn-out feud with poor Hugh are still in a sense sounding. But the point of view in the narratives has usually been Rolfe's. Fred told the story well, and he of course sympathized with Hugh's torments; but Fred had a strong streak of malice in him, and his enjoyment of the monstrousness of Rolfe's antics as the feud rolled on, tends to push Hugh into the background. Arthur also happened to be at Tremans on the occasion of Rolfe's first visit; and Arthur, as one might expect, left nobody in any doubt at all about the very active distaste he felt in the company of Hugh's new chum. Ben, still not prepared to turn her thumbs down, noted in her diary that though Arthur did not take to this seedy lunatic he was 'quite nice to him', but her honesty compelled her to add, 'a mind that works in such a very different manner is not favourable to unfettered talk'. From Ben these were strong words. She thought perhaps it would be better if Rolfe came again when Arthur had taken his brusquerie back to Magdalene with him. Ben was a trier.

And Hugh, in spite of everything, was quite alarmingly enthusiastic. Before the Tremans visit he and Rolfe had gone off on a walking tour together. How Hugh's infatuation survived the rigorous testing of a longish walking tour will never properly be known. Perhaps his enchantment with his new role of priest— the role so passionately desired by Rolfe but for ever denied him —had something to do with it. Perhaps Rolfe asked him to receive his confession, and in the course of it recited to him infamies that stupefied the innocent and basically childlike Hugh and set huge and hitherto unknown excitements racing round in his blood. . . . These are matters that have to be guessed at, but there can be no doubt that Rolfe, with his insane ingenuity, knew the exactly right square inch of Hugh's person to press in order to send him into an ecstasy of devotion and discipleship. They decided, during the tour, to write a book together, and later wrote to each other about it and came to practical arrangements. It was to be a life of Thomas Becket—St. Thomas of Canterbury, a figure much revered by English Catholics—though it should not be forgotten that Henry II's fury towards his high-handed minister was very far from idly motivated. It is odd, by the way, that Arthur manages to write a biography of his brother without so much as mentioning Rolfe (*Hugh: Memoirs of a Brother*, 1915); but Arthur does speak in his book of 'the curious intensity and limitation of Hugh's affections'. It is true that the remark is made apropos of Hugh's devotion to Maggie's collie dog, Roddy. But Roddy or Rolfe—for Arthur it came to much the same thing.

The arrangement come to between Hugh and Rolfe went like this. Hugh was to do the actual writing; Rolfe was to research and stock Hugh up with brightly coloured, saleable medieval detail. There are many today of course who would maintain that Rolfe was by far the better writer of the two. But what Rolfe, in his usual dire circumstances, must have been fully aware of was that Hugh, like his brothers, had the art of writing books that sold plentifully. A third of the royalties on a book with Hugh's name on it would amount to vastly more than three-thirds of the royalties on a book composed by Rolfe on his own. So, for the time being at any rate, Rolfe swallowed his pride. Hugh probably did not give the matter very much thought. It would have been wise of him though to give the matter the closest and most prolonged thought of which he was capable.

Rolfe was a slow worker—not idle, but slow. He wandered down bypaths; he brooded; he thought much of necromancy and the occult. Emphatically he was not as other men are. To Hugh on the other hand—how hugely he differed from the British industrial zealots of our own day—productivity came as easily as breathing. He would think nothing of polishing off Thomas Becket in a couple of months if suitably primed. Given six months he would probably have quite happily tackled a whole history of the Papacy from Peter to Pius the Tenth. The scheme and synopsis were settled by August 1906, and Hugh started writing to his partner in these terms. 'Please send comments some time *soon*, as I am beginning to warm up about it. Please also remember that my method, when once begun, is to work like lightning and then take a rest. I can't plod at all. . . .'

But earlier Rolfe had been concerned with another piece of collaboration. Colonel Owen Thomas—'an obese magenta colonel of militia with a black-stubbed moustache and a Welsh-tongued proposition'—had asked him to put into publishable form some findings of the Colonel's about farming possibilities in Rhodesia. No fixed sum was mentioned for Rolfe's work on this, but when, the work done, the Colonel offered him £50, Rolfe considered that he had been cheated as so often before and took legal advice. The lawsuit dragged on, as lawsuits have the habit of doing, and the case was not heard till December 1906. Rolfe's being busy with this probably slowed even further his work as provider of raw material for Hugh. Furthermore, during the hearing of his case, Rolfe made a very bad showing during cross-examination. The heat slowly ebbed out of Hugh's passionate involvement with his Baron. A note of hysteria crept into his letters to his tardy collaborator. 'I haven't done a word since I last wrote. I tell you all my enthusiasm is evaporating. I shall soon be immersed in other things, unless something comes from you. You know, I can't write except at full pressure. I cannot dribble. Just off to town. Nearly mad!'

It was during this visit to town that the suggestion was put to him that perhaps it might be better if his name was not so closely and openly allied to that of Rolfe—someone who was, to put the very best possible face on it, a very rum character indeed. Robert Hugh Benson, old Etonian, son of an Anglican archbishop, ordained priest of the Roman Catholic church, and Frederick Rolfe, Baron Corvo, born in Cheapside in 1860, the son of a piano manufacturer in reduced circumstances, and, since youth, an itinerant confidence-man not unacquainted with workhouses— would a partnership of these two names, announced on the title-page of a new book, do much good to Hugh? This was the question. And Hugh, his impetuous unworldliness strengthened —or at any rate made more formidable—by a quite tough disregard for the feelings of others which he inherited from his father, most dictatorial of headmasters in a century which teemed with them—Hugh was immediately prepared to give that question careful consideration.

He put things quite plainly to Rolfe. He (Hugh) was a popular author. His name, standing alone as biographer of Thomas Becket, would ensure respectable sales and a certain profit. Hugh would make acknowledgement of his indebtedness to Rolfe at the beginning, and the original financial arrangments—one-third of all profits to Rolfe and two-thirds to Hugh—should stand even though Rolfe was absolved from all further labour. (Up till then, of course, Rolfe had not done all that much, but Hugh kept silent on this, choosing to let his earlier imploring letters for material to work upon stand in Rolfe's remembrance. Or so he thought. And certainly he was right in supposing that Rolfe had a long memory. What Hugh did not properly realize then was that

Rolfe's memory was passionate, unforgiving, and endowed with a rarely exceeded capacity to magnify, minimize or distort in deference to Rolfe's immediate needs.)

Surprisingly Rolfe did not straight away become venomous. Not unnaturally he did not like the change of plan. Leaving the profit motive out of it—and Rolfe in self-lacerating mood was always perfectly prepared to leave the profit out of anything— *why* should his (Rolfe's) name not appear alongside Hugh's as co-author? Hugh never liked being checked. He was upset. He wrote another letter which was at once headlong and calculating. He would hand the whole thing over to Rolfe. All Hugh had written, all he had researched, should become Rolfe's to do what he liked with. Let Rolfe go ahead, find himself a publisher, and make himself a profit.

A generous gesture? At first glance one might think so. But Rolfe, as Hugh expected he would, took a second glance. Rolfe was a slow worker. How could he support himself while he laboriously shaped his lush and fanciful phrases? How, at the end of it all, without Hugh's backing, would he find a publisher? Rolfe needed Hugh far more than Hugh needed him. So Rolfe wrote again to say that he accepted one-third of the proceeds and total obliteration from the title-page.

Hugh was probably pleased. Since June 1905 he had been curate at the Cambridge Roman Catholic church, a grand example of Victorian Gothic which you pass on your long trek from the city proper to the railway station. 'A little too gorgeous and complete,' Hugh told a fellow-priest, and indeed so it still is. But he liked the accommodation. 'It is HEAVENLY,' he wrote. 'I have nice rooms . . . in the red clergy house next the church. Three windows look into a big garden all over-grown with trees and flowers, and one on to the east end of the church, with angels and griffins grinning at me (the angels do not grin), and the heavenly chimes every quarter-hour day and night. (They play the Alleluia out of the "Exultet" of Easter Eve, and continual plain-song hymns.)' How many thousands of undergraduates have listened to those heavenly chimes, especially on warm, sleepless nights shortly before the Tripos, and cursed all that clangorous devotion.

What Hugh did not realize—he was never good at anticipating the reactions of other people to his promises and purposes—was that he had flung open the door of his snug little pad, and that a basket of scorpions was about to be deposited in his sitting-room. Along with numerous other aberrations Rolfe suffered from persecution mania. The longer he brooded over Hugh's sly little letter, with its hint of a twisting of the thumbscrews, the more he was persuaded that he, as so often before in a thwarted life, had been most monstrously abused. More letters passed. Hugh made the mistake of insulting him with charity. Rolfe wrote a long soliloquy-letter to Mrs. Pirie-Gordon in which he held up for her to see his mauled and tattered pride. '. . . The only ambition I have is to be independent. . . . The new proposal kept me a sponger on other people's charity. . . . And so now, finding myself quite without means, and quite without means even of continuing my work, I reluctantly fell back upon him. He tells me that to take me in will break his heart and cause him strong personal inconvenience; and in the roughest possible manner he offers me the situation of caretaker in his lonely house two miles from Buntingford at 8/- a week. There I am to be quite alone, to look after the place, do the gardening, and fowls, and be two miles walk and a train journey from Mass for seven months. . . .' Rolfe, a caretaker! Rolfe, the insulted and injured man of genius, the scholar and artist brusquely offered a job as cleaner-out of hen-roosts! Whom did this jumped-up little convert-priest think he was talking to?

Hugh was genuinely flabbergasted by all this passion and bile—and disturbed too, in his upper-class way, to discover that Rolfe was not at all disposed to keep the quarrel a private matter between the pair of them. '. . . There is nothing but friendliness on my side . . .' he wrote. And in so saying Hugh was quite sincere. The large property he had bought at Hare Street in Hertfordshire—he was to leave it, at his death, as a country retreat for all future Archbishops of Westminster—was something precious to him always. In offering the custodianship of the place to Rolfe, Hugh was offering a part of himself. What was there, in such a gesture, to cause outrage on Rolfe's part? But Rolfe considered that he had been cheated, his talents had been scandalously misused, by those in authority or by those in league with authority. Rolfe clung to this idea. He cherished it. He would, as it were, pace barefoot and in rags up and down the Hills Road outside the Roman Catholic church on the corner in order to show to the outside world how one of the priests inside had kicked away the labours of a misunderstood man of talent.

At last Hugh began to see what a mistake all that sudden passionate friendship had been, how delusive the joys of that long, intensely talkative walking-tour. He had got himself mixed up with a loony—and what was worse, a loony with something not far short of genius. 'I see dimly what he thinks,' Hugh now wrote. 'But it is so amazingly unreasonable and so extremely wounding to oneself, to be treated as a fraudulent publisher, that I can hardly see how in decency I can go on making proposals. He will only see in them new and subtle plots against him. And all the while, in reality, from the business point of view it would be vastly to my advantage not to work with him at all. I have offered him the whole book, for that reason among others, if he will take it off my hands. I am honestly beginning to doubt, for the first time, whether he is really "fond of me" at all. I don't see at present how suspicion and friendliness can co-exist. . . .'

Rolfe, with a sort of inverted glee, set about stirring the pot. He sent letters out in all directions, letters full of calumny which vilified Hugh in the grossest terms. He began, slowly, to work on a new novel in which Hugh appeared as the Reverend Bobugo Bonson—a deceitful, treacherous priest who, like so many others of his cloth before, had wronged him. He even sent a letter to Arthur, giving him, in hysterically exaggerated terms, his opinion of his brother. Arthur sent the letter on to Hugh who displayed it on his mantelpiece. By now it seemed to Hugh that the best way to deal with Rolfe was to treat him as a joke—but he was a very painful joke, all the same. Rolfe could wound. 'The Reverend Bobugo Bonson was a stuttering little Chrysostom of a priest, with the Cambridge manners of a Vaughan's Dove, the face of the Mad Hatter out of *Alice in Wonderland*, and the figure of an Etonian who insanely neglects to take any pains at all with the temple of the Holy Ghost, but wears paper collars and a black straw alpine hat. By sensational novel-writing and perfervid preaching he had made enough money to buy a country place, where he had the ambition to found a private establishment (not a religious order) for the smashing of individualities, the pieces of which he intended to put together again. . . . He did not exactly aspire to actual creation: but he certainly nourished the notion that several serious mistakes had resulted from his absence during the events described in the first chapter of Genesis. . . .'

Hugh was not exactly embarrassed or put out by all this pea-shooting, which went on and on down the years. He did not greatly mind what people thought about him. He was not so much thick-skinned as preoccupied. He became an endlessly busy man, with his very successful but poorish novels, his preaching which was good and had a style all its own, his speaking tours abroad particularly in America, and his constant concern for, as well as extensions to, his little estate at Hare Street where he thought of himself as a Nicholas Ferrar who has finally turned away from the ambiguities of High Anglicanism to the security of the true Roman Church, and has accordingly made the necessary small alterations to the community life as lived at Little Gidding.

10

In Very Deep Waters

BEN WATCHED HER YOUNGEST SON's busy progress through
the world with interest and never with any sense of outrage that
he should desert the church of which his father had been spiritual
head. She was wholly tolerant of, if argumentative about, other
people's opinions—and equally firm and unshakeable in her own.
Tremans of course was a bit of a backwater and she fretted at that.
It was uncomfortable and draughty too, but she did not mind so
much provided that the visitors kept coming—and the visitors
never ceased to come—sons, sons' friends, her own friends—to
enjoy a beautiful house well kept and to enjoy even more Ben's
spirited conversation.

Here Maggie's rather obsessive intellectual interests could,
with Ben on hand to encourage, be properly alleviated. The livestock, the beautifying of the house and gardens—these were
responsibilities which captured her enthusiasm and which she
was good at. For some years indeed Maggie prospered. The
urge she had once had to run the whole show, to take over from
her mother and assume Edward's role, gradually faded. Her life
acquired a proper balance, and Ben looked on delighted.

But late in the warm summer of 1906 it seemed to Ben that,
rather suddenly, the pendulum that had been swinging steadily
and regularly in Maggie's mind was beginning again to lurch in
a most disquieting manner. Maggie indeed was showing signs
not of the itch to rule the hen-roost which had given so much
trouble earlier but of something much more terrifying—a desire
to return to the dependency of childhood. From Tremans in

June 1906 she wrote to Gladys Bevan: 'There's nothing the matter except tiredness. I *am* a little tired still. In fact I feel I shall have to relinquish a good deal a certain tattered remnant of pride that I retain, and not mind so much if I can't carry out things that I begin to do, and if I seem to fail you rather just when I would like to help. . . .' And then, again to Gladys at the end of August, came: 'Hugh will arrive on Tuesday with a few more novels. It is Beth's 88th birthday. Do send her a congratulatory picture post-card from somewhere. . . . I have given up chasing turkeys, and am gradually giving up fussing about anything. . . .' In September she wrote to Arthur from Ilkley where she was staying with relatives: 'I talked to mother rather fully then about the cause of my depression and I fear communicated it to her for the time.' It is true that she distressed her mother, but Ben had got herself on to an even keel a long time since and kept herself that way through all family distresses and despairs. 'I do regret it. . . . I fill the required place badly. . . . I have been conscious of a steadily growing friendship [with her mother], but there is a sort of elasticity I know I lack, which is much needed when so many people of keen and nervous temperament are brought together—who on the whole too care for each other and hold together as a family more than most. Mother has it, of course, and it is what Fred essentially demands. I fear I have little of it. . . . I know you know all the tortures of nervous depression, more than I do—but I think one gets less elastic when one can't escape by activities from the circle of oneself.'

How revealing all this is. She can't 'escape by activities'. Here is an immensely able woman of just over forty, who 'can't escape'. Because she belongs to the top class of people, because the date is 1906, and because she is a woman, no daily job which would demand the exercise of those abilities is possible for her. And so she becomes turned in on herself, and that family melancholy, inherited from her father, in her has time and room to grow till it is big enough to blanket all her mind, as a black thundercloud settles obliteratingly on the top of a high mountain. She wrote to Arthur because he too, as she said, 'knew all the tortures'. Indeed, only a year later, Arthur, snug and cosy in his fellows' quarters at Magdalene, his edition of Queen Victoria's correspondence just out and himself created a c.v.o. as reward, his books tumbling out from the publishers and prospering—Arthur relapsed into a similar netherworld for two years. He wrote about it in his diary on a Sunday in Tremans in August 1907. He lay in bed in the morning listening to the religious celebrations going on in the floor below. '. . . I don't mind their doing it . . . but yet there was a sense . . . of *their* having been engaged in some virtuous exercise, "playing at holy games" . . . while I was rather a reprobate. . . . The day is hot and wet, a steep rain falling out of the sky; the house like a vapour-bath; everything unutterably hot and languid and stuffy. It is partly that, and partly also a real disgust at life and its pretences which breeds these wholesome reflections. One could hold one's tongue about such things, of course; but it does not make them worse to write them down. . . . To me, the further I search, the wider spreads the desert and the dimness. . . .'

This first long descent of Arthur's into the darkness did not mean an uninterrupted shutting-off. There were times in plenty when people could talk to him and not notice anything wrong. From Ludlow on 7 June 1909 he noted: 'A good night; woke cheerful. A long and enthusiastic letter from Marie Corelli. To Bridgenorth, by the Clee Hills. A pretty town, with a leaning fragment of a castle. . . .' But causeless fears and agonies tormented him persistently so that no regular work was possible for him. He would return to the Old Lodge at Magdalene hopefully, only to have to retreat again—to a nursing-home, to Tremans, to secluded country life somewhere in the country. The pestilence suddenly lifted off him in November 1909 and he became his busy, companionable self. The attendant evil spirit of the Bensons still hung around in the background of the smooth prosperities of his life, and in 1917, two years after his election to the mastership of Magdalene, it descended to blight him again. This was in July at Tremans. He began to sleep poorly, and when he did sleep he suffered 'the same hideous pressure of visions' as before, and on the 18th of the next month he was writing in his diary: 'What it means to sit here, the soft wind rustling, butterflies poising on the buddleia, apples dangling, the garden [of Tremans] I love beyond, the life I love all about, and have this horror over me, can't be even faintly guessed. Yet a man may live so for years. . . . It separates one from everything and everybody. Affection fades before it; its only life is to say, "I should love this and do that, if the pain were away".' He did live so for years, for five in fact, until, at the beginning of 1923, quite suddenly as before, he was perfectly all right again and ready to plunge into the two and a half years of active life left him.

But Maggie's trouble, her 'tortures of nervous depression', beginning in earnest that summer of 1906, was on a different scale; it came on more slowly, but it came to stay. Ben noticed a difference in her daughter more quickly than anyone else. Maggie had taken to breakfasting in bed, and one morning in August or September her mother, anxious about faint signs, went in to see and found a woman prostrate with depression. Ben, knowing from long years of life with Edward that there could be no reasonable, even sane, answer to the question, still had to put it: What was wrong with her? Maggie's reply was: 'Oh, I am killing it!' Ominous words for Ben to hear because she recognized in them signs of a battle inside Maggie's head which might result in the mind's total defeat. She did not give in straight away; she fought against It—whatever It was; and for half a year after that frightening exclamation to her mother, serener moments kept supervening. Surface normality kept control on life at Tremans. But Ben's diary all through that autumn is full of dread and of petitions to the Almighty that her daughter and she might be delivered from something black and threatening hovering constantly over them. Maggie struggled gamely. She fell ill with influenza. She went to Cornwall to recuperate. She finished *The Venture of Rational Faith*. She fought to console herself with the beauty of the natural world. From Falmouth in February 1907 she wrote to Gladys Bevan: 'We have been to such an exquisite Cornish garden today, with palms and citrons, and fruiting bananas, and tree-ferns, and snowdrops and crocuses, and birds that come round and chide you if you haven't brought cake. Did you see the beautiful sunset yesterday evening? The country looked so wonderful that I dreamed of rose-tinted country, with hills and trees which I was trying to sketch.' But to Arthur the following month, from Fowey, to Arthur who in that same year, in the autumn, was to know in some measure at least the sort of torments she was going through, she wrote more frankly but still with hope: 'Yes, I believe the mists will disperse. I think they must. They somehow seem to have risen to hide what is so much better, behind them.'

When she got back from Cornwall she went to see her brother

Fred where he was living in Oakley Street, Chelsea. She spoke to him of what she was going through, and spoke, so he wrote, as 'of some mortal disease'. 'I wanted to see you again first,' she told him. And after she had gone back to Tremans, Fred, who was the lucky one whom the Benson terror spared, asked himself what that frightening word 'first' might mean. 'Why had she said "first"?' he wrote.

And soon after that they all knew. Ben and Lucy were away when she got back home, and she wrote round, more to reassure herself than others, to say how well the frail but tenacious Beth was looking, and how welcoming her dogs and cats and hens had been, and how pretty everything was looking with the blossom coming out. But when they got back Maggie seemed suddenly to find the struggle too much for her. The forces of darkness swept down irresistibly. She began to have terrible dreams (this was something that Arthur too, during his long distresses, always complained of); in the daytime world human beings, ones she knew and loved, turned into malevolent creatures. The familiar human faces were masks, masks that could be, and were being, taken off to reveal underneath something indescribable and quite appalling. . . .

Ben recognized that her fear was becoming certainty and telegraphed to London for a doctor whom she knew (Ross Todd) to come down urgently. All that day Maggie sat out in the garden, reading. The breakwater against insanity which she had painfully built up was still holding. But in the evening, resting in her room before dinner, she seemed to realize that her resistance was on the point of crumbling. She quoted some lines:

> But if I stoop
> Into a dark tremendous sea of cloud,
> It is but for a time.

Then, coming down, all the faces she knew changed. All the while they had been mask-faces, and now the masks were off to reveal underneath the real features which were those of terrifying evil and malevolence. Against them there was no defence except attack. Maggie became homicidally violent. It was lucky that Todd was there because it would hardly have been in the power of the women to restrain her. She was moved to a nursing home that looked after the insane.

Ben took it all more resolutely than anyone. She wrote to Fred to tell him that they were 'in very deep waters', and all the family assembled at Tremans. Maggie was certified. She disappeared out of Tremans, out of normal life for ever. Or almost for ever. In 1913 she escaped from where she was being kept in Wimbledon. She got to Victoria and found a train which took her to Horsted Keynes. After that came the two miles of hilly walk to the house. Although physically feeble and quite unused to such exertion she managed the distance, remembered the way. She arrived in the twilight and because it was summer the doors were open. She walked past the kitchen and saw, and recognized, an old retainer, Mary (not Beth any more. Beth had died two years earlier at the age of ninety-three). Maggie said: 'I have come home, Mary', and walked on in search of her mother. Ben was half expecting her. A telegram of alarm and warning had been sent from Wimbledon as soon as it had been discovered that she was missing. And where would she go if not to Tremans? Maggie was quite quiet and to all outward appearance normal. For Ben this made it, if possible, more eerie and terrifying than it was, because Ben knew perfectly well that she was not normal at all, that this was no lightning cure. This was simply a brief shaft of sunlight piercing momentarily the clouds that had settled irremovably over Maggie's mind, and giving her a remembrance of things past. Ben took her quietly round the house and she recognized everything—her own room, her Egyptian trophies, the outbuildings which had been her particular responsibility. That tour had been on the morning after because Ben had got her to bed, and she had slept quite quietly. And after the inspection, with a doctor now in attendance, she was quite ready to go back. . . .

The whole long nightmare of Maggie's alienation, and in particular that escapist reappearance, like a convict on the run, must have been most harrowing for Ben, yet she managed to keep herself outwardly serene, keeping her outbreaks against the plagues of life to her diary—and even there ending up with a retraction. 'But I won't go on like this. I WON'T. I WON'T.'

Elizabeth Wordsworth, who had known her since 1868, and known her particularly well during that emotional Wordsworth-Benson joint holiday at Whitby in 1869, when Edward had cast longing eyes in Elizabeth's direction and she, however discreetly, had undoubtedly responded—Elizabeth, naturally in the circumstances, had tended always to see Ben's more irritating side. 'Minnie all over the place arguing with you at every turn and insinuating herself into everything like the tooth-powder into the man's dressing-case compartments in *Somebody's Luggage* . . .' she wrote to her sister-in-law Susan in 1879. But a mellower Elizabeth Wordsworth, Elizabeth the retired first Principal of Lady Margaret Hall writing when she was well into her seventies, spoke differently of Ben who had died in 1918: '. . . it was not perhaps till after her widowhood that the full beauty of her character came out. . . .' Yes, beauty certainly—and strength and fortitude under the extremest distresses also.

In 1915 Maggie had a heart attack similar to the early one she had suffered in Egypt. For a while however she rallied from that and again, quite briefly, her mind glimpsed people and things as they were. Again, quite briefly, she wanted to see her mother. Ben the evil-visaged enemy became transformed once more into Mamma, the friend and consoler in all trials and mishaps. And Ben of course, by now seventy-four, immediately went up to see her. Briefly they could talk again as mother and daughter instead of as enemies in a nightmare. But then, with convalescence, came renewed, deluded hostility. But mercifully this too did not last long. The convalescence flagged. Maggie began slowly to sink out of life and in May 1916 she died. Once more during her last week insanity relaxed its hold. One morning she awoke and said, 'Eureka! God *is* in the world; He is love; it is all love.' And it was the sure hope of the family gathered round her that in saying this she was not, after all, deluded. She talked to Ben and Lucy Tait quite reasonably and cheerfully, re-telling old stories and behaving delightedly. She said: 'Promise you will come before I die.' And of course they promised. And later on, more to herself than to anyone in particular, she said: 'Well, I *have* had a happy day.' Well, it did not seem much—one or two days in nine years; but Maggie seemed pleased. And in the very early light of the next day she died. At the graveside, so Arthur remembered, a dove rose out of a tree nearby and flew off to where the trees grew thicker. Words from Chateaubriand came to him: 'Fly hence, happy bird, to the shadow of the pines!' It is characteristic of Arthur that at such a moment he should remember something melodious and sweet and literary—and not really in any way appropriate. What sort of happy bird had Maggie ever been?

But a verse from the Bible also occurred to him which came much nearer the mark. 'My soul is escaped even as a bird from the snare of the fowler; the snare is broken and we are delivered.' The grim sobriety of this could have been a foreshadowing of what was in store for him. In the next year, 1917, he was to undergo a very long spell of his own particular kinds of self-torment. The occasional letters Maggie wrote during her long shut-up period have the pathos one associates with the utterances of a good mind surfacing briefly from the dark depths. On 15 January 1910 she wrote to Nettie Gourlay, the friend of her heart: 'My dearest, I don't forget that tomorrow was the day on which I first saw you. We had some happy times after that, at least I thought them happy. I wish I had behaved more worthily, and not brought such sorrow upon you and others. I thought I saw you out the other day and tried to get to you. . . .' After Hugh had died, and Arthur had brought out his usual commemorative cautious book in 1915, she wrote in March to thank him for having sent her a copy. 'I know he was sometimes vehement in argument . . . I am sorry he felt that he had deficiencies which made him shy with other people. . . . He was *very* good to me. I think you give the picture of a most vital personality, as he was—in fact life seems to have died out of the world now. . . .' And later in the same letter: 'Fred has been good in coming to see me. He told me you were going to Tremans for Easter. . . . How one longs for the old days, imperfect as they were—but one has no confidence that one would live them better. . . .'

* * *

Fred. He weaves his way in and out of the Benson story, and outlives them all by far. He was the lucky one. He will have had his desolating moments because who can possibly escape them? But the awful Benson melancholy scarcely ever touched him. He was a Sidgwick rather than a Benson. Like his mother he was sociable, talkative, argumentative, witty. He liked the grand world, its gossip and its high secrets; he loved being accepted into it—just as intensely as Ben regretted having to leave it after Edward had died and she had ceased to be wife of the Archbishop of Canterbury and had to make do with being a country lady. He adored his mother more unstintingly than any of them because he understood her better. Their minds worked the same way.

They had the same tastes. She would have liked to flit from grand country house to grand country house as he did. She would have liked travelling abroad as Fred did. It would have been so unlike the industrious slog that Edward used to force her into once they had crossed the Channel. Fred liked to laze in the Italian sunshine with a friend of the same sex whom he was fond of; that was what Ben, given the opportunity, would have liked also.

This begins to sound as though Fred was a decadent playboy. Perhaps there was a streak of that in him, but a streak so faint as to be hardly detectable. He could work as all the Bensons could. The list of his writings is very long. His books made him famous quite early. None of them has supreme excellence, but they did get better as he went along, and when, in his last dozen or so years of life, he turned from the quick and easy novels to memoirs and biography, he produced work which still retains its vitality. And besides being the busiest of authors he was also the staunchest of family men. The Bensons, who could so easily come to grief, relied on him when it was a matter of handling the practical affairs of life. And he was a great consoler. In 1891, for example, when he was twenty-four, he accompanied his father and mother, Lucy Tait and Maggie on a winter holiday in Algeria. The Archbishop was in one of his moods of deep depression. The Queen had not much liked the thought of the Primate being so far away from England—she had forebodings, and indeed was proved right, because Prince Albert Victor, Duke of Clarence, died of influenza while he was away; and what were Archbishops for, if not to conduct royal interments? At all events Edward could not get back from a place as remote as Biskra, and that may have increased his melancholy. Furthermore he was beginning to feel the chest pains which six years later were to destroy him. It was good, in all this, to have youth on hand in the presence of Fred. True, Fred did not stay the whole course; at Tunis he left them for Athens, going by way of Malta and Brindisi. And why, one might ask, did Edward want to drag them all so far—to places which in those days were flyblown and insanitary? The answer to that of course is that he yearned for a sight of Carthage—or rather a sight of the site of Carthage. Carthage was the place where Cyprian had been bishop, and could he, Edward, plod on towards the conclusion of his literary life-work, the biography of St. Cyprian, without ever having seen the place where the saint had passed his days? Of course not. So Carthage was one consolation, but Fred, when it came to it, proved an even greater one. 'It was not a satisfactory pain,' Edward noted in his diary, 'but it was an acute pain which in the evening gave me some little torment. Fred read aloud everyone's favourite piece of *In Memoriam*. . . .' Fred was like that.

And during the last terrible near-decade of Maggie's life, it was Fred who was the most constant visitor at the nursing home in Wimbledon where she passed the greater part of her seclusion. Fred always felt that the curtains shutting off her mind were thin, that they might, at any time, be pierced. There was with him, on these visits, the spooky feeling of almost getting through. And here it should be remembered that, quite apart from his genuine love of his sister, there was always in Fred an interest in the occult, and in spookiness generally, which was obsessive. (His turning of Arthur's Eton fireside tale into *The Luck of the Vails*, a creepy book and one of his best, provides written proof of how strongly irrationality and causelessness fascinated him.)

Psychical research had become indeed, as early as the 1860s, something which claimed the interest of many first-class minds. It was very much a Cambridge movement to set against the earlier Oxford one, and its leaders were Henry Sidgwick, Fred's uncle, and F. W. H. Myers, born in 1838 and 1843 respectively. Others of the party were the Balfour brothers, F. W. Maitland and Walter Leaf. It was a line of investigation which steered them away from the neck-or-nothing orthodoxy which characterized Lightfoot, Westcott and of course Edward Benson himself a decade or so earlier. Walter Leaf put their thinking like this: '. . . I simply recognised that what I had been taught to say that I believed had no meaning whatever for me. This did not mean that I became irreligious. No sort of materialism ever made any appeal to me: I was at best a theoretical agnostic, but with a strong bent to theism of a rather intimate sort. We at Cambridge were still under the dominant influence of Mill.'

This really does describe quite accurately (except for a pause to consider exactly what he means by 'at best') the intellectual stance of many of the next generation of Cambridge men—like Arthur and Fred Benson. Both of them were a long way from being believers after their father's hook-line-and-sinker fashion, yet both were concerned not to make a clean break. Both wanted (Arthur especially) to keep in touch with the numinous. Both

liked to feel the presence of muffling curtains which alone
impeded, rather than blocked, their access to some other world.

Fred's Marlborough was a school blown out of the doldrums
by two forceful Arnoldian headmasters, George Cotton to begin
with and then, from 1858 to 1870, George Bradley, who left in
1870 to become Master of University College, Oxford, and then,
in 1881, succeeded Stanley as Dean of Westminster, where his
ministry lasted for twenty-one years. Both were strongly inno-
vative men, not content by any means to be Arnoldians and
nothing besides. Cotton's preliminary shake-up enabled Bradley
to break away from an undiluted diet of classics in the curriculum.
Natural sciences mattered, modern languages mattered, and games
assumed an importance which would have caused Arnold to open
his intensely staring eyes very wide indeed. Bradley watched
matches. Bradley considered it important that his boys should
win them. If any boy got damaged, well, all the more reason why
he should carry on. That would show he had guts—and guts, in
Bradley's view, constituted an important element in the human
male. He set a pattern which was followed by the vast majority of
English public schools in the last three decades of the nineteenth
century. It was the pattern which novelist Morgan Forster so
loathed when as a boy he came to set foot in Tonbridge in the
early 1890s.

It suited Fred very well however. He enjoyed games and was
immensely good at them. He was tall (not quite as tall as Arthur),
handsome and powerfully made. He entered eagerly into the life
of the school; he enjoyed the playing-fields. '. . . [Schoolboys]
can go for any number of pleasant walks when they are fifty: at
fifteen (given they have not got some corporal disability) it is far
better for them to run and to kick and to hit and to sweat. . . .'
And as for living for long periods in an exclusively male society
during adolescence, well, Fred had what would now be considered
extremely unfashionable things to say. 'For twelve or thirteen
weeks three times a year they live exclusively among boys, and
that at a time when their vigour is at its strongest. . . . Naturally
there is a danger about it (for what emotion worth having is not
encompassed by perils?) and [a] strong beat of affection may
easily explode into fragments of mere sensuality, be dissipated in
mere "smut" and from being a banner in the clean wind be
trampled into mud. But promiscuous immorality was, as far as I

am aware, quite foreign to the school, though we flamed into a hundred hot bonfires of these friendships, which were discussed with a freedom that would seem appalling, if you forgot that you were dealing with boys and not with men.'

Fred's particular hot friendship was with Beesly. Their parting, when it comes to be Fred's time for going on to Cambridge (Fred was the elder), is described by Fred, in one of the auto-biographical passages which pop in and out of his many books of personal reminiscence, with a tight-lipped sentimentality—hot chocolate poured on ice-cream—which turns the modern stomach. ' "It's been ripping anyhow," he said. "Did two fellows ever have such a good time?" Quite suddenly at that, when the passing-bell should have been loudest, it ceased altogether. The whole of my dismal maunderings about days that were dead and years that were past, I knew to be utterly mistaken. Nothing that was worth having was dead or past at all: it was all here now, and all mine, a possession eternally alive. "But did they?" he repeated, as I did not answer. "Never. Nor will. And there's chapel-bell. Get up." ' There is more of this conversation, some of it more embarrassing than the passage quoted; and why Fred, in his fifties, should have thought it worth the semi-permanence of print is a question that has to be answered.

He certainly preferred the company of men to the company of women—as, indeed, did Arthur. But Fred paraded this taste with much more openness and sang froid than ever Arthur did. It is probably true to say that deep down he actively disliked women. The very lengthy list of his novels provides plentiful evidence of this dislike.

Fred was only in his twenty-sixth year at the time of *Dodo*, but *Dodo*, in some form or another, had been on the stocks for a considerable time before that. Years earlier he and Maggie had written a story together in which a woman somewhat like the ultimate Dodo played a part. Then, after his First in the classical Tripos, and after his father had agreed to his staying on for a fourth year in order to take up archaeology for a second Tripos, the idea of a Dodo girl surfaced again. '. . . one morning at Cambridge, where I had returned for a few weeks before we went out to Switzerland in August, I desisted from the perusal of Miss Harrison's *Mythology and Monuments of Ancient Athens*, and wrote on the top of a piece of blue foolscap a word that has stuck to me all my life. For a long time there had been wandering about in my head the idea of some fascinating sort of modern girl, who tackled life with uncommon relish and success, and was adored by the world in general, and had all the embellishments that a human being can desire except a heart. . . .' This was in 1889, and he scribbled rapidly in the Benson way. 'I wrote with the breathless speed of creation,' he said, and then pushed the whole thing into a drawer.

He duly got his first in archaeology, went off to Chester in search of Roman tombstones, and interested Gladstone not far away in Hawarden. Gladstone explained to him in detail the only way to make squeezes, and then, after six weeks, Fred returned to Cambridge. Here he took up the blue foolscap pages again and 'had the conviction that they might amuse others . . .'. He showed it to his mother, who approved. She thought it worthwhile to send it to one or other of her many literary friends to find out whether professional opinion might be prepared to give backing to what she and Fred thought. She sent it to Henry James. Always the least censorious of men, James kept the untidy, handwritten manuscript a long time before squeezing out of himself something which would be tactful and at the same time not dishonest. 'I am such a fanatic myself on the subject of form style the evidence of intention and meditation, of chiselling and hammering out in literary things that I am afraid I am rather a cold-blooded judge, rather likely to be offensive to a young storyteller on the question of quality. I'm not sure that yours strikes me as quite so ferociously literary as my ideal. . . . Only remember that a story is, essentially a form, and that if it fails of that, it fails of its mission. . . . For the rest, make yourself a style. It is by style we are saved.' Fred had the sense to see that this was James's way of telling him that he loathed *Dodo* quite heartily. Fred pushed the whole thing back into its drawer and went off to the British School of Archaeology in Athens. He loved Greece and 'in archaeological intervals [there were plenty of these] I speared mullet by the light of a flaming torch on moonless nights with the fishermen of Nauplia, and ate them for early breakfast, broiled on the sea-shore, before the sun was up.' And when he got home, refusing to accept wholly James's politest of rejections, took *Dodo* out again. He thought he spotted 'certain gleams of vitality', and Ben thought it might be a good idea to let Mrs. Harrison see it.

(Mrs. Harrison was a more than competent novelist who wrote successfully under the name of 'Lucas Malet'.)

Mrs. Harrison did not hum and ha in the Jacobean manner. She told him crisply what was wrong, and how to put it right. Fred, who was self-confident but not over self-confident, studied her advice and revised his book. He then sent it to the publisher Mrs. Harrison had recommended. The publisher accepted it without delay. And when Fred came back from a second visit to Greece he was met by Ben at Victoria and she told him he had a best-seller on his hands. People were finding it pleasingly startlingly that the son of an Archbishop should produce something so 'frankly unepiscopal' as Fred puts it. Edition followed edition. On the whole the press did not find it worth reviewing, but that made no difference (it never has); people talked about it, and people bought it (two volumes at a guinea a volume). Fred, with no money worries to start with, found himself suddenly very well off indeed. When the book became such a triumphant success the press felt it had to notice him and sharpened their knives in readiness for the next one, which he called *The Rubicon*. 'Another Unbirched Heroine' was the heading under which six columns spread themselves in the *St. James's Budget*: 'It might have been supposed that the son of an Archbishop was hardly the sort of person to shine in this kind of literature, but Mr Benson has taught us better than that. Yet our thanks are due to him for one thing: his book consists of only two volumes; it might have been in three. . . .

How they mate in the "Hupper Suckles". . . .
Languor, Cigarettes and Blasphemies. . . .

We conclude this enthusiastic appreciation of Mr Benson with the bold avowal that we regard *The Rubicon* as almost truly perfect of its kind, and probably unsurpassable. . . .' Then Fred was taken to pieces with a ferocity which we have quite lost the habit of in our reviewing.

Fred laughed. He was doing very well, and had no false notions of himself. His father laughed too, threw his head back with a shout, slapped him on the back, and told him: 'You've got shoulders broad enough to stand that sort of thing'. And indeed he had. So had Arthur. All the same though, when Max Beerbohm skewered Arthur to the dissecting-table in *The Christmas Garland*,

Arthur was pained. Max of course was a very skilful *banderillero* and placed his darts accurately. Perhaps that was it. You could gracefully dodge the wild swipes of the *St. James's Budget*'s blunt instrument. Given a going-over by Max, perhaps even Fred would have squirmed.

Fred was content that his novels should be read by all the best people, and indeed they were. You could demonstrate how securely you were in the know by identifying the real people under Fred's fictitious names. Everyone for example felt sure that Dodo was Margot Tennant, and when the time came for her to write her autobiography she had this to say: that before her engagement to Herbert Asquith, HHA was walking in Rotten Row with Lord Rosebery when she [Margot] galloped past. 'Anxious to warn his Home Secretary against a courtship . . . fraught with danger if not with disaster he said, "That was Miss Margot Tennant, I believe. My dear Asquith, I advise you to read *Dodo* if you have not already done so—there's a great deal of truth in it." *Dodo* was a novel that made a sensation at the time of publication as the heroine—a pretentious donkey with the heart and brains of a linnet—was supposed to be myself. The author denied it, but his brother, Arthur Benson—the Eton master—and Randall Davidson came to see me to express their regret for what had occurred, and both my friends and my enemies embarrassed me and amused themselves by calling me "Miss Dodo". I told everyone I could not have been the heroine, as I was not beautiful, and did not hunt in summer; nevertheless the exact description of my sitting room and other details . . . proved that the author had me in his mind when he wrote the book. . . .'

Unlike Arthur, Fred enjoyed the fuss and Margot, in spite of her retrospective huffiness, being the kind of woman she was, probably enjoyed it too.

Dodo, and all Fred's early novels, are by now so dated as to be almost unreadable. He was none the less by far the best writer of all the Bensons, and here and there, amongst his vast output, you find passages—whole books even, which succeed in being something more than books for the moment. It is in the work of his last decade or so (1930–40) that Fred is at his best. Tiring of his fiction, which aimed low and hit the target, he turned to biography and reminiscence. Books like *As We Were*, *As We Are* and *Final Edition*, in which he looks back at his own busy, and outwardly at least highly successful life, are done with an urbanity and ease which make them as entertaining now as when they were written. He wrote biographies too—of Charlotte Brontë, of Queen Victoria, Edward VII and the World War I Kaiser—and these too, especially the royal ones in which, by accident of his birth, he was able to write from the inside, have strong merits.

Why did he write so much when he must have known, with that almost first-class brain of his, that what he produced fell very far short of achieving permanent value? The first answer to this is that Fred had the Benson itch for covering blank sheets of paper with words; the second is that he felt, quite rightly, that a man must work hard to make the most of what talents he has— and Fred's talents as a writer cannot be in dispute. Take this passage from *Final Edition*, for example (it starts, as so much of Fred's work does, with his mother): 'Her three sons, one from Cambridge, one from London or winter resorts in Switzerland, and one from Hare Street or preaching tours in America, were often with her in the years preceding the Great War. On a ludicrous occasion they were there together, each madly writing, one a reflective volume of essays, another [himself of course] a story of modern life, the third a propagandist romance. Somebody suggested that they should suspend their important literary labours for a day, and that each should devote himself to paro-dying the work of a brother. . . . So, like three Cains . . . they borrowed copies of each other's books from my mother's collection of them, studied them closely, and sharpened their dagger-pens . . . Arthur began. He had been studying *The Light Invisible* [one of Hugh's bits of popish, fictional propaganda] . . . and he laughed so much himself as he read the impression it had made on him that his eyes streamed and he had to wipe his spectacles. . . . My mother by this time was laughing helplessly and hopelessly, with her face all screwed up, but Hugh sat, leaning forward, so as not to miss a word, puzzled and inquiring, and politely smiling. . . . Then it was my turn to read. I had skimmed through several of Arthur's books and presented the musings of a wise patient wistful middle-aged gentleman called Geoffrey, who sate by his mullioned window and looked out on the gracious flowing meadow below. . . . Once again my mother was helplessly giggling, but, as I read, I became aware of a draught or a frost or something inclement in the room, and, looking up, I saw a pained expression on Arthur's face. . . . "Now for Fred," said Hugh, and then it was my turn to know what a brother thought of me. Hugh's composition seemed to me to miss its mark. Those babbling puppets with their inane inconsequent talk had no individuality; there was nothing in them. Really this composition made no impression on me: I could not see the point of it. . . . But here was my mother for the third time wiping tears of joy from her eyes, and Arthur and, of course, the author were much amused. "Oh, you clever people," said my mother. "Why don't you all for the future write each other's books instead of your own? You do them much better. Give me all those stories. I shall read them when I feel depressed". . . .'

This is a good passage. Fred makes it look easy to do when of course it is not. The sense of a close family community, basically on the right terms with each other, is conveyed; Fred's pain when it comes to be his turn to undergo scrutiny is just like Arthur's a little earlier, but it is switched off at exactly the right moment, and self-mockery takes over. It requires talent, and many years of practice, to write in the way Fred writes here.

The third point to be made about Fred's writing, and about his novels in particular, is that he is not simply a confectioner; a certain seriousness of purpose underlies the tart chattering of his characters, the busy stratagems they employ in the furtherance of futile objectives. What emerges principally—and Fred, in spite of the airy flippancy of his tone is in deadly earnest about it—is his intense dislike of women. Dodo, Lucia, Elizabeth Mapp—they are all a sisterhood though the last two make no appearance in his pages until nearly thirty years after that first one whom Lord Rosebery took such a dislike to. They are all bitches—and of course the important question to ask is why? He had a closer understanding with his mother than any of the others. He loved her deeply, and this is apparent in page upon page of his writing. He starts to glow whenever he has to find words for her. Maggie too he loved. He visited her faithfully all through the years when she had to be under surveillance, he would take her home to Oakley Street, he would take her for a blow in one of his flashy new motors—why then Lucia?

At this point the question of the Bensons and homosexuality asks itself insistently. Ben and Lucy Tait, Arthur and—George Mallory, perhaps, who was lost to him somewhere near the summit of Everest? But for Mallory a number of other names might be substituted; Hugh and Frederick Rolfe; Fred and Ellingham Brooks, or perhaps Fred and Francis Yeats-Brown; Maggie and Nettie Gourlay—the pairings are numerous. The fancy can roam. It needs to be remembered however that in the late 1970s the word homosexuality has become something of a battlecry, something really quite fashionable. In the Benson's time, whether of the first or the second generation, sodomy was something you may have thought about, but also something you kept very quiet about. There was poor Oscar standing there, right in the middle of the period, to offer himself up as a fearful warning. For most of the younger Bensons it is doubtful whether there was ever any question of heeding—or even needing—the warning which sounded loud in the ears of all possible deviants after the humiliating retribution willed upon Oscar by society in 1895. Arthur in his right mind—and there were long spells when he was far from being in his right mind—was simply a comfort-loving man who preferred the company of men of his own class and who shared his own tastes—Percy Lubbock, perhaps, or Howard Sturgis, or Herbert Tatham—to that of any woman whatsoever. Arthur examines himself endlessly in his vast diary, but the feeling the reader of it is left with is that he never, in any fixed and positive sense, succeeded in understanding himself. On the last day of January 1907, when he had been three years fellow of Magdalene and was thoroughly at home and comfortable there, he takes up the woman-question as it affects him—not by any means for the first, or for the last, time: '. . . reflected sadly today how I tended to squabble with my women friends. Here have I dropped out of all or nearly all my feminine friendships. I never see Lady P., I hear nothing of Countess B. I have lost sight of B.M. I have insulted M.C., alienated Mrs L., shut up Mrs S.—and so on. Yet I do not squabble with my men-friends. I think it is a certain bluntness, frankness, coarseness, which does not offend men, but which aggravates women. The thing which has tended to terminate my women-friendships is that at a certain juncture they begin to disapprove and to criticise my course, and to feel a responsibility to say disagreeable things. One ought to take it smilingly and courteously; and one would, if one liked the sex—but I *don't* like the sex. Their mental processes are obscure to me; I don't like their superficial ways, their mixture of emotion with reason. One's men friends never criticise, they take one for better or worse. One gets plenty of criticism from foes, and one supplies the harshest condemnation oneself. My own feeling is that one's duty to a friend is to encourage and uplift and compliment and believe in him. Women, I think, when they get interested in one, have a deadly desire to improve one. They think that the privilege of friendship is to criticise; they want deference, they don't want frankness. I don't want to excuse myself, because I think it is a vital deficiency in me; but it is *so* vital and so instinctive that I don't see how to cure it, and I cannot even frame an effective desire to do so.'

So Arthur ruminates, and the most important phrase is 'a vital deficiency'. For Arthur the pressing importunities of sexual desire never seem to have existed. He was simply undersexed. Friendships with men, because these were easier, more predictable, less bothersome, were the friendships he liked. There was no problem about loneliness. He lived, for the greater part of his life, in communities of men; there was almost always someone intelligent to talk to—and Arthur was an incomparable talker without ever, somehow, being a man of thoroughly settled views.

With Fred it was never quite like this. His dislike of women was more positive. His friendships with men were less timid, had much more of an emotional quality. During the Edwardian years and up to the war, Fred spent long spells on Capri, sharing the tenancy of villas, the longest being that of the Villa Cercola, with Ellingham Brooks. Brooks, for reasons which remain obscure, had married Romaine, an American lesbian painter. Soon after the marriage Romaine inherited a fortune and left Brooks immediately afterwards, making him an allowance of £300 a year. In his villa, as far inland as in Capri it is possible to be, Brooks lived comfortably, taking care not to over-exert himself. He played his piano, not particularly well, and devoted himself to the translation of the sonnets of Hérédia. As well as Fred, Somerset Maugham paid something towards the rent of the Villa Cercola, and there were regular summer visits on the part of both of them, with careful forward planning so that there should be no, or at any rate a minimum of, overlapping. Compton Mackenzie recalled Brooks's coming to see him one day in a great flutter to tell him that Maugham had got himself involved with a married woman and that he was going to have to marry her. 'I don't know what I shall do if Maugham brings a wife to the Cercola,' he said. 'I don't think Benson will like it at all either.' But in the event Maugham never brought Sirie to disturb Cercola's male peace. Before the war also, Fred developed a very warm friendship with Francis Yeats-Brown, whose family owned the castello at Portofino. 'I settled down with him,' Fred wrote, 'from May to August in that enchanted castle of Portofino. . . .' And he went on to talk of the 'long ritual of swimming and basking, and in the afternoon a rambling climb through the wooded hills, or . . . a scudding across the bay in the red-sailed boat. . . . And then came dinner . . . and afterwards hours of serious work . . . fatigued and exhilarated we brought the quires of scribbling paper. . . .' How Yeats-Brown saw Fred and Fred's friendship he put down in June 1909, writing in Portofino: 'I have made great friends with EFB. He is a most remarkable man: living vividly in the present and talking cleverly. His manners are truly perfect: he has square shoulders and looks boyish [Fred was forty-two]. His forehead is magnificent: he is strong and well-built. He likes his work, but perhaps he likes the world still better.' This friendship continued after the war, and when Yeats-Brown had finished his *Bengal Lancer*, which in the end grew to be a vast success, Fred helped him in placing it—a job which neither of them found easy. By then, though, Yeats-Brown's estimate of Fred's usefulness as a literary mentor had gone sharply down. His suggestions about writing, he said in 1927, 'seem to me sterile'.

Was Fred a thoroughgoing homosexual? In his case it is impossible to say No with as much certainty and confidence as it is when talking of Arthur. Brooks was certainly a homosexual, and Fred's liaison with him was long—and Fred was quite willing to defend what appears on the face of it to have been Brooks's pretty futile life. Even to write the sonnets of Hérédia does not strike one as a way of achieving a perfectly fulfilled life; to spend one's days simply trying to translate them seems a pennyfarthing pastime. Yet Fred is prepared to speak up warmly for Brooks. 'He was short in stature,' Fred says, 'and clumsy in movement, but his face was very handsome. His mouth had a fine thin upper lip priestlike and ascetic in character, but below was a full loose lower lip, as if the calls of the flesh had not yet been subdued. . . .' This does not sound like the portrait of a charmer, but Fred seems to have got on with him splendidly, and to have enjoyed the company of all the other cranks, oddities and minor talents with which Capri in those pre-war years was crowded: Count Fersen who liked his pipe of opium and who had, people said, been involved in the celebration of the black mass. Norman Douglas incubating *South Wind* and Axel Munthe living at Anacapri and still busy with the *Story of San Michele*, American spinsters aged, wealthy, and, so Fred thought, 'adventurous', Scottish Mrs. Frazer who spent long hours in the sea in an outfit designed to keep out any possible cold. . . . Fred was fashionable. He led the life of the *beau monde*: the winters in the Alps taking a prominent part in winter sports, beginning now to be modish after the tough preliminary work done by Leslie Stephen, Edward Whymper and their like; the summers in Italy, with Venice the favourite place next to Capri; the first weeks of the autumn in Scotland where, as he was a notable games player, he could get his birdies in on some of the finest courses in the world; and for the rest in London where, once he had ceased to make Tremans his home (round about 1900), he always had his *pied à terre*.

He insisted that he had no dislike of Arthur, but it is not altogether easy to accept this. 'I think we really liked each other,' he says, 'though sharply disagreeing, better than anybody, and though our lives lay widely apart, we were strongly and fundamentally united.' This is not much more than whitewash. Arthur, in his dying moments at Magdalene in the summer of 1925, said he saw no reason why Fred should be sent for. Fred came none the less, and got there in time to see his brother alive. But he was candid about his own emotions. 'I felt no real sense of personal bereavement,' he says. '. . . for except for those few days at Lamb House every year [they had shared the lease of Henry James's Rye house since 1922], we saw nothing of each other. Our ways of life, our diversions had little in common, and never, since we were boys had we spoken of things that intimately concerned us as we spoke of them to our friends. . . .' And later he goes on: '. . . He shunned emotional experience'—rather implying that he (Fred) did no such thing, and one wonders just how far this implication is justified. Fred was the likest of all to his mother, and Ben was cold. She was plenteously and gaily affectionate in a dutiful sort of way, but deep down underneath the melting tip there was the iceberg.

11

The Last of Tremans

ARTHUR'S LAST SEVENTEEN YEARS, from 1908 to 1925 really
only amounted to ten, because for seven of them (1908–09, 1917–
1922) he lived shut off from life, enclosed in an impenetrable
melancholy. The long second attack began at Tremans at the
beginning of July 1917.

Ross Todd, the doctor who had had charge of Maggie and
who therefore knew the family trouble, advised him to leave
Magdalene and install himself as a patient in a nursing home near
Ascot. Fred came down for Christmas to Tremans, but it was a
dwindled party: no Maggie, no Hugh, no Beth, no Arthur, Ben
getting really old by now; deaf, and more critical than ever. Fred
consoled himself by thinking that the better she loved the more
critical she became—but was that, perhaps, exactly right? He
showed no reluctance when the time came for him to hurry back
to his war work in London where he was busy at the Foreign
Office, helping, as he was thoroughly competent to do, in the
thorny business of Turkish affairs. He must have wondered; first
his father of the daemonic passions and protuberant eyes, then
the quite terrible alienation of Maggie, and now Arthur. When
would it come to his turn? It is not difficult to understand why
Fred was at pains to keep himself at something of a remove from
the rest of his family. He could have looked upon them as a
doomed and stricken lot—except for his mother for whom, so
far as Fred was concerned, there was always only an extremity of
adoration which bordered on the unhealthy. But for the others,
what curse was on them that they should sparkle bright and early

and then be snuffed out, either utterly or else partially in ways variously unpleasant? Martin the brilliant and impeccable taken off while still a schoolboy, Nellie, the most natural, the best balanced of them all, strangled by diphtheria when she was just twenty-seven. And Hugh; what sense was there to be made out of Hugh? His brief life—he died in October 1914 of something they called 'false angina'—had been, viewed from Fred's standpoint, that of an insanely activated puppet. He had a lack of any strong human affection; he had phobias—about being buried alive, for example; he worked in a kind of perpetual frenzy; novels poured out of him, all of them dashed off, all of them the work, you felt, of someone who could have done so much better; he scurried about the world pulpiteering, and his sermons were a vast success—made him, indeed, famous; he laboured, during brief respites from public appearances, at his little Hare Street estate, seeing it as a Little Gidding community *in utero* and seeing himself as a Nicholas Ferrar quite properly divorced from Anglicanism and a fully fledged, passionately committed Monsignor of the Roman Catholic Church; and then he died, in gloomy Salford, while on a preaching mission, too obsessively preoccupied even to make a proper will, so that Cardinal Bourne had had quite a job getting his hands on the Hare Street property and the quite false legend had grown up that the remaining Bensons were trying to do him out of his promised legacy: Was not all this—again from Fred's point of view—a fretful, feverish, misguided existence suddenly obliterated in mid-career? And Maggie, when that grim, rationed 1917 Christmas came round, had been only two and a half years dead. It was all very well for Arthur, writing of her end, to quote Chateaubriand in his mellifluous way—'Fly hence, happy bird, to the shadow of the pines'— Fred knew that Maggie's life had been a horror; he knew that better than any of them, better than Ben herself because he had kept faithfully to his visiting through all the years of her insanity. So Fred went back to London, and Whitehall, and Turkish deviousness, and public horrors—and went, in a way, with relief because the public horrors of December 1917, dire though these were, were not thumping down on his particular head alone, whereas the private Benson horrors were by now his alone; Ben was visibly ageing and making her preparations to sail away from them for good, Arthur was in his Ascot nursing home.

Yet Arthur was to rally, to re-emerge blinking from his dark night, so that indeed it could be said that his last ten years, from 1915 to 1925—in 1915, on Donaldson's death, Lord Braybrooke, seventh of his line and Visitor of Magdalene, had immediately offered Arthur the Mastership of Magdalene and Arthur had accepted to the great delight of everybody—were years of quite remarkable achievement. And this is the point at which the remarkable tale of the rich American woman of vast wealth, who lived with her husband and family in Switzerland, begins to be important, as will shortly be seen.

When Arthur had been elected fellow of Magdalene in 1904, the college had been very small and financially rather cramped. He came from a family very comfortably provided for—the salary of the Primate in those non-inflationary days was very large indeed. In addition the income from his books was handsome, and his rate of production swift. He was not a spendthrift man. His personal needs were small. He was a stay-at-home. 'All his migrations,' in Goldsmith's lovely phrase, 'were from the blue bed to the brown.' He was perfectly suited therefore for the role of benefactor, and it was a role which he enjoyed. His first two years at Magdalene somewhat lacked the tranquillity he always craved for; because of his dithering, hot-and-cold response to the hypothetical question: Did he, or did he not, want to succeed Warre as Headmaster of Eton? He had always felt that Eton's teaching had been far too limited in scope; he would want to widen the curriculum—make drastic changes, in fact. Was he the kind of man to institute, and carry out, drastic changes in the face of numerous and powerful opposition? His father, with his intense and concentrated masterfulness, could certainly have done it; but could he? He had doubted it and after much agonizing had indicated as much.

But once the agitations brought on through Warre's resignation had subsided, Arthur settled quickly to life at Magdalene, and began to enjoy it. He moved into the Old Lodge, and enlarged it at his own cost. He delighted in the civilized company of the dons; he had Hugh to consort with at the Cambridge Rectory; and he had all the Magdalene young men to get to know. Few dons of his generation were as assiduous as Arthur in entertaining, and getting on to terms of close friendship, with Magdalene men *in statu pupillari*. His talk was good; it was apt and ready without

ever showing any over-eagerness to take charge; he could pull
stories and illustrations out of the air to fit any topic. After hall,
in the combination room, port and coffee went down smoothly
when Arthur was there—and he usually was. And because he had
a quite extraordinary readiness of tongue the conversations did
tend—although, it must be repeated, there was never any overt
over-eagerness; he was much too well-mannered for that—to go
Arthur's way.

After the first dark period of 1907–08, he plunged again into
college and university life. Just before his attack he had been
invited to join the board of governors of Gresham's School,
Holt, and during the five years before the war he took an active
part in the school's management. The widening of the curriculum
which he would have wanted to put into effect at Eton was more
readily received at Gresham's—more especially, perhaps, because
this enlargement came in the form of suggestions from Arthur,
who had for some while been a Liveryman of the wealthy and
honourable City Guild of Fishmongers, by whose providence the
school was enabled to flourish. Arthur therefore, in a modest
way, had the chance of becoming an educational reformer; and
he took it.

The flow of his published work began again to run swiftly
between 1908 and 1914. He was 'blessed and afflicted', Percy
Lubbock thought, 'with a facility which he has not the weight to
stem'. In his diary Arthur told himself: 'I live first to shape
thought into word . . .'—but here he was deluding himself. In
1923, two years before his death, he wrote again in his diary of
Mallory, this time critically—he was well able to criticize his
friends—'[Mallory] believes too much in his power of inspiring
second-rate people by somewhat incoherent thought. . . .' Arthur,
who could, as we have seen, laugh at himself in public and refer
to his books as 'twaddle', was never really fond of hearing other
people talking about them in this dismissive way. When *Punch*
laughed at him he was not amused; when Max Beerbohm
laughed at him he was not amused either. But if Mallory ever
got to hear of this little swipe, he might with ample justice have
replied with a *tu quoque*. Arthur's writing lacks purpose; it
wanders; it has no guidelines. So far from its thought being
'incoherent', it suffers from not having, in any positive constant
sense, any thought at all. He would have felt himself insulted if

he had been told so because he was a man fully conscious of, and enjoying, his very real authority, but none the less if someone *had* told him so, Arthur would have been hearing the truth. *At Large, The Silent Isle, The Leaves of the Tree, The Child of the Dawn, Thy Rod and thy Staff, Along the Road, Joyous Gard, Where No Fear Was, Watersprings*—nobody reads them now.

But as they came out, plenty of people read them. The very substantial royalties, and the floods of letters from comforted and uplifted persons male and female but more female than male were proof of this. And in 1915, two years before his second breakdown and in the year of his election as Master of Magdalene on Stuart Donaldson's death he received this best of all the letters he ever got from a stranger—the one from the American Suissesse. She derived comfort from what he wrote, she told him, and Arthur answered, because his pen was never still and he answered everything. There was no self-seeking ulterior motive in this habit of his; a blank sheet of paper was something to be filled. But this time, with the American lady, his scattered crumbs brought unimaginably rich returns. Having elicited Arthur's customary ample response, the American lady went on to talk business. She knew that he had plans for the expansion of his small adopted college because he had told her so. What would he say to a contribution from herself towards this? She might be in a position to add a touch of splendour to what he had in mind. Arthur wrote back immediately to say that this was not to be thought of. It would be improper, and Arthur never countenanced the improper. The American Suissesse was not to be put off, however. She said she would simply be doing what she liked with her own. Her family approved. Not for one moment was Arthur to think of himself as a pensioner. He told close friends, Stephen Gaselee, Percy Lubbock, of this remarkable offer; how should he respond? Well, obviously, these told him, he would not be looking on this little gift as a means whereby he could gratify personal hankerings; he would be, as it were, the administrator of a little trust fund, and as such, why not say yes?

Arthur did say yes, and received, *as a first instalment*, funds to the value of about £45,000. In terms of buying power this would represent, in today's minuscule pounds, a sum of the order of three-quarters of a million. Arthur was himself already a rich man. He had already shown considerable generosity to his adopted college. Now he became a benefactor on the largest scale. He built, he beautified, and most important of all, he gave largely so that boys could come up to Magdalene, boys who otherwise would not have had the means to come up to Cambridge at all, and show their gratitude by getting Firsts in the Tripos. The college flourished. It had never had such a Master.

The strange thing about all this is that Arthur and his bene-factress never met. For him she remained always no more than a signature on a cheque; for her he was the author of his books and a letter-writer as punctual as he was enchanting. Fred wrote about this strangest of relationships long after Arthur was dead. Many had spoken of it before, because there was no sort of secrecy about it. But Fred's tone was a little unkind. Even when one was old and the other dead, the two brothers still did not manage to get on. 'After this constant and intimate correspondence,' Fred said, 'either or both may have felt that personal contact might involve anti-climax; in any case this bodiless relationship entirely satisfied each, so why run the risk of the minutest disenchant-ment?' But why at least, one might ask, did he not invite her to Tremans? There are two answers to this. The first is that his second, more terrible, breakdown was not far away, because in 1917 the awful dreams began again: '. . . a large green bottle, hanging in space by a series of linked chains—no meaning whatever. There was no terror or agitation about these. Suddenly without any warning an awful access of horror and despair, so that I wondered if my end was come. I got up, lit the lights, and almost instantly felt that I was all right again—as if something had repelled the invasion and, so to speak, sealed the sepulchre. . . .' The second answer is that in 1915, Ben was seventy-four, and beginning to be very deaf. Perhaps at last she was beginning to be less readily sociable. Her long reign at Tremans had only three more years to run.

* * *

Ben had lived a very grand life. For fourteen years she was second lady in the land. She had personal maids and kitchen maids and housemaids and nursery maids. She had a family which, with reservations, adored her. Of all the eight principals involved in this story she was the one with the swiftest intelligence—Martin we shall never be sure about because he died too soon. For the last twenty years of her life she lived in a lovely house in Sussex, a county which in her time was beautiful and tranquil, and yet, thanks to the admirable train service of those days, handy for the Army and Navy Stores and for Lucy Tait's occasional small town house in Barton Street, Westminster. If a history claims the right to a heroine, then she unquestionably is the one to fill the role in this one. She could reign in two palaces, Lambeth and Addington; she could move confidently and easily in the grand society of what was then the most powerful country in the world; and when the time came for rustication and comparative seclusion, Ben knew that people would come to her wherever she was. There was no need for her to take Royal Lodge, Windsor Great Park, which the Queen had offered this illustrious widow; for one thing, the costs of upkeep would have been far too great.

Yet, although a heroine as of right, Ben must be considered a tragic heroine. Her marriage was a disaster, although, except for one lapse, she contrived not to make it seem so. Proposed to when she was a child, married when she was scarcely more than a child and certainly totally ignorant of what was meant by the sexual life between man and woman, she received a shock right at the beginning which scuppered for good the full and proper development of her emotional life. Edward, himself clumsy and ignorant, would have rushed at her. He would not have understood that in most women the sexual response is something that has to be gently coaxed, that it comes to fullness much more slowly than in men. In effect, Ben was raped. And in Edward there would have been afterwards the feeling of guilt which his upbringing and outlook would have made inevitable. Post-coital depression— common to many people, but fleeting—would in him have taken the form of massive, long-lasting depression. He took her to Paris for the honeymoon—'How I cried at Paris,' she said. After the birth of Hugh in 1871 there came the feeling that she could stand life with Edward no longer. She probably did not frame it in this blunt way even to herself. She was suffering from— nervous exhaustion, or from something else equally unscandalous. She went to stay with Bishop Wordsworth in his palace at Rise-holme. She and Elizabeth, the bishop's daughter, were much of an age, and after that Whitby holiday Ben felt affectionate towards Elizabeth—more affectionate than Elizabeth felt towards her because Elizabeth had felt Edward's eyes fixed admiringly upon

her, and was uncomfortable about the Bensons. Ben, it is probable, would not have minded how admiringly Edward had fixed
his eyes on any woman; what a relief in so many ways that would
have been. His insistence—how he could insist—that she return
to Wellington in time for Speech Day did nothing to alleviate the
'prostration', and she went to her brother-in-law, Christopher
Benson, a crippled man, who lived with his wife, who had been
Agnes Walker, in Wiesbaden. This flight to Wiesbaden, arranged
by her brother Arthur, is the one from which, it seems likely, she
was determined never to return. The children? Well, she had
great affection for them certainly, but there was always Beth, and
Ben was never a woman maternal in the fullest sense of the word.
She preferred her daughters to her sons—though Fred was a
favourite, but there was a distance between them, a sort of
mockery. She had the hard bright mind of the Sidgwicks. She
did come back though, early in 1873, but only after many wheedling letters from Edward. He had no talent for wheedling women,
no talent for wheedling anyone really. He wrote one on Christmas
Day 1872, at seven in the morning. 'I shall write you but a few
lines because it is Christ's birthday, and I find none like one of the
ancient anthems for the eve—"Sanctificamini, filii Israel, dicit
Dominus:/Die enim crastina descendet Dominus,/*Et auferet a
vobis omnem languorem*" '—what a way to ask a woman to come
back to him, even with the third line underscored: 'May he take
away the sickness of your head'.

But then she did come back—and there, at Lincoln, was Mrs.
Mylne, her beloved Tau, not the first of her close women
friends, but the most intensely close to date and Tau gave her a
sort of religion. It was not at all Edward's sort of religion; it had
no rigidity, no dogma, no Articles of Belief either less or more
than thirty-nine. It was more a sort of private hot line to God, to
a God she could talk to direct without the intermediacy of
bishops, priests and deacons. Someone who would tell her what
to do when there were problems. Someone who would give her
comfort and quietude when the problems, in human terms, were
not soluble. It was a religion she stuck to for the rest of her life.
At Tremans she gave it outward forms in deference to Edward's
memory, because he so loved ritual and ceremony and glittering
copes. She could not give it quite these, but she did insist on
Compline on Sunday evenings—and Arthur, however furious,

had to bear with it. She, Ben, at last, was going to have Rules, and Arthur, who came so frequently, and who so enjoyed the comfortable self-indulgence which the place afforded, would have to conform to them. She was no bigot. Hugh could have his papistical chapel up in the top storey, Fred could mock as he mocked at everything and she still loved him because he made her laugh. Her religion would keep her straight—in the way, she now guiltily and unnecessarily felt—she had not been in Edward's time. As at Wellington, when she had been so young, she would be punctual; she would get to meetings on time, she would fight the good fight over money matters so that her financial affairs would never again get into a tangle, she would not *over-eat*.

Lucy Tait became on and off a member of the Benson family as soon as her father, Archbishop Tait, died in 1882, and Lucy Tait proved to be the last and longest of Ben's close friendships with women. Now, after sixty years, she is not an easy person to get to know. She came from good stock, she was intelligent, she had a strong will, it might be said that she played the male role in the relationship—although, almost certainly, it would be wrong to give that relationship a sexual flavour. But it is quite certain that unwittingly she was the cause of the tragedy which shadowed Ben's Tremans years, just as Edward, not quite unwittingly, was the origin of the tragedy which overshadowed her youth and prime. (Of course it would be totally unjustified to make out that Edward was an archfiend rather than an Archbishop. Both Edward and his Minnie were in some measure at least victims of the ways of thinking of their time—a time which popped sex and sin and secrecy all together into a black bag and stowed it under the bed. And the Edwards and the Minnies of the 1970s are equally victims of ways of thinking which put sex and casual fun and exhibitionistic openness together, only then to find that this also is a mixture that does not quite work.) But none the less the shutting-out of so-called 'respectable' Victorian women from any knowledge or understanding of the value, importance—even primacy—of the sexual life was utterly monstrous. In every village and town there was a Berlin Wall for women; on one side of it lived the whores, outcast non-human spreaders of the clap and the pox, on the other side lived the ladies dreading what was going to happen to them when the hour for going to bed came round. Bertrand

Russell, sexually a forward-looking and in no way inhibited man, wrote in his *Autobiography* (1967), when he was speaking of his first marriage to Alys Pearsall Smith, the sister of Logan: 'She had been brought up, as American women always were in those days'—that was 1894, and the remark applies to Englishwomen with equal force—'to think that sex was beastly, that all women hated it, and that men's brutal lusts were the chief obstacle to happiness in marriage.' Ben was like Alys Pearsall Smith—and with far more cause, since the sexual eagle, flapping his (to her) dirty wings, swept down on her when she was scarcely more than a child. No wonder she turned for relief to the gentler emotionalism of Mrs. Mylne, and the others, and finally to Lucy Tait.

But, understandable or not, her fidelity to Lucy Tait, obstinate and unshakeable as it was, brought her disaster. Maggie's resentment of this intermediary between herself and her mother was neurotically intense. And what more natural, given the unnatural circumstances? Maggie had to have, in common with everyone else, an outlet for her emotions. But the care of pigs and poultry, the writing of deeply touching little vignettes with titles like 'The Soul of a Cat' quite certainly failed to satisfy Maggie's emotions which were tempestuous like her father's—and she had no small boys' bottoms to beat although these, dutifully presented to him, may have provided him with an outlet, a relief, which was most certainly not consciously formulated. Maggie had only her mother. Only her mother could really satisfy because Nettie Gourlay and Gladys Bevan were, compared to Mary Sidgwick of the formidable intelligence, rather mouse-like really—although this thought too, like her father's in his fiercer, more disciplinary context, was never given admission into her private thoughts. And what was Lucy Tait, everlastingly there, at mealtimes, at not too strenuous exercise, at quiet diversions going on and on through long winter evenings—what was Lucy Tait up to, making a stiff satin barrier of herself to stand between Maggie and the only person into whose arms Maggie could, without impropriety, throw herself? Small wonder that tensions were there. Arthur, with his intelligence and his quick schoolmaster's nose for any whiff of emotional unease, for something 'not being quite right in the house', would undoubtedly have been aware of it. But he would probably not have given it the thought it so urgently needed. He would come down from

Magdalene for long stays with his books to write, his troops of friends to chat to sharply and amusingly—not at all the Arthurian voice you find in the easy-going chunnerings of *Thread of Gold* or *From a College Window* (both published in 1906)—and he would decide, for the sake of his own, so insecure, peace of mind, that this was women's business, something fussy and only marginally important, something that in time would right itself if left unregarded. And Fred, more concerned, more perceptive, was much less frequently at home. He belonged to the great London world, the world his mother had left and still regretted, and he could amuse her with the gossip and her eager laughter was strong enough to overcrow the rumblings of the volcano which for all that never ceased to threaten.

What happened on that night, when Maggie came down to dinner and went for her mother, or for Lucy, or for both of them, with a carving-knife, we shan't know quite for certain. Dr. Todd was mercifully there with male strength enough to hold down female frenzy. For the others it was, naturally enough, something not to be spoken of.

Arthur, in his life of his sister, speaks of it only in the vaguest terms. He knew that his mother, for some considerable while, had been 'almost alarmed by her [Maggie's] insistence on some detail, and her tendency to recur to certain lines of thought'; but in the same year confesses (1906): 'I for one had really no idea that there was anything seriously amiss with her.' For Ben though, who was always, or nearly always there, and who recognized Arthur's airy 'nothing seriously amiss' for the nonsense it was, the terrible climax must, even though foreseen, have called upon all her fortitude and sanity to endure.

Maggie at first was removed to the Priory, Roehampton—'a house for such cases', Arthur says: but briefly before that— whilst it was still hoped that her mania would be temporary— she had been in the charge of nuns. Arthur visited her while she was with the nuns, and was shaken by the sight of dementia. What made it in a way worse was that Maggie even then could show concern for others. She begged Arthur, for example, not to come again 'because it would be bad for him'. And bad for him indeed it was, because Maggie's plight was undoubtedly in some measure the cause of his own nervous breakdown in 1907–08.

The greatest torture for Ben was the occasional visiting—she held this to be her duty—to see her daughter in Roehampton. Ben for Maggie was still a treacherous figure who had deserted her elder daughter in order to consort, in such intimacy as to be an insult to the Benson blood, with Lucy Tait. And so Maggie had been removed to a nursing home. There were two chief ones, at Roehampton and at Wimbledon; one was much more expensive than the other, and it was Fred who always stood out for the expensive one, and Arthur who grumbled and thought that the cheaper would do very well; an odd little insight into the characters of the two men, a symptom of their basic antagonism, because nobody could ever argue that Arthur was not the most generous of men—and when he died he left £120,000 which would represent at least a million and a half in terms of today's purchasing power.

Maggie had always to be coaxed into seeing her mother in these sad places, but Ben never failed to go bravely visiting, though the sight of a beloved daughter blinded by horrifying delusions must have been a torment to her. Fred was the only one she would see with pleasure. And this is odd, because Fred is, if in only the discreetest of ways, the black sheep of the family, the least Bensonian. Of her sons he was the one whom Ben most loved— she saw the Sidgwick in him. But in Maggie the Benson influence was much the stronger—and yet in the long years of her misery it was always Fred she took pleasure in seeing. Fred, then, was the favourite of both; and this is odd, because Fred's dislike of women as a sex shouts itself out of all his novels; and Fred was much less frequently at Tremans than Arthur, because Fred was always on the move, visiting notables here, visiting notables there, visible and welcome at gatherings for winter sports at the appropriate places, welcome also when the season was right among his dashing friends gathered somewhere or other round the shores of the Mediterranean. Perhaps it was that they all saw in Fred a streak of practical worldliness that the inbred unworldly Bensons could turn to and lean on.

Arthur's collapse in 1917, so soon after Maggie's death, must have made Ben's last years hard indeed. Nellie was gone; Maggie was gone; stuttering Hugh, the one who went his own way and broke the biggest hole in the Benson family net, had been four years dead. Yet Ben was never one to mourn and wail. It is the most delightful of all her many delightful characteristics. She was an accepting woman, yet never a docile one, but gay, sharp and argumentative, conscious always that the strength and agility of her intelligence would make her mistress of the situation. By now she had stopped longing for London lights and the social round. Tremans would have to do and she would be cheerful in it. Always bothered about diet, she took to eating charcoal biscuits, but she did not worry about herself and the dire blows struck at her family could not shake her inward serenity. She had her *petite religion à elle* which supported her solidly. 'Faith is not a bundle of mere spiritual truths,' she wrote, 'but a *condition of soul* which I should describe as eternal life.' This condition of soul was not to be shaken, and gave her a stoutness of heart which was proof against anything the world might do to her. She died, without any long lingering, in 1918, and Percy Lubbock expresses what people felt when it happened as aptly as anyone. 'Her last years,' he wrote, 'had brought her many sorrows and anxieties, but her spirit to the end was quick with youth, and her friends mourned for her and missed her, not as one dying in the fullness of age, but as one whom old age could never touch.' And this is true. She was a very young girl when Edward married her, and, in her widow's cap, greatly overweight, confidently authoritative, with brains enough for half a dozen and the habit of command acquired over many years, somehow a very young girl she remained to the end. With serene and total certainty she believed in the life to come in a quite literal way. This may sound, to the materialist ears of the 1970s, as if Ben was vague and soft-centred. No woman was ever less so. She took no part, showed no particular interest in, the women's movement that was running so high and strong through her middle and later years, yet no woman of her generation could be more appropriately chosen as figurehead of the movement. She was terrifyingly clear-sighted. Towards her children she was affectionate and loving and understanding—and candid. There was always that certain hint of coldness, of mockery, which prevented the relationship from becoming the usual hot, mindless, maternal one. She had a backbone that refused to be bent or broken.

Without her Edward would not have been much more than nothing. In his early days as headmaster of Wellington she was very young, not grown yet to her full strength and certainty.

Edward's headmastership was by far the least successful of his undertakings; and when she left him at the end of it, he, with all his arrogance and self-certainty, suddenly realized that without her he was going to be nothing. She *must* return to him from Germany. It was as near to imploring as that stiff man ever came. And she did come back to him, and Edward White Benson was enabled to fulfil himself as a consequence. Her relations with her youngest son, Hugh, too, are most revealing in what they tell us about the sort of woman she was. Hugh was the most independent, the least clinging, of her children. Human relations were of small consequence to him—as the tragic, deplorable Rolfe was to discover in due time. Ben knew that Hugh would always do as he chose, and she had the intelligence—very rare in any woman— to recognize that in his case *la douce tyrannie de la mère* would get her nowhere. She did not repine about this. She thought he was wrong, and pointed out his mistakes to him with an intellectual clarity which anyone but Hugh would have found unanswerable. Yet still he argued—because here was a woman with whom one *could* argue, and enjoy the process still even when she got the better of it. He could say everything to her, and he knew she would never try to influence him by bringing feeling into it. Did she approve of his becoming a Roman Catholic? Certainly she did not; it did not fit in at all with her own private and peculiar brand of Christian faith. But never, at any time, were there such familiar appeals such as look what he was doing to his loving mother. Arthur said that between Hugh and his mother relations were 'absolutely tender and chivalrous'; he says also that they were 'wholly candid, natural and open-eyed'. That is right. Hugh saw and admired the cold iceberg Sidgwick quality in her, and recognized it more readily than any of the others except Fred, because he had more than a touch of it himself.

Fred was probably her favourite son because there was more of the Sidgwicks in him than in any of the others. He lacked the Benson intensity which could be so tiresome. In him there were no smouldering fires deep down. Or at any rate, if there were they were fires kept permanently banked. That was the right treatment for fires, Ben always thought. Arthur, once he was elected Master of Magdalene in December 1915, she naturally saw rather less of. He seemed to have shaken off Maggie's long tragedy and death. His writing was coming out again in torrents. Being

Master did not shake his certainty that for him being Author was what mattered above all things. 'It's the *congenial* thing,' he told himself in his Diary. 'I tend more and more to group my life round it; and all the other things are simply diversions or distractions or contrasts or reliefs. This applies to all my college work and administrative work. The truth is that writing is a *passion*, and it is worth while sacrificing everything else to it. It's a hard mistress in some ways, and it gets me into rows; but it is more and more clear to me that it is my real life, through which I see and view everything else—even friendship, even death . . .' He wrote a life of Maggie, which is evasive on the whole though there are moments of deep pathos which he does not seem quite to be aware of. He spoke of how delightedly she would bring other folk's children to Tremans. 'Maggie knew exactly how to treat children and how to talk to them. She devised the most delicious surprises and treats for them and loved to make plans for them as she had done in old days for herself and me. She often wished her brothers would marry that she might have children about her. "Sometimes say *our babies*, when you write of them," she said to me. "Oh, why should some families be so rich, and others have nary a child to their name?" ' It is hard, reading a passage such as this, not to wonder whether Arthur was ever capable of recognizing heartbreak when he saw it.

He also studied with great interest Father Martindale's two-volume life of Hugh which came out in 1916 and which provoked him into illuminating comment. (Arthur, of all the family, was the one closest to Hugh, the only one with any understanding of that difficult, buttoned-up man.) 'His [Hugh's] intensity comes out,' he commented, 'his extraordinary lack of insight about people, his power of extrication. Hugh's hardness was a strange thing. . . . He was an artist of a fiery amateur kind; he wanted to express himself in a dozen media. But it was the expression he liked. . . . His prayers, offices, meditations were, I believe, all part of the game. . . . He loved Catholic controversy; but his religion was one of artistic values, I believe.' This gets as close to Hugh as anyone is ever likely to. But did Arthur understand the horrible parallelism with himself of that phrase, 'It was the expression he liked'? In the spring of 1916 he finally made up his subterranean quarrel with Eton which had been, if ever so mildly, rankling for upwards of ten years. Cornish, Vice-Provost since 1893, paralysed now and with not long to go, had said he wanted to see him. Arthur had a delightful time—oysters, cutlets and macaroni for lunch—and, writing it up afterwards, looked at himself pretty squarely in his diary. '. . . the old affair: twenty-seven years of my life—i.e. exactly half, so far—spent there. I had some hard times there as a boy, but no experience, and as a master some experience and not much happiness. But it isn't my native air at all. It represents an aristocratic life, a life pursuing *knightly* virtues—chivalry, agility, honour, something Spartan. I am not like that at all; I like the poetical, epicurean, tranquil, semi-monastic life. I haven't the clean fresh sinfulness of the knight; I am half-bourgeois, half-monk. I was never big enough to embrace and overlap Eton. This could be done by a large-hearted and fatherly man, because it has the petulant and inconsiderate faults of youth; and such an one could have extended to it a fatherly and amused tolerance. But I was always a little afraid of it. . . .' Nobody, seeing him there, Master of Magdalene, a generous and constant benefactor to his adopted *domus* by virtue of his own generosity as well as that (to the end constantly maintained) of the unseen, admiring Suissesse, easy, authoritative, shrewdly combative in conversation, swift and effective in the quashing of opposition from the argumentative however eminent, affable, gracious, apparently so sure of himself —nobody could have imagined that, yes, he was 'always a little afraid' of life, at any rate of life in the larger sense. Arthur was an elegant fish who swam well in the snug pools he was used to. He shrank from being pitched into the wide waters where the currents tugged and the big fish with bad manners idled alertly around. Nobody could have imagined that in less than a year after that visit of reconciliation to Eton he was to be plunged into a state of mental misery and instability which would bring him to a state of desolation as complete almost as Maggie's had been. He could not then face Magdalene; he offered to resign, but the Visitor and fellows refused to accept this. He went to live in a nursing home near Ascot, there to endure a cushioned, private hell.

And so it was that when Ben came to die, quite suddenly in June 1918 on the anniversary of Maggie's birthday, only Fred, of all her six children, was alive and well. And even he was not present at her passing. He was busy, of course, with his war work in London. A brief while before he had written to tell her he would be able to manage a short break at Tremans, and she had answered in delighted expectation. He had come. She was fat, she was deaf, she was old. Of all those closest to her only Fred and Lucy were left, because Arthur was under his cloud and no use to anyone, least of all to himself. Yet in this house she had never really wanted to come to, crammed and cluttered with the accumulations of busy lifetimes but short now on people, he had found her fortitude and her gaiety unimpaired. Not even the fact that she was living through the fag end of a war ghastly enough to deprive all life of sense and purpose was sufficiently strong to break her or even to diminish her. Fred's cab had scrunched away taking him on his first stage back to London, and she had waved him good-bye, and a few days after that, in her sleep, she had set off for a destination she was absolutely certain about.

Of all the Bensons, Mary Sidgwick, who became a Benson by marriage, at an absurdly early age, is beyond question the most brilliant and the most gifted. She accomplished nothing that you could put down on a score-sheet or note in a book of reference. But she had power. She was not herself properly conscious of it, yet it was there, and, in a sense, strong enough partially to destroy all her children save Hugh, who was impervious. This 'destruction' is perhaps too strong a word. It was, of course, in no way willed, yet it was there, a sort of barrier which prevented highly gifted people like Arthur and Fred and Maggie from finding their own full identity, so that their achievements, not by any means to be dismissed as of no account, fell short of what such talents ought to have been capable of. Gladstone's dinner-table remark that she was the cleverest woman in Europe may have been half-jokingly said. Yet it has to be listened to. Gladstone was old when he said it, with a vast experience of human beings and human affairs, and badinage was never his line. Edward's fourteen years at Wellington stand out as by far the least successful period of his life. Minnie was only thirty-one when he was ready to leave it—and she was ready to leave him. She was fully adult by now, tired of his passionate imperiousness, warped also by his inability to bring tenderness and understanding into sexual relations. She would go to Germany, and—vaguely—be apart from him. Edward had the shock of his life. He was suddenly jolted out of his certainties into an awareness of his dependence on her. He had written imploringly, and she had come back. From then on he soared unceasingly. He was an undoubted success at Lincoln

even though clever, old, dried-up Dean Blakesley failed to warm
to all that limitless enthusiasm. He did a splendid pioneering job
in the new diocese of Truro where the Celts had turned their
backs on cut-and-dried conventional Anglicanism. From Truro
to Canterbury was a mighty leap, but he made it, and, for another
fourteen years, did all and more than was required of him as
Primate. The Queen came to rely on him—how admirably he
coped with her difficult eldest son—and he died, appropriately
and even gloriously, in the arms of his Prime Minister in the
Prime Minister's own parish church of Hawarden. In all this
Minnie was his prop. She had dedicated herself to him. Her
intelligence, her tact, her subtlety were all far stronger than his,
and they were at his disposal. Without her he would have been,
not a nobody certainly, because he had great abilities, but not a
top man either. She was his kitchen cabinet; you could call her
his *éminence grise*, only grey was never her colour. Never at any
time was she at pains to tell him what to do. He simply came and
asked what he should do.

And yet he had destroyed her as a woman. There were no more
babies after Hugh in 1871. She saw to that. And Hugh himself,
the last of the Bensons, was always something of a changeling.
She had come to hate the physical facts of maleness. She turned to
women. To her own sons she gave affection certainly, but not
love in any maternal sense. Beth would have to do for that. It was
this undoubtedly which led to the decidedly unorthodox sexuality
both of Arthur and Fred. Hugh has to be left out; Hugh was sex-
less, as Frederick Rolfe was to discover during that 'ascetic' (the
adjective is Fred's) walking-tour of August 1905. For Arthur the
problems of the sexual life could always be solved in a quite
gentlemanly fashion. He could experience throbbings in the
company of a good-looking undergraduate, but comfort, for him,
was always a primary consideration, and there was plentiful
evidence that throbbings, if given their head, could lead to sharp
discomforts. He was content therefore to sigh, and be regretful,
and consider himself well out of entanglements which could so
easily disturb the flow of the kind of busy, ordered life which he
loved. Upon Fred the effects of his mother's early shock and
disenchantment were more serious. He loved her, of course, but
he wanted her to love him more, to love him, perhaps, in a way
that was not wholly natural. He gives the impression always of

wanting exclusivity to come into it, and it is because of this that
his dislike of women in general—Miss Mapp sitting at the bow
window of her house in Rye, keeping track of all the comings and
goings of her friends and neighbours and being woundingly
mischievous about them, Lucia who turns snobbery into a profession—becomes obsessive and almost hysterical. It was this that
made his homosexuality more positive, more defiant than Arthur's
—yet there is a quality of pose about even his. His Capri co-
habiting with Ellingham Brooks has really nothing more unorthodox, reeks no more of carnality, than Arthur's ruminative bicycle
rides with Herbert Tatham. Yet Arthur disapproved of Fred, saw
in his high society butterfly-flutterings a rakishness that was not in
fact there, and entirely disapproved of unmentionable people like
Brooks. Fred, for his part, was quite candid about his inability to
get on with Arthur. 'Our ways of life, our diversions had little in
common, and never, since we were boys, had we spoken of things
that intimately concerned us as we spoke of them to our
friends. . . .' Yet Fred goes on (he is speaking of the time of
Arthur's death) '. . . Close blood-relationship certainly implies
dutiful instincts. A man who does not stick up for his kin nor is
ready and eager to help if they are in trouble is wanting in
normal decency, but it does not imply any warmth of friendship. . . .' 'Normal decency'—that is the phrase to latch on to
here. In the case of both Arthur and Fred emotional development
was thrown out of gear because their parents possessed powerful
but totally incompatible personalities. Arthur was perfectly aware
of the parental clash. 'She was afraid of papa,' he notes in his
diary, '. . . they were two very vivid people utterly antagonistic
in temperament and probably ought never to have been
married. . . .' From there it was a short step for him, and for Fred
as well, to come to the conclusion that nobody ought ever to get
married. About Minnie's being afraid of her Edward though,
Arthur is far out. Certainly in those early Wellington days, when
Arthur was too young to understand much of what was going on,
there was a certain terrified submissiveness about Minnie, called
upon to play the woman's part before her childhood had slipped
away, but never afterwards. From the time when she came back
to Lincoln what she gave Edward was affectionate tolerance and
the unfailing support of a nature much stronger than his, yet of a
nature quite prepared to be selfless in all outward matters because

the important things for her lay outside the bounds of his understanding. If there was any fear about in Lincoln or Truro or
Addington or Lambeth that fear was Edward's. He was terrified
lest he should lose her because he knew that losing her would
demonstrate to him the impossibility of living out his own life
adequately.

Fred, with that candour which makes us like him, is willing to
say that he and Arthur lived in no brotherly closeness. What also
makes us like him—and this too comes out in the passage just
quoted—is that he was the man for family emergencies. When
disasters happened, it always seemed to be Fred who was on hand
to smack the cheeks of hysteria and to ensure that life with its
insistent practicalities went somehow on. It was Fred once again
who had to decide what to do about Tremans once his mother had
died. Arthur was away in his Ascot nursing home, struggling
with the longest and most severe nervous breakdown of his life,
useless to himself and to everybody else. All the other members of
the family were dead, leaving not a single new-generation Benson
to be consulted. For Lucy Tait, parted for ever—if that was not
an unChristian way of putting it—from her beloved Ben, the
house had become a derelict place with its character taken away
from it; she bought a smaller place and her sister, and her sister's
husband, Archbishop Davidson, saw more of her. (Fred was not
very fond of Davidson and wrote an essay about him, comparing
him with Balfour, in the early 1930s. This is very polite and suave,
but as full of sharp little darts as a banderillero's quiver. Fred
had always a great talent for this sort of demolition-work.
'. . . Immensely too,' Fred said, 'did he [Davidson] enjoy being in
touch with great affairs, and pleasure in such cases is always a
whetstone to wisdom. . . .'

And so, in 1919, Fred decided to give up the remainder of the
lease, and to rid himself (and Arthur) of most if not all the
Bensoniane (going back, some of it, to the mid-nineteenth century)
with which the house was crammed. He did not want the place.
He preferred a fashionable Brompton Square house for himself in
London, with one or two familiar nesting-places abroad to be held
in reserve for when people of the better sort were out of town. He
did not want either to hug to himself letters and documents and
material objects that were three-dimensional and out of date. He
preferred to keep family memories in his head, and, in his own

very private and personal way, refashion them by putting them down on paper. And so there were bonfires, and there was an auction. He destroyed a hoity-toity correspondence between Lord Derby and his father when Edward was a young headmaster and prepared to tell an eminent Governor that he would run Wellington as he thought fit or else resign without pause or pang. He destroyed wild and reproachful letters written by Maggie during her insanity to her mother, which would now make interesting reading if they had been preserved. He got rid of the organ which used to get on Arthur's nerves so much, especially on Sunday nights. But he kept Maggie's Egyptian treasures. Egypt was a place which had very painful, as well as loving, memories for him. Altogether though, it seemed as if the Benson clan was being dismantled, reduced from corporate stateliness and grandeur to the humdrum anonymity which the twentieth century seemed to prefer for those who had survived 1914–18 and the plague of Spanish flu that followed. Fred himself still survived of course, but he was never a man given to overvaluing himself and the literary success he had undoubtedly gained seemed to him to have been won on the cheap. And there was Arthur as well. But Arthur, all sixteen stone of him, seemed reduced to nothing. The Master of Magdalene was showing no signs whatever of making a comeback. Arthur could be written off. And perhaps on this score Fred's regrets were more superficial than was seemly. Through Fred's relations with his brother there ran a well-disguised but obstinately enduring streak of envy. Arthur had reached academic eminence; Fred, of his own free will admittedly, had chosen the role of novelist-entertainer and had done very well out of it. Yet he too had got his First, and would have liked to have been called Master in a college of his choice. Were not his abilities, after all, at least commensurate with Arthur's? This itch to have it both ways was quite irrational of course and not consciously admitted even to himself. Yet now, in the summer of 1919, he felt the ambiguous triumph of being the sole survivor. He disposed of Tremans; he destroyed on his own initiative a great deal of the accumulations of a numerous family of the highest importance and distinction; in October he would take over the sub-lease of Lamb House, Henry James's home in Rye. And to be master of Lamb House, leaving it in the winter for the south of France which would be kinder to his rheumatism, could count as almost as great a distinction as being Master of Magdalene. Especially as, this time, poor Arthur seemed so seriously stricken that any return to Cambridge as Master of anywhere had the look, at best, of an outside chance.

12

The Survivor

ARTHUR, HOWEVER, WAS NOT YET DONE FOR. In 1922 he
began to get better. At the beginning of 1923 he was back in
Cambridge, Master of Magdalene, master of his faculties, and
busy as ever. It was strange how Arthur in mental sickness and
Arthur in health were two completely different, tightly compartmentalized men. When he was down he was down, and when he
was up he was up. Arthur hiding away in the depths of torment
at Ascot had no influence whatever on Arthur the distinguished,
commanding, endlessly busy man, with more books in his head
than even he had time to write. He had the college to set to rights
after the confusions and neglect of wartime. The lady from Switzerland saw faithfully to the money supply. Soon it would be his
turn to be Vice-Chancellor. As liveryman of the Fishmongers'
Company he was climbing from dignity to higher dignity; in 1924
he would be Renter Warden. True, he no longer had Tremans for
the vacations, but he and Fred came to an arrangement about
Lamb House. They would, on a Box-and-Cox basis, share the
tenancy. What it came to roughly was that Fred should be at Rye
in term-time and Arthur during the vacations. Arthur liked Lamb
House as much as Fred. He had only two years to go, but they
were probably the happiest of his life. On 24 April 1923 he noted
in his diary: 'I enter my sixty-second year in good spirits, not
remorseful, interested in life and work. *Thank God!* I had a pile of
letters, mostly from kind but relentless women . . . At 11.0 Peel
[a don] came, and we walked round, looking at small details—
the old pleasure returns. At 1.0 College Lunch. . . . Walked with

F.R.S. [F. R. Salter, another don], who was enchantingly nice—
his very best. . . . Wrote. Hall, very friendly. Committee about
Reading Room, Ramsey [President and Tutor of Magdalene],
Peel, Morshead [another don] in my study . . . I offered £1500;
this a small thank-offering to my dear kind colleagues. I drew up
a report. . . .' Everything was coming right for Arthur's brief
Indian summer.

'Wrote': the single word should be noted. The dominant
passion of Arthur's life remained tenaciously with him after five
years of obliteration. He produced four books during his period of
resurrection, as well as much of a fifth in manuscript. Two of
these, *The Trefoil* and *Memories and Friends*, are probably the best
things he ever did. Both are, directly or indirectly, about himself
and about the people he had known. As a memoirist he is always
at his best. In *The Trefoil* he evokes the scenes of his childhood
and youth in Wellington, Lincoln and Truro. *Memories and Friends*
describes itself. Arthur gives us eighteen portraits of interesting
people he has known, and these are done with a perceptiveness and
insight that make them wholly delightful. Eton notables figure
largely in it because Arthur, although he turned his back on the
place in a huff for twenty years, was always inextricably bound up
with it. But there are others too and these save the collection from
becoming a coterie-book. Arthur came to know Henry James as
early as 1884, when the great man was in his early forties and still
had his short pointed beard. At that time Arthur says 'he had not
yet acquired, or he did not display, that fine conversational manner
of his later years. . . . He talked little and epigrammatically'—
which is a startling reminder of what the years succeeded in doing
for Henry James. The essay—only twelve pages long—succeeds
admirably in conveying the slow Jacobean evolution. James and
Arthur never lost touch with each other. 'The last time that I saw
him he was lunching at the Athenaeum, and I went up to him—
he had a companion—and said that I only came for a passing
benediction. He put his hand on my arm and said: "My dear
Arthur, my mind is so constantly and continuously bent upon you
in wonder and goodwill that any change in my attitude could be
only the withholding of a perpetual and settled felicitation." '
That catches James III beautifully. 'It was like being present,'
Arthur says, 'at the actual construction of a little palace of thought,
of improvised yet perfect design.' Perhaps because a third of the

pieces in his book were written for periodicals, he is forced to abjure his besetting sin; that of spreading himself too thinly. He shows that he can produce sharp, tight phrases—like 'the mental dilapidation which comes from the habitual practice of deference'. A tight editorial rein was always good for him. The little monographs he wrote for Macmillan's 'English Men of Letters' series are all admirable, more especially the one on Edward FitzGerald where he is able to touch—delicately and sympathetically as one would expect—on FitzGerald's homosexual need for Kenworthy Browne.

His busy life went on. He dined well and frequently with ceremony. He now weighed nineteen stone, which was altogether too much for him to carry around. His geniality increased—the real-life Arthur, as opposed to the book-Arthur could lash out woundingly, especially at his closest friends. Percy Lubbock, for example, suffered from this, as did the viperish Gosse. But at the end of 1924 he is able to note in his diary: 'My breeze with P. blown over. . . . My friendship with Gosse has revived. I have made many speeches and entertained endless undergraduates. Lamb House has been an unspeakably delightful haven of refuge. . . .' Lamb House, indeed, because joint tenancy and total apartness were turning out in practice to be quite unworkable, was bringing Arthur and Fred closer together than they had been since distant Truro days. In March he entertained Asquith and Margot to dinner in Combination Room before they drove to Guildhall. Asquith was 'pleased, I thought, at being an Earl'. Margot came up to him before the platform stuff began, 'clasped my hand, and said, "Good-night, old *friend*!"' Were Arthur and his brother kept strictly separated in her memories, or had she forgotten how Arthur's brother, all that long while ago, had called her Dodo, and made her the unsympathetic central character of the most successful of all his countless novels? Arthur was working now on the memoir of his mother. That completed, he would have composed *oraisons funèbres* on most of the Benson clan: Hugh, Maggie, his father, his mother, and his own personal diary already amounted to more than four million words. 'I find my Memoir *pours* out,' he now noted when he was at Lamb House on 21 March. After such a long experience of fluency it is odd that he should sound surprised. On 20 April the Suissesse came good with yet another gift. '. . . I can carry out all my schemes without anxiety,' he wrote. 'It is like a romance: and it fills my mind with affection for the dear donor, who has brought so much sunlight about my path of late and asks so little. Though I have not seen her, I feel about her as I did for mamma and Beth—an unsuspicious love. It is wonderful. . . .'

But it was not given to him to carry out many more schemes. Early that June he returned from a single-day visit to London feeling poorly. The doctor called at Magdalene the next morning and told him he had pleurisy. Lacking antibiotics he then left, leaving Arthur's mighty frame to conduct its own defensive campaign. In 1925 there was nothing else a doctor could do. He seemed to resist the attack satisfactorily for a few days and on the 10th he got up and sat in his armchair in the study. There one of his coronary arteries got blocked and his heart almost stopped. They were afraid to move him from his chair until the next day but one. Still, it had not been a massive blockage, and on the twelfth they were able to get him back to bed. But the further outlook was unpromising. To cope with pleurisy now developing into pneumonia, and the after-effects of a heart-attack as well was too much to ask; and at midnight, on Tuesday 16 June 1925, Arthur died. The memoir of his mother remained unfinished. Fred took it over, completed it, made alterations the extent of which it is not possible to know, and then published it under his own name. The diary, surely the longest ever put together by one single man, would now hang suspended. The last entry in it concerns a visit Arthur had recently made to a reception given by another Head of House. He is sharply critical, as he so often was when talking to friends or to himself and not addressing his large and faithful public in priced and printed pages. A pity about the wife of this Head of House, Arthur mused. Quite a lower-class sort of person, and not having at command the easy dignity which her station in life was now requiring of her. . . . So was Arthur a snob? This was a question which, not for one single moment, would it ever have occurred to him to put to himself.

*   *   *

So, by the summer of 1925, the Bensons were reduced to one. Fred stood alone except for collaterals. He could not mourn; he felt too far away from Arthur for that to be possible. But now he again carefully carried out his duties—of tidying up and destroying—which he had carried out seven years before after his mother's death at Tremans. Arthur had left him the Old Lodge at Magdalene to do with as he saw fit. The tumbling cataracts of books; what was he to do with them? He invited Arthur's friends to take their pick, but in such plenteousness they made no noticeable inroads. Gosse came poking around, looking for rarities but had no luck; Arthur had never been a collector in the professional sense. Fred had them crated and sent to institutions.

Boxes upon boxes of letters had to be gone through and then, for the most part, conveyed to the college boiler-house in a clothes-basket. Amongst all the thousands there was, according to Fred, a packet 'of very dangerous stuff, and one to be burnt unopened'. In what way these were dangerous can only be a matter of pointless guesswork, because, although Fred was on the whole candid both about himself and about the family as a whole, he could, when he judged it necessary, be impenetrably discreet. It is good to know though that Arthur, some time, somewhere, in the course of an irreproachable, if emotionally deviant life, got himself involved in something so hot that it demanded instant incineration. Fred discovered Hugh's letters too among the jumble, but none, regrettably, from Rolfe; Arthur himself, no doubt, had tip-toed down to the boiler-house with these. Fred took long laborious days in stripping and for the most part destroying. Then the big stuff was sold and Fred hobbled back to Rye. 'I felt no real sense of personal bereavement,' he says. There he arranged for the unveiling of a stained-glass window in Rye parish church in memory of the unseen lady who lived in Switzerland, who had enjoyed Arthur's outpourings in print so much, who had been such a large benefactress and who had now died. Her name? Not Cornucopia, but Mrs. de Nottbeck. Lord Davidson, recently retired from his record quarter of a century as Primate, came down, still active and full of quips, to perform the ceremony; and after that, his family duties done, Fred felt it was time to look to his own future.

He had just short of fifteen years left to go; a long time, and he made good use of it. Arthritis in both hips was beginning to slow him down. Winter sports at Pontresina held diminishing attraction. Brooks wrote from Capri; his health was bad and he was short of funds; would Fred, from his plenty, be willing to set him up in a new house on the island? Fred sent him a small sum of money but was careful not to write encouragingly. Rye had a splendid golf course, but although he was a good and enthusiastic player, he began to find pivoting increasingly difficult. From being a gadabout Fred was gradually becoming a stay-at-home.

He scrutinized his rows of published novels and came to the conclusion that they did not amount to much. This self-examination was not an immediate consequence of Arthur's death. It began, really, soon after the selling up at Tremans. He had too much of the damned Benson fluency. He ought to write more slowly. He ought not to write so much. It was a pity to play so many variations on the same tune. A great war had crushed the life out of the civilization he had been brought up in. He must stop writing novels about fashionable Edwardian society in which he could indulge his misogyny in sharply amusing, but repetitive little scenes. Could he not look out of his bow window in Lamb House and study the small world of Rye as it sauntered past? Could he not become a provincial to his own and everybody's benefit?

Sir Osbert Sitwell recalled a scene—it must have happened in the very early twenties—when he and Gosse were lunching in the Marlborough Club, and Fred by chance was sitting close at hand. 'Was that Fred Benson I saw in the dining room,' Gosse said in a calculated stage-whisper. 'Was it really? If so, he looks much older, oh, *so* much *older* than when I saw him last. . . . But then I recollect, his father died at the same age . . .' 'Be careful. Be careful,' Sir Osbert warned. 'He's just near you.' But Gosse, knowing perfectly well of course that Fred could not possibly be near his father's total sum of sixty-seven years, continued to fire his little darts at Fred. 'Quite a nice chap, I'm told, if you get to know him. But how can one do that? One never sees him anywhere . . . and besides, I could never get on with a man who sees *spooks*.' Fred said nothing. Perhaps he could not trust himself. Perhaps it was only a short while before that he had read all those viperish letters from Gosse to Arthur before casting them into Magdalene's furnaces. Perhaps he considered that he had sufficiently mastered the ghost story; was not *Visible and Invisible*, published in 1923, on hand to prove it?

But it was perfectly true, as Gosse had roundly put it, that Fred was no longer to be seen much in town, was no longer a frequenter of the best houses. He was staying at home and writing books about Rye and its mischief-making females who lacked sufficient to do. *Queen Lucia* had come out as early as 1920; *Miss Mapp* in 1922; and he kept up this novel-series, at intervals, until 1939, by which time he was indeed well past his father's sixty-seven and had not long to go himself. These novels are a great improvement on the ones of his younger days. They are malicious, amusing, and still hold the reader, but still Fred accepts too readily the wisdom of Browning's thrush who sang each song twice over. He also wrote, in 1932, a novel called *Secret Lives* which is about the unique Mary Mackay who called herself Marie Corelli. This is one of his best novels and affords him yet another opportunity to enlarge upon his dislike of women. Why did he hate them so much? Probably because he kept comparing them with his mother, and kept finding them wanting. Probably also because he thought—and here Fred's neurosis comes to the surface— that even she did not love him in quite the way he would have liked. In the summer of 1918, quite a short while before she died, Fred managed to disentangle himself from diplomatic affairs at the Foreign Office and wrote to say that the chance of a few days at Tremans offered itself. She wrote immediately back: 'Oh Fred! a whole week! Lovely! Come to your foolish but ever-loving Ma.' It had not been quite the response he would have liked. It was too jokey. Mary Sidgwick had always kept a tiny little distance between herself and her sons. And as for her daughters, Nellie had died so young, and Maggie had driven herself insane because she rejected the right of Lucy Tait to be admitted to the family circle.

But it was above all at Rye that this new and soberer Fred discovered where his most valuable gifts as a writer lay. He had always been of course, like all of them except Hugh (always the loner) obsessed with his family—the tiny group set apart from the world even though sometimes united in disunity. He would do as Arthur, amongst so much besides, had done; he would write about his family. Arthur's manuscript life of his mother, not far from finished, he had brought away from Cambridge. He took it out, completed it, and published it under his own name, calling it simply *Mother*.

All through that final decade and a half between Arthur's death and his own, Fred was taking himself more seriously as a writer. 'I feel that a day is wasted on which I haven't written a

9

thousand words or so. . . . I don't enjoy it as much as I used. I take
more trouble than ever. I tell myself that this time there will be a
masterpiece. But I'm not quite as convinced of that as I used to
be. . . .' Certainly when he spoke of a thousand words a day he
was scarcely exaggerating. No fewer than ninety-three titles
stand under Fred's name in the final records. Not an output quite
on Arthur's colossal scale, but considerable none the less. He
turned to biography. The lapidary-inscriptive, two-volume type
of stuff common in his father's day would no longer do. Lytton
Strachey had seen to that—and so had Gosse, who, as long ago as
1907, had so cleverly and spitefully angled the truth about his
relations with his father in *Father and Son*. Between Strachey and,
say, Arthur's commemorative tomes about their father, there
might, he thought, be a middle way. Fred wrote a life of Drake,
which is no more than moderate; but he also wrote a life of
Charlotte Brontë which is very good indeed. There was so much
wrong with Mrs. Gaskell's admired biography; she had been so
intent upon making a heroine out of Charlotte and a villain out
of Parson Brontë. He strove for, and found, a better balance.

But he also, like Arthur, turned to memoir-writing, and, like
Arthur again, turned his eyes inwards for the most part—upon
himself and upon the remarkable family he belonged to. As early
as 1920 he had written *Our Family Affairs*, which is a bit too
smooth and sticky with his own adolescent passions. But then in
1930 and, also in 1932, he produced successively *As We Were*, and
As We Are. The first of these is not quite his masterpiece, but
runs it a close second. Family memories have their place in it, but
here the portrait-painting is much firmer, much more perceptive,
than ever before. He also ranged more widely. By 1920 Fred had
had the entrée into the very best of English society for upwards
of thirty years; he had pointed stories to tell—of the Queen herself, of Gladstone, of hostesses like the Duchess of Devonshire,
Lady Londonderry and Lady Ripon, of Cambridge dons both
worldly and other-worldly like Oscar Browning and Walter
Headlam, of scandals like the Tranby Croft affair, of poets conventional and unconventional—and he told them with incomparable vivacity so that his pages came alive, peopled with gorgeous
creatures who had flitted about before the calamity of 1914 which,
for good and grievous reasons, had snuffed all the brightness out
of life—for Fred and for so many others of his generation. *As We*

Are is an odd book. Not as successful as its predecessor, but interesting and revealing all the same. Fred is here seen picking himself up and dusting himself down after the terrifying storms and fires of 1914–18 had quietened and dimmed. He recognizes that he has to face a ravaged and not very brave new world. But the novelist in him is still strong so that the book becomes a mixture of fiction, prophecy, and social commentary. Fred imagines two aristocrats from the world that has gone, Lord and Lady Buryan, living at Hakluyt Park where the grounds are plenteous and from the walls of the house Botticellis and Titians stare down at you, shedding the warmth of genius. But after the war the Buryan ways change. Henry, the heir, marries Helen. These are a pair—typical Fred implies of their generation—for whom the old morality has given place to *Fay ce que voudras*. Helen has two sons, but her sexual inclinations are lesbian. And Fred has this passage—a strange one in which he is perhaps fictionalizing his beloved mother's trouble. 'To Helen the call of the flesh meant very little: marriage had not ripened her, nor yet maternity. She had done her duty in bearing two healthy sons, and that, she considered, was all that could reasonably be required of her in fulfilment of her marriage-vows. Men with their gross contracts and insistent, intrusive needs rather disquietened her, and her intimacies were those of her own sex. She wanted Henry to leave her alone; as long as he did that she did not really care whether he took his ardours elsewhere, provided that he behaved with discretion and did not make . . . her appear in the truly ridiculous role of the slighted wife. . . .' Thoughts of his adored and elusive mother must have been in Fred's mind as he wrote this; but of course the notion of infidelity on Edward's part was inconceivable. Fred would have been too young to remember the days at Whitby long ago, when Edward was certainly ardent, even if Elizabeth Wordsworth was not.

Two-thirds of the way through the story—or parable as he liked to call it—of post-war life, Fred packs it quickly away in order to become portraitist and rueful commentator. Arthur Balfour and Randall Davidson are compared and the suggestion persuasively made that they might both have been happier had they exchanged roles. He looks at the literary world—the new one springing up around him, and argues that Henry James has already done better what Virginia Woolf is trying to do. And finally—a man of sixty-four in 1931—he looks sadly at his England after thirteen years of peace. '. . . the nation was tired. . . . It wanted to forget and amuse itself, to have its cup-ties and league-matches. . . . A little relaxation. . . .' Seriousness, especially among the working classes, had departed. And Fred, to do him justice, could quite see the reason why. A broad-minded sixty-four-year-old in 1958 could have, and probably did, come out with the very same words. *As We Are* is an odd jumble of a book, but interesting still.

Increasingly through the thirties he became a fixture at Rye. His joints creaked and although he sought energetically for cures, they kept on being agonizingly painful. Golf, which he loved so much, got to be impossible. Travel—to town, to anywhere, from being an easy routine became a burden. Still there were compensations. Friends called. Yeats-Brown, remembered from that strong friendship in Portofino in 1909, came down, and Fred, the arch-professional, showed him how to turn *Memoirs of a Bengal Lancer* into a best-seller. Ethel Smyth, nine years older than he, a Dame now, and still very formidable, came down. And then, in the autumn of 1935, Captain Dawes, the Town Clerk of Rye, rang him up to ask whether, if the Council elected him Mayor for the coming November, would he be willing to stand? Fred was staggered. He was still his own particular sort of busy man; he was determined still to get 'some sort of status again as a writer'. True, he was on the bench, but he knew nothing of local government. Drains and elementary schools, and council houses—they moved in a mysterious way their beneficent functions to perform, and Fred took them all for granted. And all the farcical mockeries of the Lucia-Mapp novels; surely Captain Dawes knew, as well as anybody else, that the town of Tilling where these harpies lived was really the Ancient Cinque Port of Rye itself? Yes, Captain Dawes, and the council, knew that, but they still wanted him for Mayor.

Fred thought deeply. This was recognition of a sort, if not quite the sort he had been working for. And at all events his writing work could go on. He accepted. He organized celebrations for King George V's Jubilee. He was, indeed, a triumphant success. He was voted in for three successive years. He was in office when the old king died and when the new one abdicated. He spent his mayoral expense-account in the first three weeks of each of his terms and for the rest fell back on his own not meagre resources. They elected him Speaker of the Cinque Ports, and when Lord Willingdon, accompanied by Lang, by now Archbishop of Canterbury, came down to be installed as Lord Warden, it fell to Fred to speak up for the Boroughs. He did it admirably. All his life he had been hob-nobbing with Archbishops—and ex-Viceroys as well, come to that. He was that rare creature, a Mayor who remains unawed through all pomp and circumstance.

Then in 1937, Magdalene elected him into an honorary Fellowship, and this pleased him much. In view of all that Arthur had done for the place one might have thought that twelve years was a long time for the College to take before making up its collective mind to honour Arthur's distinguished brother. If such a thought passed through his head he made no mention of it. At last he was making headway in a direction that had always called him; he was beginning to catch up with Arthur in the academic field.

Fred had moved from Oakley Street, Chelsea to 25 Brompton Square not long before the beginning of the First War. This remained his London headquarters till the end. There was much visiting of course until the war came, but after 1914 war work kept him more closely tied to his handsome property which was furnished and decorated with easeful grace, and had a grand piano on which he performed with greater spirit and accuracy than most amateurs.

In 1916 Charlie Tomlin was taken on at Tremans as general assistant about the place. He was only a boy, but remained thereafter constantly in Benson service until the line finally petered out in 1940. After Ben's death and the break-up of Tremans Fred took him on as permanent henchman. Charlie is still alive and well and living in Rye, and playing golf to a handicap of fifteen, which, for a veteran, is very good indeed, and reflects the quality of the coaching which Fred, with his outstanding aptitude for games and for physical skills in general, must have given him all that long while ago.

Charlie nursed Fred through his final illness, going in every day, and for most of the day, to University College Hospital in Gower Street where the last of the Bensons lay incurably stricken. He remembers Ben herself—the 'lovely lady'; he remembers Arthur, who could never bring himself to meet his beneficent Suissesse face to face because, being past his prime and weighing nineteen stone, such an encounter 'might destroy the illusion'; he remembers Lucy Tait who was gracious even if at moments she could be a bit acid. For Charlie indeed all those members of the Benson family and their close adherents who remained above ground in 1916 remain as resplendent and kindly luminaries shining still in a firmament unchanging and defiant of the unimaginable touch of time.

A little of the Benson melancholy used to descend upon Fred especially during that last decade when arthritis gnawed and there was no remedy save two sticks—no *Indocid,* no plastic hips. When the Mayoralty of Rye was offered and accepted—it was a gesture on the part of the Town Fathers which he greatly appreciated—he had got to the stage of being uncharacteristically frightened at the inevitable prospect of a succession of public occasions and an endless number of public speeches both long and short. 'I can't do it, Charlie,' he used to say. And Charlie would roundly answer, 'Of course you can, sir.' And once Fred had plunged in, of course Fred could, and of course Fred did.

Then he was free again. 1938 came in. Hitler ranted, fixed his hypnotic glare on the German people and drove them mad, and for Fred 'still the masterpiece beckoned'. And there was still time left to write it. He called it *Final Edition,* and subtitled it 'informal autobiography'. He delivered the manuscript to his publishers in February 1940, but he never saw it in print because, on the last leap-year day of that month, Fred died in University College Hospital. He was seventy-three. *Final Edition* was, and remains, an enchanting book, alive with happenings long past but vividly remembered, peopled with characters we have most of us heard of and presented here truthfully but without malice—Henry James, Marie Corelli, the second Viscount Halifax, arch-champion of the Anglo-Catholics—but best of all is the account he gives of his own strange, and strangely gifted, family. There are gaps; Martin died when Fred was too young to know him, his father, who was feared when he did not want to be feared, he skates gingerly round. Poor Nellie too, the direct one, had so small a time in which to assert herself. But of Arthur who combined in himself such opposites, of Hugh who darted off on his own to Rome, to Hare Street, to world-wide Roman Catholic evangelization, of Maggie, who strong-mindedly drove herself into insanity he writes so that they come alive. And, of course, of his mother, of

Mary Sidgwick. It is she who is the true leading character in the hundred years of Benson history. It is she who says in her diary that the material she was given to work with had to be fashioned 'into a garment of praise, not into a cowl of heaviness'. It is she who, after numbing blows, refuses always to accept that life can never be more than a matter of glum acceptance.

Select Bibliography

Askwith, Betty. *Two Victorian Families*
Arthur Christopher Benson as seen by Some of his Friends
Benson, A. C. *Life of Edward White Benson* (2 vols.)
                Life and Letters of Maggie Benson
                Hugh: Memoirs of a Brother
                The Leaves of the Tree
                Memoirs of Arthur Hamilton
                The Trefoil
Benson, E. F. *As We Were*
                As We Are
                Final Edition
                Mother
                Our Family Affairs
Benson, R. H. *Confessions of a Convert*
Lubbock, P. (ed.). *Extracts from the Diary of A. C. Benson*
Martindale, C. C. *Life of R. H. Benson*
Symons, A. J. A. *The Quest for Corvo*

Index